THE
HOME DESIGN
G U I D E

Planning, Building or Buying Your Dream Home

JAMES SHEPHERD AND
G. ALAN MORLEDGE

**Real Estate
Education Company**
a division of Dearborn Financial Publishing, Inc.

While a great deal of care has been taken to provide accurate and current information, the ideas, suggestions, general principles and conclusions presented in this text are subject to local, state and federal laws and regulations, court cases and any revisions of same. The reader is thus urged to consult legal counsel regarding any points of law—this publication should not be used as a substitute for competent legal advice.

Acquisitions Editor: Christine E. Litavsky
Managing Editor: Jack Kiburz
Editorial Assistant: Stephanie C. Schmidt
Interior Design: Lucy Jenkins
Cover Design: Paul Perlow Design

Published by Real Estate Education Company,
a division of Dearborn Financial Publishing, Inc.

Printed in the United States of America

95 96 97 10 9 8 7 6 5 4 3 2 1

Library of Congress Cataloging-in-Publication Data

Shepherd, James M.
    The home design guide : planning, building or buying your dream
  home / by James M. Shepherd and G. Alan Morledge.
        p.   cm.
      Includes index.
      ISBN 0-7931-1283-4 (pbk.)
      1. House construction.   2. Dwellings—Planning.   3. House buying.
  I. Morledge, G. Alan.   II. Title.
  TH4811.M59   1995
  643'.12—dc20   94-46243
                                                          CIP

CONTENTS

■ **PART TWO** ■
Exterior House Design

■ PART THREE ■
Interior Home Design

■ APPENDIXES ■

INTRODUCTION

This book has been developed to give you insight into the most important factors of house design. Its lessons will be equally rewarding, whether planning a new house, reviewing the drawings from a catalog of house plans or considering a house already built. It also will be useful to broaden the knowledge of those selling houses and lots.

A house plan should be based on current and foreseeable needs, but consideration also should be given to future living. For example, the plan should be right for the family at present but should project ahead for the time when more children are expected, or when children are older or even after they leave the nest. If a house is well planned and the time factor is considered, the house will work well for the family over a wide span of time.

Another related matter to consider is the future resale value of the house. The pattern of many American families is to move several times as their situations change during their families' lives, and it is advantageous not to be stuck with a white elephant when it is necessary or desirable to sell. To be salable, the best plans appeal to a broad range of prospective buyers.

■ DEFINING THE OWNER'S SITUATION

If you are planning a starter home, your budget will dictate most of your decisions. The house will be relatively small, either one or two stories, with a living space of from 900 to 1,200 square feet. It will have a living or family room with one conversational grouping, a dining room seating six to eight, a kitchen, a bath or bath and a half, two bedrooms for single beds and a good-sized master bedroom. All rooms and closets will be small and storage limited. Your main emphasis is to obtain efficient use of this space, and style usually is not a major consideration, even for resale.

If you are thinking of a medium-sized house, living space will comprise 1,300 to 2,200 square feet. This house will have three to four bedrooms that are larger than in the small house, a larger living room, a dining room seating from eight to ten, a family room or den, a larger kitchen, and two to two and a half baths. For this size of home, the budget is not as tight, and you may choose to include such luxury features as built-ins, crown moldings and chair rails. The house can be one, two or more stories, with its size proportional to the size of your family. If this house is not to be your ultimate home, the design should take into account the potential for its future sale. For example, a permanently installed swimming pool is expensive, and in many cases buyers will not want to pay an asking price that includes the cost of the pool.

Planning for the more spacious house—from 2,500 to 4,000 square feet or more—is even less tied to tight budget requirements. It includes more generous-sized rooms and often specialized spaces such as a recreation room, a library, a sewing room, a workshop and an exercise room. In addition, houses of this size often include such luxury features as a his-and-hers master bath, a whirlpool or hot tub, lots of built-ins, more expensive finishes such as marble and more elaborate heating and air-conditioning systems.

Finally, if this is your dream home, you are most concerned about getting just what you want in nearly every reasonable respect. Cost, although always important, is usually secondary. This house size will be dictated by your wishes, and it may not necessarily be large. The main concerns in this highly customized house are to satisfy you and your dreams. For example, some traditional-inspired owners may go to great lengths to achieve the utmost authenticity in historic design, or art collectors may incorporate a display of artwork collected over the years.

■ HOW TO USE THIS BOOK

The fundamentals of house design are contained in Chapters 1 through 24. The appendixes contain in-depth, additional design details on such matters as doors and windows, electrical systems, insulation, heating, air-conditioning and so forth.

It is suggested that you read the entire book to get a feeling as to the information it contains. Then reread the book at a slower pace and focus on points that are important for *your* house design. It also will be helpful to make an appropriate checklist of those special points to compare with your finished plan.

PART ONE

The Site

Finding the Lot

■ LOCATION

In planning a home, the first important consideration is location. Location affects property value, especially resale. *Usually it is wisest to pick the best location which you can afford.* A good location will appreciate over the years. Your real estate agent and banker can offer advice in this respect.

Factors to check when buying a lot are numerous but thorough study at this stage is well worth the effort to avoid surprise or disappointment later. The remainder of this chapter will help you determine *how* to identify your best location.

Affordable Lots

At an early stage you should determine how much you can afford to invest in building. Usually a lot is only a fraction of the cost of the finished overall home investment in a range between one-tenth and one-third. The financial ability of most people in their earning years continues to improve and should be taken into consideration. Many people are in a position to buy a lot several years before taking the bigger step of building. Later, should you find the lot unsuitable before building, it could be a good down payment on a better one.

Quality of the Subdivision or Neighborhood

What is the reputation of the area? Has it been around long enough to earn a rating? Is it stable or on an upswing? How much investment has the developer made in streets, recreational facilities and other amenities?

Subdivision Character

Is the area attractive? Does it have interesting topography and nice landscaping? Are the homes already built there attractive? Are lots a good size? Is a reasonable degree of privacy possible? Do lots have good views that can be enjoyed through the windows of your planned house?

Streets and Traffic

Are streets nicely laid out, safe and convenient to outer roadways? Will traffic in the neighborhood vicinity be relatively light and not noisy? Are any of the residential streets major traffic ways?

Nearby Amenities

Are good schools nearby? Are shopping centers, places of worship, parks and recreational facilities in the vicinity? Can children walk or bicycle to these areas? Is there a neighborhood association with ownership and control of a clubhouse, swimming pools or tennis courts? Are use fees in your range?

Utilities

Are utilities—electric power, gas, water, sewer, storm sewer, cable and TV—in place. Find out which are public and which are private. Are wire systems underground, since this makes a subdivision more attractive than overhead wires? If you should need a septic system, will the soil in your lot satisfactorily absorb the sewage waste? Check with the local health department.

Public Services

Inquire about fire and police protection, garbage and trash pickup and recycling. Where do school buses run?

Neighborhood Mix

Is the neighborhood's age mix balanced or does one age group predominate? For neighborhood stability, an age mix is often desired. For an interim home, the age mix may not be as important, and predominately younger families may be preferred from the standpoint of common interests. For a long-term home, however, a healthy mix of age groups is preferable. Neighborhoods with ownership primarily in one age group tend to deteriorate more rapidly. When looking at older urban areas, keep this in mind.

Objectionable Conditions

Are there noise problems such as a nearby airport, trains or interstate highways? Is the area downwind from a smelly industrial area?

Surrounding Areas

If vacant land is nearby, how is it zoned? If it is zoned industrial or commercial, this could create possible future problems. Other nearby residential subdivisions offer protection.

Lot for All Seasons

If you have ample time to search for a lot, look at the subdivision in all four seasons. In the winter, when trees are bare, you see everything. Do you like what you see? In the summer, the subdivision usually is at its best; this usually is a good time to judge the degree of privacy that lots afford. This also is the time when neighborhood activity is highest, with children playing, lawns being mowed, dogs and cats romping and barbecues in action.

Corner Lots

Sometimes corner lots are preferred, since they usually are larger. The intersecting street, however, may carry busy traffic and noise, and you may find it more difficult to position your driveway for safe and convenient access or exit, and lights from turning cars may be a distraction. A corner lot may be less flexible regarding orientation of the house and may offer less privacy.

■ DEVELOPER POLICIES

Does the developer permit or make it easy for you to plan or arrange to build your new home? Can you buy a lot outright or must you buy a finished house and lot package? Some developers require that you use their builder rather than one you might choose. Are there restrictions or requirements as to house style?

Landscaping Standards

Are you a garden-and-yard person? Will you be able to clear enough trees (assuming a wooded lot) for good sunshine? Alternatively, if you like the naturalized look such as wildflowers and mulch with low maintenance, is it permitted? Ask the developer. You also may be concerned about privacy. Are fences permitted, and if so, are there height and style restrictions?

Restrictive Covenants

Many subdivisions contain restrictive covenants that apply to lots within the subdivision. These are privately stipulated by the developer, become a part of the deed and may affect such matters as the following:

- Location of the house on the lot
- Minimum house size
- Style of the house
- Garage requirements—for example, doors may not be allowed to face the street
- Exterior finish materials for the house, such as roofing, siding and color

- Prohibitions on storing boats and recreational vehicles on the lot unless garaged
- Type of driveway, including paving material
- Sizes and types of fences
- Operating a business from your house
- Offering rooms for rent
- Cutting down trees
- Preservation of scenic easements

You may be required to obtain approval of your proposed plans and specifications from the developer before beginning construction.

■ FINANCIAL CONSIDERATIONS

Lenders

Does the developer offer or arrange for financing and is he or she held in high regard by private lenders? A bank or savings and loan might be able to give you a better rate and with fewer strings attached.

Taxes

Learn in advance what your real estate taxes will be. Find out how property is assessed, tax rates and when bills are paid. Information is available through the local jurisdiction.

Lot Prices

Cost figures vary widely from area to area, but within any one area there will be a range of prices. Lot prices are based on the developer's costs and profit, and competition with other developers. If lot prices seem unusually low, be alert; there must be a reason. Perhaps the developer is in financial difficulty, or a major highway construction or shopping center is planned nearby that may adversely affect the subdivision.

On occasion, a difficult hilly lot may be found in a good subdivision at a lower price. With ingenuity, you may be able to take advantage of the bargain by adapting a house plan to fit that lot, but recognize that the hilly lot may require added cost to build, or it may limit your choice of design and layout.

■ PROPERTY OWNERS' ASSOCIATIONS

Associations are typical where certain property, such as a lake, tennis courts and recreational facilities, is held in common. Regular maintenance on these facilities is performed by the association, as well as on other common property, such as streets and walks when they are not public property. Usually the lot purchaser is required to become a member, pay an initial fee and continue to pay annual assessments. In a planned unit development where security personnel are employed and the maintenance of common property is included, the annual assessment pays for these services as well. The property owners' association probably will be controlled by the developer until a certain percentage of the lots is sold, usually over 50 percent (one lot equals one vote). If the developer has agreed to furnish certain amenities, find out if he or she has fulfilled the commitment.

■ YOUR PRIORITIES

As you become more familiar with lot hunting, it will be helpful to set priorities of importance to you. A systematic written list will be useful and should include both the subdivision and the lot. Many judgments will have to be made and this list will help you get the best results.

Zoning Ordinances, Easements and Building Codes

In addition to restrictive covenants imposed by the developer, many governing jurisdictions (city or county) impose regulations that apply to lots within a subdivision and various zoning districts. Such regulations affect how you may use your property. Check with your developer or the city or county offices and obtain a copy of regulations affecting your property.

■ ZONING ORDINANCES

These generally regulate the use of the property (such as for single-family houses), permitted accessory buildings (garage, storage shed, swimming pool and so on), yard requirements and building heights.

Included within zoning ordinances are subdivision ordinances that govern requirements imposed on the developer, and hence indirectly on the property owner. Examples are requirements pertaining to streets, public utilities, storm drainage and sidewalks. Zoning ordinances also may specify the minimum number of off-street parking spaces required.

Setbacks

Most zoning ordinances stipulate the minimum setback from the front property line; minimum side yards, that is, distance from the side property lines to the building or buildings; and minimum rear yard. Although you own the entire lot, you are restricted as to where you may place your house and accessory buildings. Typical setback lines are shown in Figure 2.1.

FIGURE 2.1 ■ Setback Lines

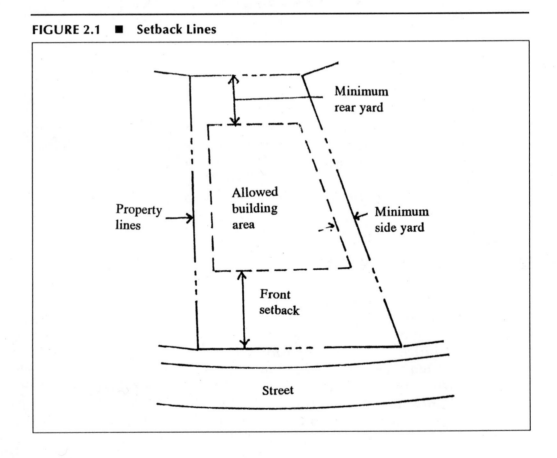

■ EASEMENTS

Easements are reserved areas on the property giving the government or other regulated authority certain rights for specific purposes. For example, power and gas companies may have easements for their lines and pipes, or a drainage easement may require unimpeded flow of the surface storm drainage. These easements are often ten feet wide and may also extend along neighboring lots. Examples are shown in Figure 2.2. Scenic easements usually include restrictions on changing the landscape on part of your lot as seen from other areas, such as regulations on cutting down trees or limiting the placement of the house.

Most easement holders or authorities have the right of access not only to install but to repair and maintain whatever their easement calls for. Generally the property owner is prohibited from building on an easement except for a driveway, walks, landscaping and fences. Retaining walls may not be allowed if they change drainage patterns.

Driveway paving across an easement could be a problem. Assume that you build a concrete driveway to the street that crosses an easement along the front of your property. If it has to be broken up to repair a damaged water line under it, you may be left with the responsibility of restoring the driveway unless the easement specifically requires the water company to do so. Easements are legally part of the property and transfer with it upon sale of the property. Normally they do not have much impact on resale value. Rarely are easements legally eliminated, unless the authority holder is agreeable to abandonment, which is unlikely.

■ BUILDING CODES

Building codes are a separate body of regulations that govern minimum requirements for construction of buildings and associated features. Some building code provisions affect the use of the property such as fence heights; and features affecting safety, such as railings on steps, porches or decks, or design of swimming pools and protection around them to prevent a toddler from accidently falling in. In locations of high fire threat, some codes prohibit use of wood shingles or shakes for roofing, unless treated to become fire-retardant. Some codes or ordinances also require minimum distances between septic systems and buildings or wells.

FIGURE 2.2 ■ Easements

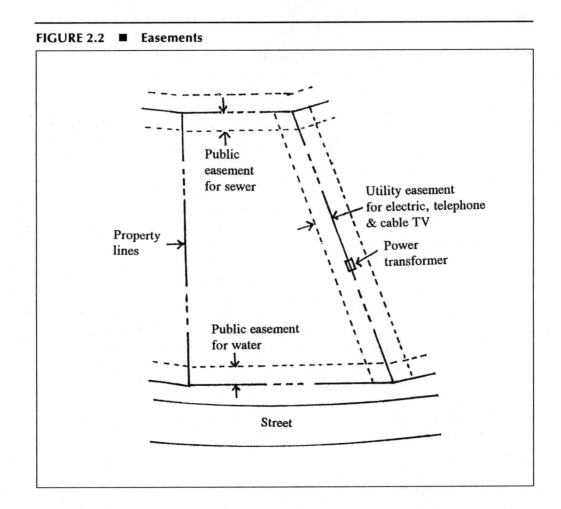

Building codes also regulate certain minimum requirements. For example, one room in the house used for general living purposes must have at least 150 square feet of floor space; other habitable rooms, such as bedrooms, must be at least 70 square feet. Habitable rooms also must have a ceiling height of not less than seven feet, six inches for 50 percent of the required minimum floor area. One entrance door must be at least three feet wide. Usually, it is not difficult to meet these requirements.

Other building code regulations may govern types of materials used, such as safety glass at potentially hazardous locations and the use of fire-safe types of insulation. If the garage is attached to the house, the adjoining walls and ceilings of the garage usually must be covered to protect against the spread of fire. Smoke detection generally is required in or near sleeping areas. In addition, sleeping rooms often must have one window to meet requirements for emergency egress of occupants

In most government jurisdictions, a building permit is required before construction is started. When application for the permit is made, the local building department requires that a set of plans be submitted. At this time, the plans will be reviewed for conformance to the building code. Your familiarity with the code will speed approval and help to avoid unexpected surprises.

Applying the House to the Lot

■ MATCH THE LOT AND THE HOUSE

It is very important that the house plan fits the lot properly. If you have your heart set on a particular style of house, select a lot that will permit an attractive placement of that house on it, based on the following considerations.

■ HOUSE ORIENTATION

Orientation is the position and direction of the house on the site. For example, the size or shape of the lot may dictate the location of the house, especially considering the required setbacks and restrictions imposed by topography. Usually one orientation and location will be obvious, especially on a small lot.

For small lots, houses commonly are located parallel to the street. Larger lots may offer further possibilities, such as a deeper building location or better placement to the lay of the land. If you have a lot with a scenic view of a lake, river, mountain, golf course or the like, the house design, particularly the orientation of windows and rooms, should capitalize on this asset.

If you have a choice of lots that share many of the same characteristics, such as topography, landscape and lot size, the two planning factors of most immediate interest are privacy and close-by views. For privacy, you should have the fewest windows, especially picture windows, facing a neighboring house. If neighboring lots are unbuilt, assume that a house will be built there eventually. Unless you buy the neighboring lot, you cannot control what is done to it.

Decide where you want living areas and the bedroom or private areas to be. Until you actually start a floor plan, these locations may not be obvious. Most people tend to prefer living areas on the front and bedrooms on the back, where privacy is better. Examples of house orientations are shown in Figure 3.1.

FIGURE 3.1 ■ House Orientation

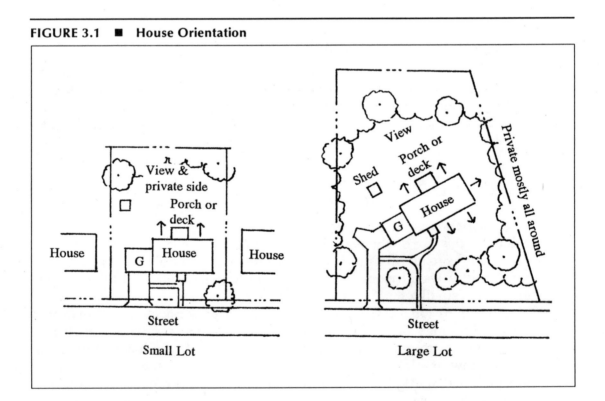

Larger lots usually offer more flexibility. A house placed deeper on a lot makes the front more private than if close to the street, and even bedroom privacy may be easily achieved if located on the front or side. This offers the opportunity of placing the kitchen, breakfast area and family room to the back where a nice indoor-outdoor relationship can be established with outdoor privacy.

If you already have a lot, check how the proposed floor plan fits and is suited to the lot.

To accomplish this check, take a copy of your plat (it shows property boundaries) and draw the zoning setbacks (front, sides and rear) and any limits prescribed by restrictive covenants and easements. The house must fit into this area.

Based on the proposed floor plan, draw the house outline or footprint on a piece of tracing paper (to the same scale as the plat) and slide it over the plat. If the house plan fits, you can go ahead with your project. If it doesn't, see if minor modifications can be made to your plan to fit the lot. Try to keep any floor plan reduction to not more than 5 percent. If this doesn't work, your best alternative is to select another house plan, or you may want to consider a different lot.

If you intend to buy stock plans, most catalogs show basic plan dimensions, so go through this exercise before buying house plans that you may not be able to use.

If you do not have a lot, select your house plan on a preliminary basis and then follow the previous exercise as you begin to look for lots.

■ TOPOGRAPHY

If the lot is flat or nearly so, you will be relieved of some anxieties. If it is not flat and topography is a problem (vertical differences of several feet or more along the building length), you will have to investigate further. Just walking around the lot can be deceiving. Slopes may be significant enough to adversely affect the size and shape of a floor plan, especially for a spread-out one-story house. Slopes also may limit or determine the driveway approach from the street, and the location of the garage or carport.

Topography generally is not shown on the plat, but your planning is more accurate and easier to deal with if you have a topographic map showing the slopes and major trees. A topographic map is almost essential to assist in good siting and to plan for drainage around the house. Ask the developer or lot seller for a topographic map or consider hiring a surveyor yourself to produce one. A surveyor's fee is usually much less than the added expense to correct difficult house drainage later. For an example of a topographic map, see Figure 3.2.

FIGURE 3.2 ■ Topographic Map

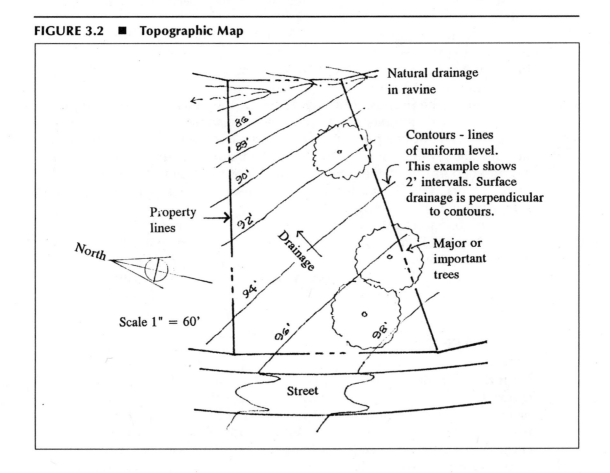

Drainage will be apparent from the topographic map. The main problem is control of the surface water. It is undesirable to have surface water flow toward or collect on any side of the house, regardless of whether it has a basement.

Lot shape also may be critical if it is not a simple rectangle. For example, a pie-shaped lot that is narrow at the street entrance may require positioning the house farther back than the minimum front setback. One of the most difficult lots to deal with is one that slopes both sideways and front to back. Here your creativity will be tested and you probably should consult an architect or landscape architect to provide recommendations for siting and necessary remedies.

Hillside Location

On a hillside lot, it is better to orient the long direction of the house parallel to the level of the ground line and have the narrow direction go up or down the slope, as shown in Figure 3.3a.

FIGURE 3.3 ■ Hillside Location

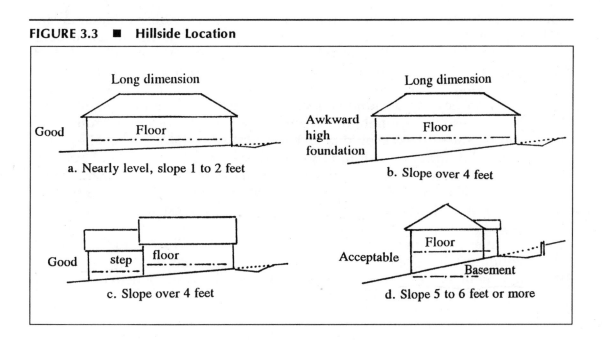

a. Nearly level, slope 1 to 2 feet

b. Slope over 4 feet

c. Slope over 4 feet

d. Slope 5 to 6 feet or more

A hillside lot is usually unsuitable for a large, spread-out single-level house if ground drop-off within the plan of the house is three or four feet or more. High foundation walls will result at the lower side of the slope.

Such foundations are not only more expensive but awkward in appearance. (Figure 3.3b).

If the building slope area down the narrow direction is four feet or more, a lower floor at the lower grade may be a solution, as shown in Figure 3.3c. For slopes of five or six feet or more, adding a basement may solve the problem (Figure 3.3d). Generally, such a lower level or basement can be built at minimum added cost, since comparable foundation walls will have to be built anyway. Another solution is to place the garage in the basement, which, although not as convenient, may be the most economical use of space. In this case, fumes from cars will have to be vented away from the rooms above.

■ SOLAR ENERGY

Solar design definitely should be considered in house orientation and lot selection. Where site, size and topography permit, position bedrooms on the easterly side for pleasant morning sunshine, because westerly bedrooms retain heat late in the summer day and are less pleasant. East and west windows are difficult to shade from low sun angles except by evergreen shrubs and deciduous trees, which are effective in the summer yet permit desirable sunlight in the winter. Largest glass areas (windows and sliding glass doors) should be in a southerly direction. The smallest glass areas should face north to minimize heat loss in the winter. Southerly glass areas are pleasant in the winter with desired solar gain, while in the summer they can be shaded by roof overhang, deciduous trees or both, as illustrated Figure 3.4. Deep roof overhang above east and west windows has little value except for rain protection.

Even with insulated glass, some heat will be lost at night through windows and glass doors. Fitting these glass areas with pull draperies having insulating characteristics will reduce this heat loss. Solar energy is discussed in more detail in Appendix G.

FIGURE 3.4 ■ Solar Angles and Shading

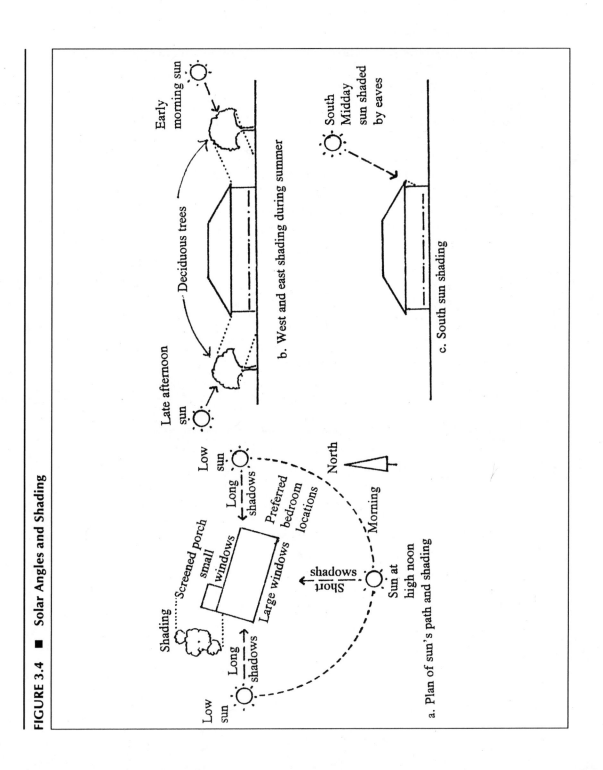

■ ═ **C H A P T E R   4** ═ ■

Basic Construction
at the Site

■ TYPES OF FOUNDATIONS

From the standpoint of method of construction, there are two types of residential foundations in general use: slab on grade and crawl space.

Slab-on-Grade Construction

In this type of construction, the main floor of concrete is placed directly on the ground, as shown in Figure 4.1. A second floor of wood joist construction usually is compatible.

Slab construction requires a relatively flat and well-drained lot. On a sloped lot, extensive fill will substantially increase construction cost by requiring compaction to avoid settlement and the enclosing high foundation walls. Slab construction accepts most types of finish flooring such as tile, resilient sheet material, parquet and carpet, but conventional strip wood flooring usually requires installing wood sleepers first. Perimeter insulation under the slab edges is required in moderate and cold climates, and the area beneath the slab should be treated for termites before the slab is poured. A moisture barrier beneath the slab also is necessary to avoid ground dampness.

FIGURE 4.1 ■ Slab-on-Grade Construction

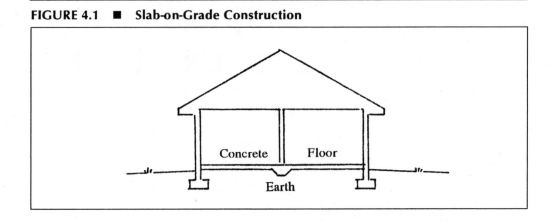

Following are some of the advantages of slab-on-grade construction:

- No special under-slab venting is required.
- Entrances are at or near ground level and thus require no long entrance ramp for disabled persons.

Some disadvantages include the following:

- After the slab is poured, it is difficult to make changes.
- Under-slab repairs are difficult and costly, and additions may be more complicated.
- A concrete slab can be tiring to stand on, and one's feet may feel the cold in climates where crawl space construction would be more comfortable.

Slab construction is not recommended where the water table is high, or in areas where there is a threat of flooding (low coastal areas and in a river flood plane).

Crawl-Space Construction

In typical crawl-space construction, the main floor is supported two or more feet above the ground on a system of joists (narrow beams), plus related girders and supporting piers, as shown in Figure 4.2. This crawl space usually is vented. In making this choice, consider the following advantages:

FIGURE 4.2 ■ Crawl-Space Construction

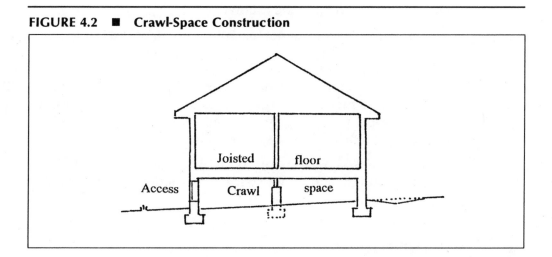

- This is the most popular type of construction because it is more forgiving of topographic irregularities than slab on grade, and it is more flexible.
- The wood-framed floor of a crawl-space construction is more resilient and more comfortable than that of slab-on-grade construction.
- Insulation is easily installed between the floor joists.
- It is easy to run heating ducts, plumbing and electrical cables in the crawl space.
- Dampness from the ground is less of a problem than it is for slab-on-grade construction.
- Repairs and future alterations to the house plan are more easily incorporated.
- Many house designs, particularly many traditional designs, look better if elevated above the ground by a crawl space.

Disadvantages include the following:

- The cost of the foundation usually is greater than it is for the slab-on-grade foundation.
- Five or more entrance steps may be required.
- If a house occupant has mobility impairment, an access ramp will be needed. By modest enlargement of a garage, an access ramp can be built inside, providing an all weather protected entrance and avoiding a difficult or awkward ramp on the outside.

Many house designs use both types of construction: slab-on-grade for basement or garage, and crawl-space construction for the principal living areas.

■ SOIL CONDITIONS

Soil types vary widely. Sandy clay generally is satisfactory to support house foundations. Soil should be firm and drain well. The best time to evaluate drainage is during and after a substantial period of rain. Is there much standing water in depressions or does it dissipate quickly?

Some sites are rocky; successful building requires knowledge of how to deal with these conditions. Inquire locally about soil conditions and how the experts deal with them. If houses are already built in the area, find out if any have foundation or dampness problems. During prolonged drying conditions, heavy clay soil shrinks substantially; if the drying is not uniform, differences in shrinkage can cause foundation cracking. This is more likely to occur when part of the foundation is close to the surface of the ground and other parts are placed much deeper. Some localities have soils that become loosened and slide on hillsides after heavy rains, resulting in catastrophic damage. If soil conditions are questionable, consult a soils engineer or architect for recommended action.

Generally, a good house site is on high ground, ideally draining on all sides. If this is not possible, drainage problems can be solved with appropriate construction and grading to control surface water.

If the lot is wooded, tree stumps and other organic matter should be removed from the construction, since dead, woody material attracts termites.

On some lots, the topsoil is relatively deep and it should be moved aside, then repositioned when construction is complete. On other lots the topsoil is only a few inches thick and during clearance of trees for construction it gets mixed with the underlying clay and is virtually worthless to regrade as landscaping work is done. In this case, it is usually necessary to haul in additional topsoils after the house is completed.

If house design and placement on the lot require excavation of considerable amounts of earth, it is usually more economical and advantageous to reuse the earth to build up certain areas for better drainage rather than to have it hauled away.

Be alert to possible problems when the outside of the foundation walls is backfilled during construction. The greater the fill depth, especially adjacent to a basement, the greater the likelihood of settlement of the fill in the future, which will result in the collection of water. To minimize settlement, the fill should be placed in layers about six inches to one foot thick and packed in the process.

Approaches and Entrances

The driveway, walks and landscaping visible at the house front have visual as well as functional roles. They not only should be attractive, but also should help a visitor find the entrance you prefer to be used.

Where the house is close to the street and visitors park in the street, an attractive, landscaped entrance walk between street and house usually is desirable. If the house is deeply set into the lot, establish a direct view of the entrance as the house is approached. A driveway or obvious walk usually will be adequate. The intended entrance should be nearest the guest parking. Secondary entrances such as a kitchen door can be hidden by a fence or planting if on the front or located where they are not in full view.

■ DRIVEWAYS

Where off-street parking is required, a driveway is necessary. For economy, it should be kept to the minimum length and a width of nine to ten feet. Wider drives may be appropriate if several cars are to be parked. Examples of driveway layouts are featured in Figure 5.1.

On hillside lots, a steep drive and walks will be dangerous during icy conditions, and drainage control may be difficult. On a steep lot, it is

FIGURE 5.1 ■ Representative Driveways

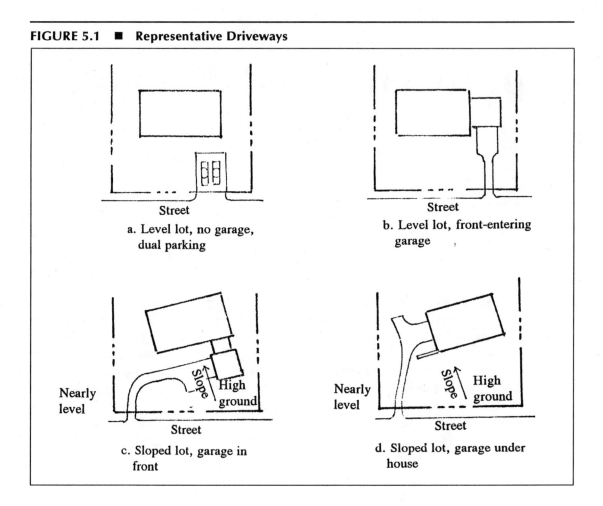

a. Level lot, no garage,
   dual parking

b. Level lot, front-entering
   garage

c. Sloped lot, garage in
   front

d. Sloped lot, garage under
   house

better to run the driveway and walks nearly parallel to, rather than per-
pendicular to the slope, unless for short distances.

If driveway parking is needed, the area should be level enough so that
cars do not accidently roll away, and it should accommodate necessary
drainage. If a short drive goes straight to the garage or carport (front
approach), cars can be backed to the street; therefore, a turnaround usually
is not required but is safer if street traffic is heavy.

Where the garage has a side or rear approach, provide sufficient maneuvering space in the vicinity of the garage doors to allow the car to turn around. Examples of standard driveway approaches are illustrated in Figure 5.2. In backing out of a garage, the front end of the car should clear the door opening before turning, requiring about 25 to 30 feet. This depth can be reduced if wide garage doors are used, or if you don't mind backing and filling to turn. The maneuvering may be T-shaped or boomerang-shaped to provide for additional parking.

Restrictive covenants may require hard-surfaced driveways. Gravel over a prepared gravel base is the least expensive, but also has the highest maintenance due to rutting, washing and weeds. Other driveway materials include concrete (plain or exposed aggregate finish), blacktop or asphalt, brick and patented pavers. Hard-finish materials are more expensive but create very attractive results, which usually are maintenance free and can eliminate weeds. Any driveway paving should be installed over a good drainable base.

Where needed, drainpiping (noncrushable) can be installed under driveways if a nearby undrained pocket is blocked by the driveway and interrupts natural water flow. If a driveway slopes down towards the garage, a drainage swale (shallow trough between the slope and the garage) should be made crossing the driveway several feet away from the garage doors to prevent flow of water into the garage, or install a trough drain to serve the same purpose. Residential trough drains are available with grilles that will support cars. These should be installed at time of construction.

■ WALKS

Walks are a matter of convenience and individual use. Provide a paved walk at least to the main entrance from the driveway, the street, or both. A front walk should be three to four feet wide or wider. Secondary walks to side or back doors may be narrower—two to three feet in width. To be useful during inclement weather, walks should be installed with proper drainage. For safety, walks should not be steeply sloped where icy conditions are common. Paving may be the same material as that used for the driveway, or flagstones may be used where a naturalistic appearance is desired.

FIGURE 5.2 ■ **Typical Driveway Approaches to Garage**

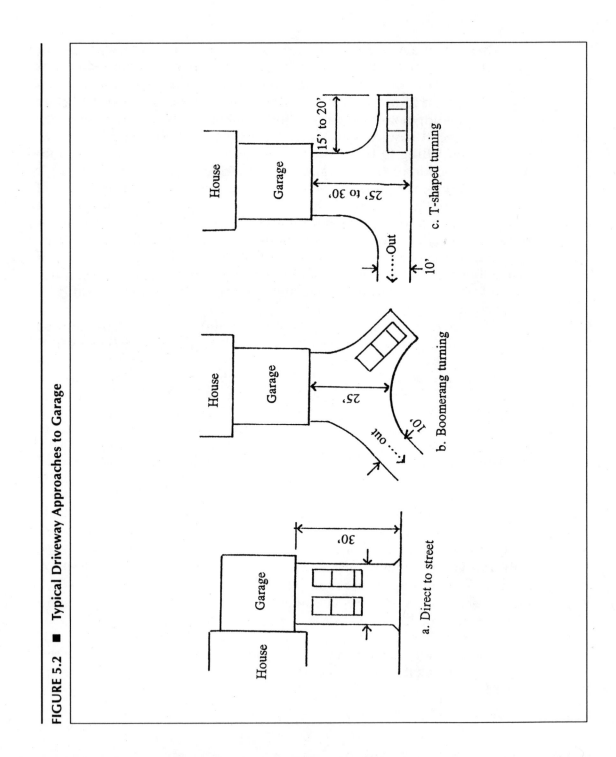

Where the slope is greater than 3 to 12 (3 feet vertical for each 12 feet horizontal), steps are advisable, especially if the walk surface can turn slippery. For safety, install a handrail on one side for long runs of steps. Also install handrails along shaded areas (particularly those paved in brick or stone) that do not readily dry out. Dampness promotes the growth of dangerous, slippery organic matter or moss.

■ PATIOS OR TERRACES

Terraces usually are built immediately adjacent to a house. Where eaves are unguttered, the terrace should be moved outward to avoid the roof drainage. Terrace paving can be similar to that used in walks installed over a properly drainable base. Where terraces are large, their surfaces should be pitched for runoff, and underground drains should be installed where needed.

Terraces usually require steps down from the house floor unless the house is slab on grade. If steps are objectionable, a higher deck or a porch is a fine substitute.

■ DECKS

Planning for decks is more flexible than for terraces, since they require little or no change to fit the topography beneath. Decks are unlike covered porches, since the porch lines must be coordinated with the rest of the house.

To illuminate terraces, decks, walks and sometimes driveways, outside lighting often is necessary or desirable. Plan this in advance and make sure that electrical cables are buried before the paving is installed, or plan routes that do not require crossing the paving later.

■ = CHAPTER 6 = ■

Sanitary Plumbing and Storm Drainage

■ SANITARY PLUMBING

In planning a house, you must give attention to the house sewer and its connection to the public sewer. This may be critical on a hillside location. It is preferable and more economical generally to have gravity flow from the lowest plumbing fixture drain—in a basement, for example—rather than resort to a holding tank and ejector pump. If this is not feasible, however, do not reject the idea of basement plumbing if in other respects the floor plan design is good. It also may be practical to have gravity flow serve all upper floors and an ejector pump for basement plumbing. If an ejector pump is used, it should have a holding tank large enough to hold sewage during times of power failure. Local codes may regulate this situation.

■ SEPTIC SYSTEMS

If a public sewer system is not available, the conventional practice is to install a septic system. It requires a large drain field in an open treeless and relatively flat area having good drainage characteristics, although a moderate hillside is possible where individual drain lines run along contours (lines of equal elevation). For more details, see Appendix H.

The design and capacity of septic systems usually is provided by the local health department. You should predetermine the type and number of fixtures that will generate waste water. Contact the health department early in your planning for assistance in designing the system and placing it on the lot.

■ STORM DRAINAGE

Inadequate attention to surface drainage causes more serious and lasting problems than any other site design factor. Hillside locations require particular attention. For examples of storm drainage, see Figure 6.1.

It is better to build on high land than in a depression. Water should not flow toward or collect along any side of the house. Where a slope occurs toward the building, it is important to divert storm water by creating a swale pitched to lead the water harmlessly away. This may require substantial regrading. The swale should be far enough away from the house to carry roof runoff away from the foundations. The object is to keep water away, no matter where it comes from, rather than have to deal with consequences of standing water and wetness next to or seepage under the house.

If space for the swale is limited, the diversion of water may be aided by a retaining wall.

For difficult-to-drain yard areas or along a walk or driveway, consider installation of a catch basin to an underground drain with the ground around it sloped for water to flow into it. This is a good solution for low-lying areas or depressions, perhaps in front of a carport or a garage door, or in a garden area where too much wetness drowns plant roots. The underground drain runout pipe from a catch basin should lead storm water harmlessly away from the house and may join with runouts from roof downspouts. Outlets should be located where surface flow does not cause such problems as water collection and erosion.

■ ROOF DRAINAGE

At the house itself, the most common way to control rainfall is to install eaves gutters with downspouts carrying the water to splash blocks

FIGURE 6.1 ■ Drainage Around the House

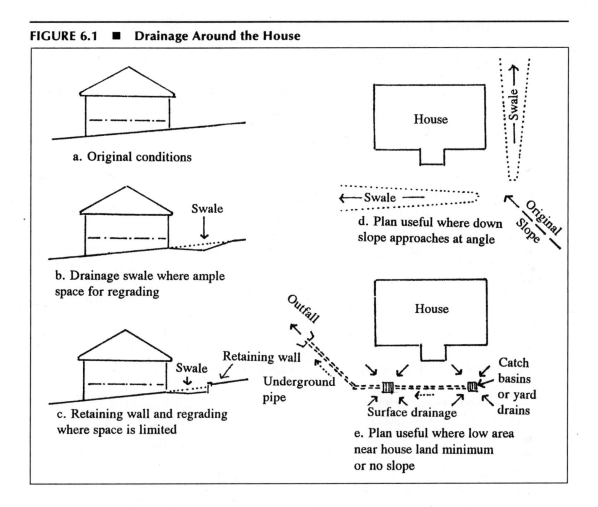

a. Original conditions

b. Drainage swale where ample space for regrading

c. Retaining wall and regrading where space is limited

d. Plan useful where down slope approaches at angle

e. Plan useful where low area near house land minimum or no slope

at the bottom to absorb the impact and carry the water away from the foundation. Such gutters are practical for an unwooded or lightly wooded site if trees are not too close to the building and thus falling leaves are not a problem. For examples of roof drainage systems, see Figure 6.2.

Splash blocks at the base of the downspout usually work fine if erosion is not a problem and the water will continue to disperse and flow away. If erosion is likely, underground drain runouts should be considered, discharging at a point that is harmless to the house, the lot or neighbors' property. Several leaders may be connected to the same underground drain. Some codes now require the ground area where water exits the underground pipe to be rip-rapped to prevent erosion. Cleanouts along the underground pipe should be provided to dislodge an occasional stoppage, especially if the pipe changes direction.

On heavily wooded sites, eaves gutters will require frequent cleaning. Overflowing gutters may cause rot and other damage to the eaves or structure. Install screening or patented gutter guards to reduce this problem. Even then screens will require cleaning, but not as often. Some patented gutter covers are nearly trouble-free.

As an option, gutters on the ground are a good solution to handle roof drainage on heavily wooded lots. These are troughs built along the foundation under the eaves to take the impact of falling water and lead it away from the house (Figure 6.2). Ground gutters can be brick, concrete, other paving materials or a gravel ditch drained by a slotted pipe installed at the bottom of the gravel area. Ground gutters must also be installed so that water does not accumulate near foundations and may require underground runouts described earlier.

With ground gutters, the accumulation of leaves on the gutter is easily cleaned.

■ BASEMENT DRAINAGE AND WATERPROOFING

To be livable or useful for storage, a dry basement is essential. An efficient system consists of the following:

- A waterproof barrier installed on the outside of the foundation walls up to the final grade along the walls.
- A moisture barrier, usually a sheet of polyurethane under the basement floor slab, plus a complete pipe drain system that carries off any water seepage to the outside of the house footings.
- A continuation of the pipe drain system at the bottom of the exterior of the foundation or footings to lead seepage away from the building.

Discuss this subject with your contractor, architect, or both.

■ DRY WELLS

Where natural drainage and runoff is not possible, a dry well can be installed to disperse water from swales, roof drainage and footing drains.

FIGURE 6.2 ■ Gutters

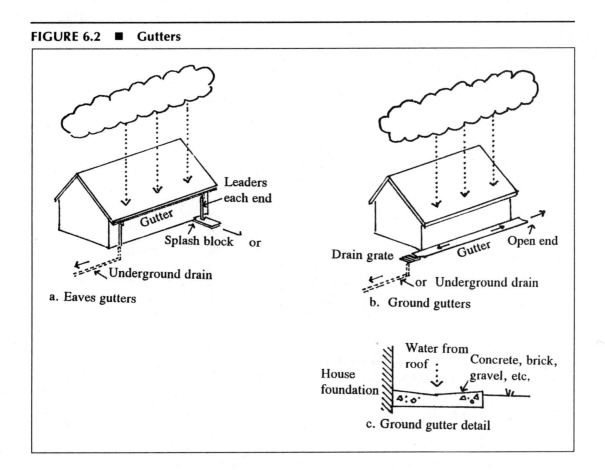

Leaders each end
Gutter
Splash block or
Underground drain

a. Eaves gutters

Drain grate
Gutter
Open end
or Underground drain

b. Ground gutters

Water from roof
Concrete, brick, gravel, etc.
House foundation

c. Ground gutter detail

Dry wells can be used only where the normal water table is below the dry well bottom. The size of the dry well is based on the volume of water drainage to be handled. For storm drainage, the dry well could be quite large.

For an example of a dry well, see Figure 6.3.

■ ACCESSORY BUILDINGS

A garage, carport, storage room or a shed usually have no need for a view or solar design but their location should not block the use of solar

FIGURE 6.3 ■ Dry Well

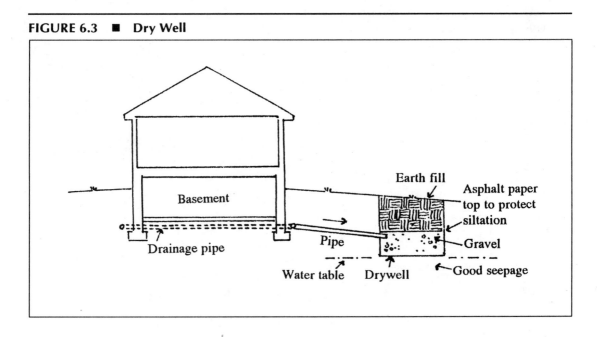

heating or good views from the house. Place them, however, where they will be convenient to use.

■ TREES

When preparing to build on a wooded lot, remove all large trees within 20 feet or so of the house. If tree roots are cut during excavation for footings and foundations, the ability of trees to stand safely in high winds is weakened. As a rule of thumb, the spread of tree roots is about equal to the spread of the branches.

The best time to remove trees is when the lot is being cleared, since post-construction tree removal is difficult and expensive.

Avoid the temptation of retaining too many trees in the vicinity of the house, especially if they are leaning, diseased or otherwise in question. Trees and large shrubs near the house will increase mildew problems due to shading, lack of air circulation and their tendency to hold moisture. Shading, if excessive, also will reduce the daylight inside the house and make the interior dark and unpleasant. Remaining trees will grow rather quickly to fill in the open space left by the felled trees. A driveway over a large part of the roots of a tree may kill the tree.

If a close-by large tree is important enough to be saved, take every precaution to protect it from damage during construction and prevent the ground over the root system from being compacted. Do not place fill over its roots or trunk. Fill will suffocate the root system and eventually kill the tree.

Small Outbuildings, Landscaping and Other Site Features

These features are a part of lot utilization and should relate to house design. For example, a detached garage, garden shed or storage building will look better if its design is in keeping with the style of the house. Placement of such accessory buildings is important and generally should be in a location beside or behind the house. Some zoning ordinances prohibit placing them in front of the house.

Landscape treatment including retained existing trees and shrubs and, in particular, foundation plantings and flower beds will have a significant impact on house appearance. If there is a historic precedent for the type of landscaping suitable for your house, follow it. Examples of landscaping elements include parterres (ornamental gardens in which the flower beds and paths form a geometric pattern), hedges, fences, garden walls, walkways and so forth.

Your lot planning efforts will be more successful if you establish definite goals. Draw a plan to include site features and the screening of objectionable items such as a power transformer and the exterior machinery for the air conditioner or heat pump. The best houses are those that show thought and attention to the site around the house, and reflect your appreciation and pride for the property.

■ FENCES

Fences may be used for privacy and decoration and may be necessary where small children and pets must be restricted. Some building codes or ordinances regulate fence heights and style and material used. Some even forbid their installation so regulations should be checked carefully.

Fences 36 to 42 inches high with narrow spacings are generally satisfactory for fencing pets in or out. Representative fence designs are illustrated in Figure 7.1. Post intervals are usually 8 to 12 feet. The most popular and generally the most attractive fences are made of wood. Wooden fencing materials should be rot-resistant or treated. Rustic fences are left natural; other wood fences are painted or stained. Brick fencing also may complement the house. Iron fences are appropriate for some period house styles. Metal fencing (chain link) is widely used, but sometimes may not be allowed by restrictive covenants.

Fences along property lines generally must be installed on your side of the line and you should check regulations for specific requirements. Be sure you know the exact location of your property line.

Neighbors might object to fences, particularly chain link fences, along property lines. This problem may be solved equitably if discussed before the fence is installed.

■ LANDSCAPING

Shrubbery and trees enhance the look of most houses. While specific plant selections for any geographic area and soil conditions vary widely, evergreen shrubs and shade trees generally are popular for the effects they create. Avoid positioning shrubs too close to the house foundation to avoid damage from ice and snow slides from the roof. Overgrown shrubs and trees often produce problems by shading desirable daylight from windows, or roots may invade foundation walls. Also, the proximity of large shrubs close to house walls cuts down air movement and may contribute to dampness and mildew problems.

Unless you are knowledgeable and experienced about the selection and growing of plants, you should seek advice from a good nursery or landscape designer on suitable plants to select, growing conditions, plant diseases and so on. Remember that nearly all plants require maintenance.

FIGURE 7.1 ■ Typical Fences

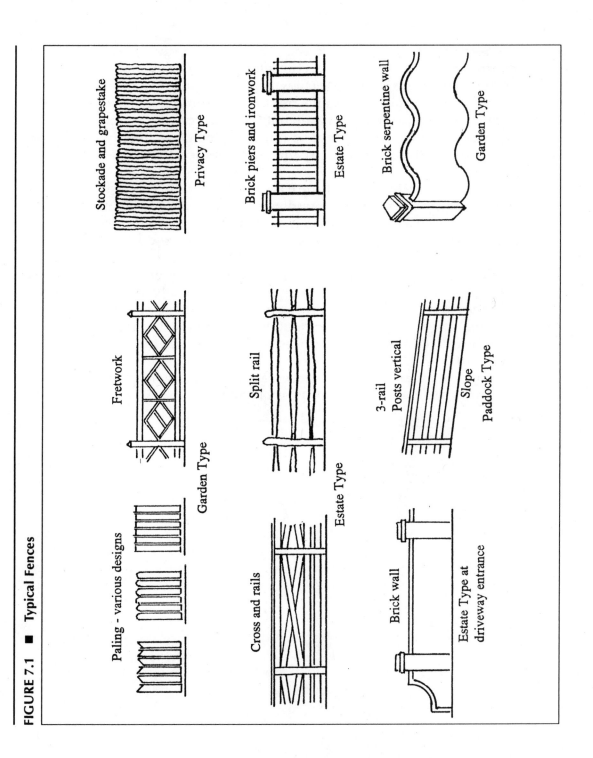

Stockade and grapestake
Privacy Type

Brick piers and ironwork
Estate Type

Brick serpentine wall
Garden Type

Fretwork
Garden Type

Split rail
Estate Type

3-rail
Posts vertical
Slope
Paddock Type

Paling - various designs

Cross and rails

Brick wall
Estate Type at driveway entrance

Some plants make good screens or shields for privacy and may help to control local wind effects. Careful selection and early planting of screen shrubs and trees will increase enjoyment of the property.

Remember that shrubs and trees require growing space. When first planted they may seem too small, but five years or so later they will fill up the space. If trees and shrubs are planted too close together, they may crowd each other or expand against the building they were intended to beautify.

To get some idea of the future appearance of the landscaping of your home, look at other homes around you. Notice scale and position of plants after a few years of growth. There is a tendency in landscaping new houses to overplant so that after a few years of growth the house looks smothered.

In summary, site planning starts with the selection of the lot. Choose one that is attractive and will be least affected by adverse factors such as noise or poor drainage. When you know the type and size of the house to be built, you will have key information for planning. Become familiar with local jurisdictional requirements as well as those controlled by restrictive covenants.

Give site planning its deserved attention to avoid problems and to enhance your goals for the best possible house.

PART TWO

Exterior House Design

Design Features

In building a new home you should consider all of the relevant factors that work together to create a pleasing and efficient house that fulfills your goals. This chapter deals with the exterior of the house, including how its design is influenced by the site and interior design.

The most visible attribute of a house is its style. Style is determined by the basic features of shape and proportion in the roof and the detailed treatment of walls, including siding, windows, doors and chimneys.

■ HOUSE STYLE

There are two basic groups of house styles: traditional and contemporary (or modern). Traditional styles are based on historical models, while contemporary styles are derived from our current times.

Traditional styles vary from almost authentic copies of historic designs to modified adaptations. For example, a southern eighteenth-century colonial may be modified to have modern conventional ceiling heights of eight feet rather than the traditional ten feet or more; a roof with asphalt shingles rather than slate or wood; or common bond brick work rather than Flemish bond.

Some traditional styles are popular everywhere, especially those from English and central European sources; others, such as Spanish Mission and Japanese, are more regional. Our discussion will be limited to widely used styles. Readers can refer to many style books in public libraries for information on other styles.

Contemporary styles basically express functional character, form and shape. These styles may include houses with flat roofs, irregular geometry, shed roof designs, nontraditional proportions and other features made possible by modern technology and artistry.

If authenticity of traditional style is important to you, limit any changes from the essential character of the style, or you may end up with a hodgepodge.

In most situations, house style is a matter of personal choice. Large numbers of new houses are built in the traditional style, yet many contemporary designs are popular for their particular advantages such as informality of floor plan or adaptation of a plan to a particular site. Choice of style also may be influenced by prevailing style in an area or restrictive covenants particular to a subdivision.

Many popular styles are difficult to pin down when architects and home designers create mixed designs incorporating features of several different styles. These so-called trend designs are popularized through magazines and newspapers and by models put up by home builders. While appealing to many people, they may later appear dated as still newer trends emerge; however, trend designs may be favored by those who are looking for the latest ideas while time-tested designs appeal to those with more conservative tastes for purer, known styles. Carefully consider the impact of your choice of style if you plan to sell the house later. Will it weather changes in popularity?

■ HOUSE DESIGNS

A good place to begin looking at house designs is the number of stories and related characteristics.

The One-Story House

The front of most houses is the style-defining side. A one-story house should look as though it is hugging the ground from the front. It looks best on a generally flat lot; however, it can be built on a rearward sloping lot when the slope is gentle. If built on a crawl-space foundation, the front of the house can hug the ground while the foundation wall toward the rear can have additional exposure height. If the slope of the lot is steep, extra space might be realized by building a walk-out basement. For examples of one-story house styles, see Figure 8.1.

FIGURE 8.1 ■ One-Story House Designs

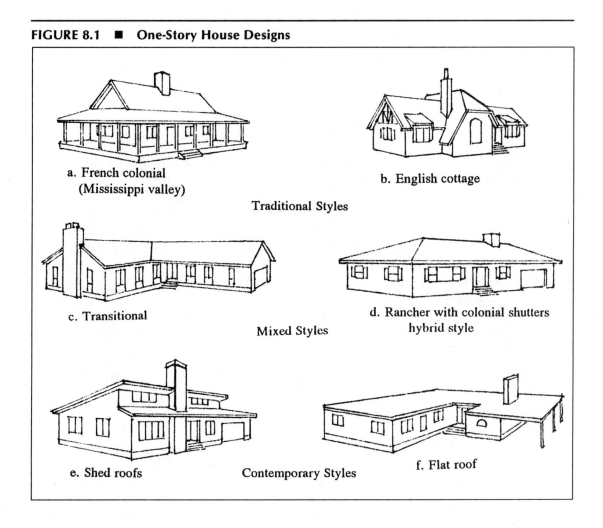

a. French colonial (Mississippi valley)

b. English cottage

Traditional Styles

c. Transitional

d. Rancher with colonial shutters hybrid style

Mixed Styles

e. Shed roofs

Contemporary Styles

f. Flat roof

If cost is the most important factor, remember that the one-story house usually is more expensive to build than a two-story house of the same size due to the larger roof area; some people, however, prefer the advantage of having no stairs to climb. Many one-story houses of either traditional or contemporary style look equally good, regardless of whether they are built on a crawl space or a concrete slab on grade. Consider the following other factors when planning the one-story house:

- No space is necessary for interior stairways to a second floor.
- It is the most advantageous plan for the disabled or the elderly.
- A one-story house needs a larger lot than a two-story house with the same size living space. Also, the slope of the lot may make a large one-story house awkward and less practical.

The Two-Story House

Consider the following when planning a two-story house:

- It generally is less expensive to build than the one-story house of the same floor area, since it has about one-half the roof size. The floor structure of the second floor creates the ceiling for the first floor. For bedrooms, the second floor location provides more privacy.
- The stairway should be readily accessible and, if centrally located, the plan usually is compact. In a large two-story house, a second stairway may be useful.
- The two-story house usually looks better if built on a crawl-space foundation.
- It is adaptable to many traditional and contemporary styles.
- The formality of a traditional two-story house usually makes the plan less flexible than one with a contemporary design.

For examples of traditional two-story house styles, see Figure 8.2

The Story-and-a-Half House

This popular traditional design with a cozy appearance features a steeply pitched roof with a partial story on the second floor.

For daylight, ventilation and view, dormers often are spaced along the roof with windows at the gable ends. Some designs feature a shed dormer on the front or rear, and others have single dormers in front and a shed dormer at the rear.

The usable floor area of the upper story will be about two-thirds of the main floor depending on the roof pitch. Limitation of the upstairs wall height is due to sloped ceilings except where a shed dormer is used.

FIGURE 8.2 ■ **The Two-Story House**

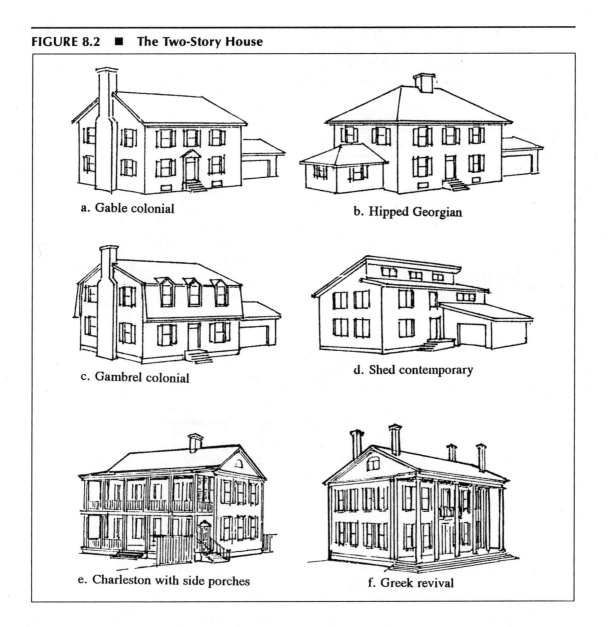

a. Gable colonial

b. Hipped Georgian

c. Gambrel colonial

d. Shed contemporary

e. Charleston with side porches

f. Greek revival

A half-story second floor, as in full two-story plans, can usually be built less expensively than an equivalent one-story house, since the roof area is less.

The contemporary-style house shown in the bottom of Figure 8.3 is a variation of the story-and-a-half plan, using a full-width clerestory dormer to add additional floor space upstairs.

For examples of the story-and-a-half house, see Figure 8.3.

FIGURE 8.3 ■ The Story-and-a-Half House

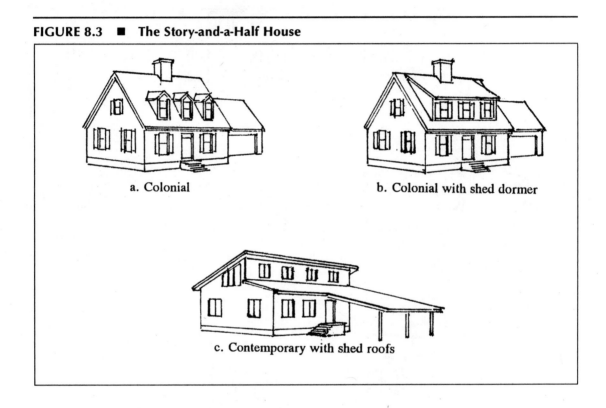

a. Colonial

b. Colonial with shed dormer

c. Contemporary with shed roofs

The Saltbox House

This traditional design shifts the roof ridge line forward (about one-third back from the front), so that the first floor has more space than the second (see Figure 8.4).

The saltbox house design provides most of the economy of the full two-story design. Historically, it is derived from a two-story to which a rear addition was added to the first floor. This cozy-appearing house plan is useful where proportionally more space is needed on the first floor.

FIGURE 8.4 ■ **The Saltbox House**

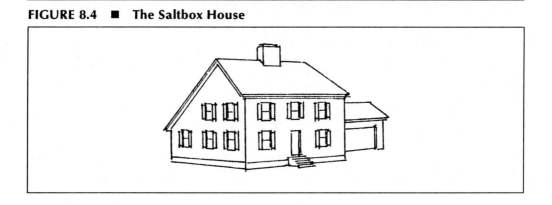

The Garrison Colonial

In this traditional design, the second floor projects about one to two feet at the front or the rear of the house, or both, making the second floor larger than the first. It is a useful design if larger upstairs bedrooms are desired; its cost is only slightly more than if the two stories were the same size.

For an illustration of the Garrison colonial design, see Figure 8.5.

FIGURE 8.5 ■ **The Garrison Colonial House**

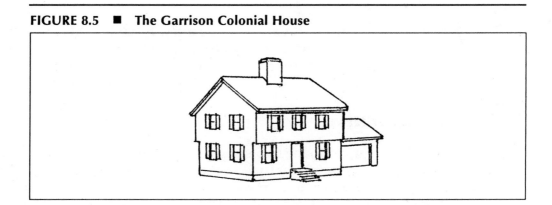

■ DESIGNS TO FIT SLOPING LOTS

The Split-Level House

This design combines features of both one-story and two-story houses with the stories separated by half flights of steps as shown in Figure 8.6. Entrances can be at either the midlevel or the lower level.

FIGURE 8.6 ■ Split-Level House

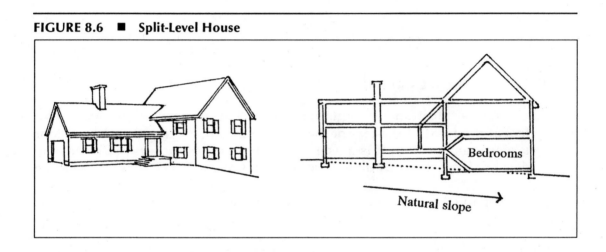

The split-level design is particularly suited for a lot that slopes from side to side. It provides more privacy to the bedroom area than the one-story house does. It is appropriate for some traditional as well as many contemporary houses.

The Split-Foyer House

This style is similar to the two-story house design except that the main entrance is approximately halfway between the two floors. The lower floor usually is partially underground, making this house suitable for building on a lot that slopes to the rear. For an illustration of the split-foyer house, see Figure 8.7.

In the split-foyer design, the lower level generally is used for kitchen and living areas, with bedrooms above. A disadvantage is awkwardness at the entrance of having to go up or down to reach anywhere in the house. This plan type also is appropriate for some traditional and contemporary houses.

FIGURE 8.7 ■ Split-Foyer House

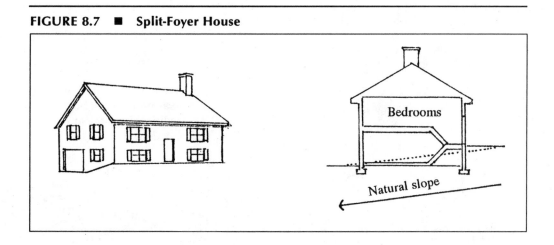

Both the split-level and the split-foyer designs require waterproof walls below ground to some extent, adding to the cost of the construction. Neither design is easily accessible for those with mobility disabilities.

■ ADDITIONAL DESIGN FEATURES AND VARIATIONS

Many types of design features can be used to enhance the house design and lot. These variations, which include glassed-in areas, breezeways, atria, porches and decks, increase house maintenance costs but usually are a decisive plus in enjoyment and resale. For illustrations of these features, see Figure 8.8.

Glassed-in Areas

Frequently the site or yard provides views that call for large glass areas. For privacy, large glass areas should be toward the rear or screened for privacy if on the side or front. On a very large lot, the front may be opened with a screened driveway approach routed to fit the plan. Large glass areas are relatively easy to incorporate into contemporary designs,

FIGURE 8.8 ■ Design Variations

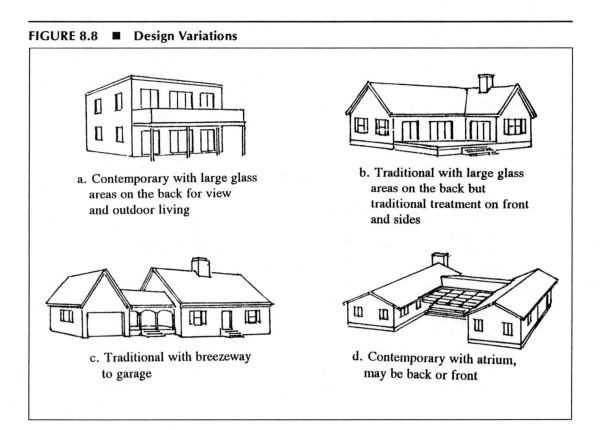

a. Contemporary with large glass
   areas on the back for view
   and outdoor living

b. Traditional with large glass
   areas on the back but
   traditional treatment on front
   and sides

c. Traditional with breezeway
   to garage

d. Contemporary with atrium,
   may be back or front

and many traditional houses also can be modified if large glass areas are
kept at the back of the house.

Breezeways

A breezeway can enhance design and livability. Breezeways can be
used in either traditional or contemporary designs. Illustrated in Figure
8.8 is a traditional house with breezeway to the garage.

Atria

The atrium or courtyard design is most suitable for the contemporary
house. The atrium is private or semi-private and provides a nice
"outdoor" room or garden.

Decks and Porches

These features may be used with contemporary or even traditional designs if judiciously placed or screened. Where climate permits, the added outdoor living space is a worthwhile asset.

Most of these design features add to the basic cost of a house, but can be well worth it. Large glass areas are more expensive than small ones and, in addition, create larger energy losses. However, if solar gain can be captured when wanted in the winter daytime and suitably controlled at nighttime and on dreary days, the overall energy loss may be lessened or neutralized (see the discussion of solar heating in Appendix G).

■ SPECIAL DESIGNS

The House on Stilts

A house on pilings or stilts is suitable where soil or topographic conditions do not permit typical wall foundations. Examples include steep hillsides where the downgrade side is quite high or low, and at the beach where the potential of storm damage and flooding may devastate wall-type foundations.

FIGURE 8.9 ■ Stilt Designs

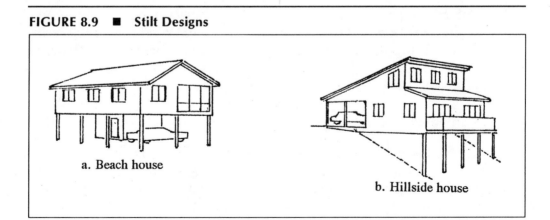

a. Beach house

b. Hillside house

These designs, illustrated in Figure 8.9, are best suited to contemporary-style houses, which may be one or more stories in height. Construction cost is relatively economical in localities where piling construction is common. Advantages include use of a site that otherwise might be unsuitable for a conventional house and where minimum disturbance to the site is desirable or necessary. The elevated living space offers especially good opportunities for views. Frame construction is most practical. Because of special structural requirements, help of an architect or engineer is advised.

The Log House

Traditionally the log cabin holds appeal as a getaway vacation house and sometimes even as a primary home. Some builders feature log construction, and kits are available from manufacturers that a skillful buyer can erect. The cost of a log house varies depending on the house's size as well as the degree of interior finish and how rustic a look is desired. For example, the interior of a log house can be just the logs, but if a plaster look is desired, the installation of the wallboard and the necessary finishing will increase costs.

The A-Frame

The A-frame design provides a unique structure and can be used either as a primary or vacation house. Its shape permits a loft above the main floor of about half the main floor area. While relatively economical to build, the slanted sidewalls reduce the efficient use of floor space. A-frames are available in kits or can be stick-built by a contractor. Examples of this on the log house are illustrated in Figure 8.10.

The Earth-Sheltered House

In this design large areas of the exterior walls or roof are in contact with masses of earth. Two examples of earth-sheltered houses are illustrated in Figure 8.11: the first has earth piled against part of the exterior walls and on the roof; the second has earth piled only partly against the exterior walls.

FIGURE 8.10 ■ Special Designs

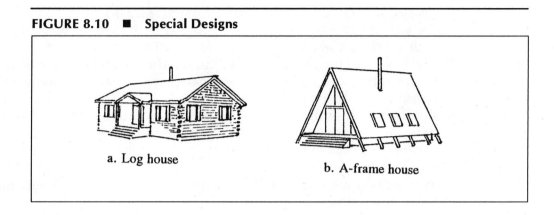

a. Log house

b. A-frame house

FIGURE 8.11 ■ The Earth-Sheltered House

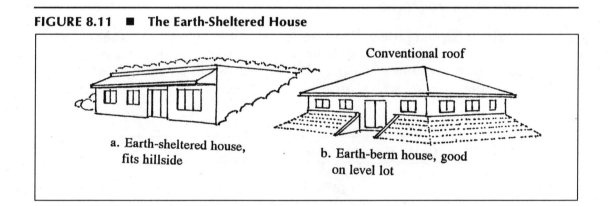

Conventional roof

a. Earth-sheltered house, fits hillside

b. Earth-berm house, good on level lot

Where covered with earth, the structure is built of concrete or masonry material strong enough to hold the weight and to compensate for the horizontal pressure on the walls. The subgrade surfaces of the house must be waterproofed effectively and drainage systems must be installed to take away the seepage water, which adds to the cost. In addition, if waterproofing is not done efficiently, dankness and mildew can be real problems.

The following are among the other features of this type of house:

■ Large areas of the exterior of the house are not exposed to the sun and the weather and, hence, exterior maintenance is greatly reduced.
■ Energy savings are possible, since contact with large earth masses makes the temperature of the subgrade walls and roof more uniform

year-round. Generally, the earth's temperature is lower than that of the outside air in the summer and higher in the winter, resulting in little need for energy to heat and cool the house.

- The design of the earth-sheltered house also is suitable for passive solar heating as the major, if not the sole, supplier of heat where sunshine is dependable.
- Building cost for the earth-sheltered house is almost always higher than for conventional construction. However, the higher initial cost can be paid back in time by the energy saved in heating and cooling.
- Since a large portion of the exterior is underground, less light is available through windows. Some rooms in the rear of the house may have no windows at all, but may have skylights.

The Geodesic Dome House

The intriguing idea of this design is based on using the geometry of the triangle assembled in combination to form a portion of a sphere that provides the exterior enclosure of the structure. For an example of the geodesic dome design, see Figure 8.12.

FIGURE 8.12 ■ The Geodesic Dome House

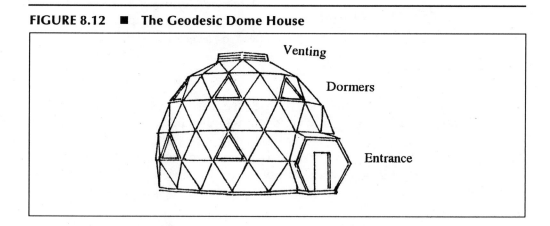

The following are some of the advantages of the geodesic dome house:

- The interior of the structure gives the occupant the feeling of spaciousness not normally found in a conventional house.
- Because of its structural shape, it is often possible to light the entire dome with just a few skylights.
- Because of the dome shape, air inside the house will circulate very efficiently.
- The dome shape provides the least exterior exposure and thus the least potential for reduced heat loss through the house's outer surface. Therefore, domes theoretically are more energy-efficient than conventional houses assuming, of course, proper sealing and adequate skin insulation, and a heating and air-conditioning system suited for the local climate.

Following are some of the disadvantages of the geodesic dome house:

- In the half- and three-eighths–sphere domes, the vertical and horizontal curvatures of the exterior walls may present a problem for the location of cabinets and furniture close to the exterior wall. This problem is less severe with the five-eighths–sphere dome.
- Windows and doors usually are custom-made to accommodate the triangular design and may be expensive; or are installed in dormers.
- Changes in temperature affect the sphere by expansion and contraction, which can cause creaking of the structure. Also, panel joints must be well designed and well installed to avoid leakage.

The decision to use this or any other nonconventional design should be carefully considered on the basis of practicality as well as your individual preference. Keep in mind that uniqueness often carries the burden of higher construction and maintenance costs, since construction techniques may not be well-proven and components may have to be modified from standard types available. Also, resale could be difficult.

■ = C H A P T E R 9 = ■

Exterior Details and Finishes

As we get into the discussion of specific features, let's review some basic practices in conventional construction.

■ EXTERIOR WALLS

Note that with slab-on-grade construction, the foundation appears very low; this effect is particularly true if the siding above the foundation is wood, shingles, plywood, aluminum or vinyl, and the foundation is brick or stone. On the other hand, if the upper wall continues with the same material as the foundation wall, the low visibility effect disappears.

The center drawing in Figure 9.1 illustrates a one-story house with standard eight-foot ceilings built over crawl space, producing a different effect, since the foundation wall is higher. This higher foundation wall is emphasized if the siding above is wood, plywood, shingles, aluminum or vinyl.

The right drawing in Figure 9.1 is a similar one-story design, but with nine-foot ceilings. Note the higher wall above the doors and windows if standard top-of-window height is used.

These differences at first may seem subtle, but they actually have a great deal to do with the appearance and style especially in traditional style houses. Drive past a number of houses and evaluate for yourself.

FIGURE 9.1 ■ Foundations

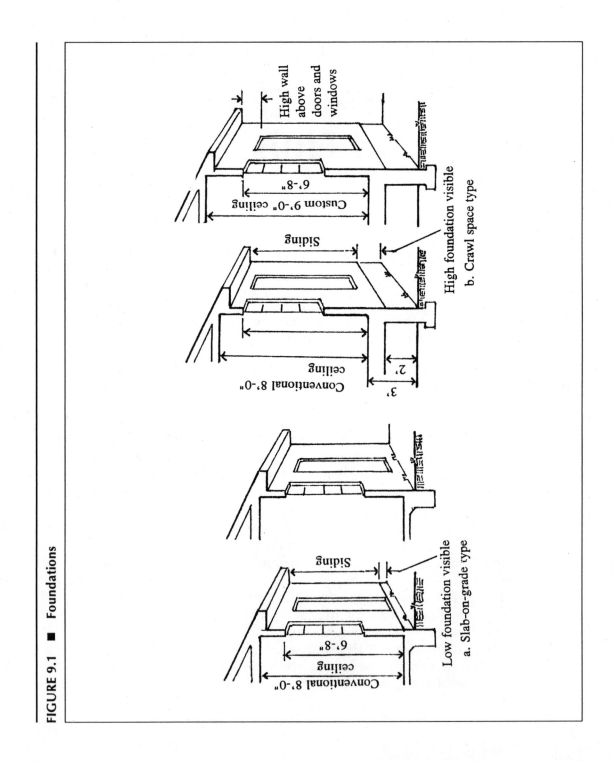

■ EAVE LINES

In most historical traditional one-and-a-half story designs, the top of the roof eaves is approximately level with the top of the flooring of the second floor, as shown at the left of Figure 9.2. With the eaves at this height, the overhang can be a maximum of 12 to 15 inches to avoid a "crunched-down" look over the windows.

FIGURE 9.2 ■ Roof Lines

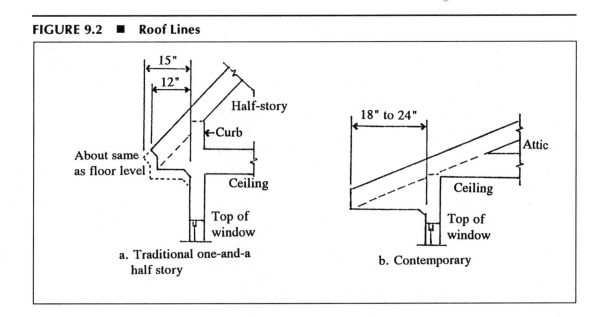

Contemporary house designs permit a greater variation in roof line height and eaves overhang to as much as several feet to provide greater protection of the windows, as illustrated at the right of Figure 9.2. However, note that the closer the window top is to the roof overhang, the more that daylight is shaded from the interior. For a house in a wooded location, this is a disadvantage.

Roof lines and roof shapes will be addressed in more detail later in this book.

■ EXTERIOR FINISHES

Brick

Brick is suitable for traditional and contemporary houses. It makes a very attractive exterior. It has a very long life and rarely requires maintenance. It is, however, more expensive than wood, stucco, vinyl, steel or aluminum. The pattern of brick work is identified by the bond, illustrated in Figure 9.3. In common bond, all bricks are laid with the long side showing; in Flemish bond, every other brick is laid with the short end showing; and in English bond, alternating courses of all long sides and all short ends are laid. The latter two patterns historically were devised to connect the outer and inner brick work when houses were built with solid masonry walls. Today, however, modern house construction uses a wood or steel frame with the brick used only as a veneer. In this construction, the Flemish and English bond appearance is obtained by using half bricks for the short ends. Flemish and English bonds are more expensive than common bond due to extra labor.

The standard masonry cement for brick is gray, but various premixed mortar colors are available to enhance certain brick colors. Check with the brick supplier to see what is best for your brick. When you choose brick, do so from actual samples, since color photographs usually are unreliable.

Although brick does not require painting, any exterior wood trim will. Trim is relatively more expensive to paint, because it takes more careful labor to do the finer work. Prefinished or preclad trim can be used in many instances to lessen maintenance work.

Stone

Stone has the durability and low maintenance advantages of brick. Stonework generally is more expensive than brick; however, this may not be true if a lot of stonework is done in your vicinity. Stone is appropriate for many traditional and contemporary house styles.

FIGURE 9.3 ■ Popular Brick and Stone Veneer Patterns

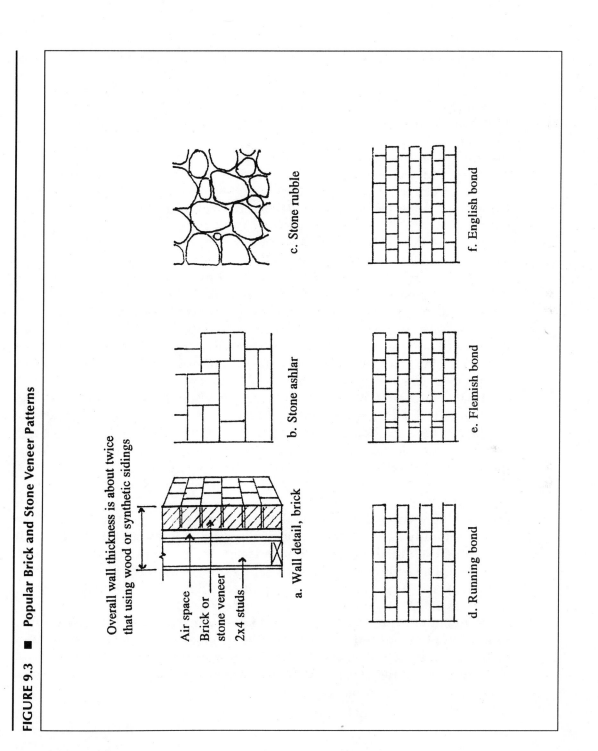

Overall wall thickness is about twice that using wood or synthetic sidings

Air space
Brick or stone veneer
2x4 studs

a. Wall detail, brick

b. Stone ashlar

c. Stone rubble

d. Running bond

e. Flemish bond

f. English bond

Stucco

Stucco is an excellent exterior finish with long life and requires very little maintenance. It is a form of cement plaster and has most of the characteristics of that material with several choices of factory-made colors. If a different color is desired, stucco can be painted with a product recommended for application over masonry. The surface finish can be smooth or textured. Stucco often is used for a traditional English or European half-timber effect with wood battens suggesting solid timbers. It also is suitable for other traditional as well as contemporary house styles.

Wood

Wood siding may be installed in several forms, as illustrated in Figure 9.4. Note the patterns that are appropriate to traditional-style houses. Most are also appropriate for many contemporary house styles.

The best type of woods to use are redwood, fir, cypress, pine, cedar, spruce or hemlock because of their durability and resistance to moisture problems. Paint finishes are the most popular. Shingle siding creates a nice rustic effect. Hardboard siding imitates wood and plywood patterns.

Board and batten siding consists of wide (8- to 12-inch) boards installed vertically with a two- to three-inch-wide board nailed over the seams between the boards. This pattern is popular in traditional designs where a barn-like character is desired, and also is used in contemporary designs. Paint and stain are popular finishes, but stains may have a shorter life.

Plywood   Plywood siding is available in many varieties of wood and patterns, generally applied vertically and usually at less cost than individual boards for both material and labor. Surfaces are available rough or sanded. Most wood and plywood can be either painted or stained. Siding and trim of traditional houses usually are painted. Several plywood patterns, known as T1-11, are available and are widely used.

Plywood with reverse board and batten consists of the standard four-foot-wide plywood with two-inch-wide grooves cut vertically about 8 to 12 inches apart to resemble a reverse board-and-batten pattern.

Plywood sidings are most widely used in contemporary house styles and usually are inappropriate in traditional styles.

FIGURE 9.4 ■ Wood and Plywood Siding Application

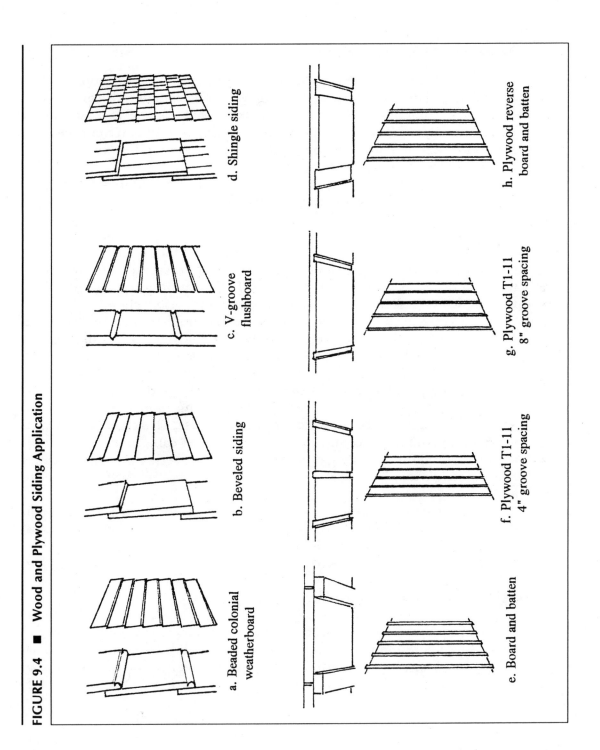

a. Beaded colonial weatherboard

b. Beveled siding

c. V-groove flushboard

d. Shingle siding

e. Board and batten

f. Plywood T1-11 4" groove spacing

g. Plywood T1-11 8" groove spacing

h. Plywood reverse board and batten

Vinyl, Steel and Aluminum

These types of siding are available in different patterns and textures for both vertical and horizontal installation. These materials can be used alone or in combination to cover most exterior surfaces. Their advantage with long-lasting factory finishes is to reduce painting and maintenance. Various imitative patterns are available for traditional designs and some are suitable for contemporary styles.

Aluminum and steel are available in a variety of colors from tints to deep rich tones. Most manufacturers offer guarantees of 20 or more years, although fading can occur in less time.

Disadvantages of aluminum are that it will easily dent if struck by a hard object such as a baseball or lawn mower, and the surface color can be scratched, exposing the bare aluminum. When scratched enough to remove the paint, steel siding will rust. Both aluminum and steel siding may rattle or creak in high winds or abrupt temperature changes.

With vinyl siding, the standard color selection is limited to white and tints. The color appears throughout the entire thickness of the material so that a scratch will do little harm. Vinyl will not dent, but it becomes brittle in very cold weather and some pieces may shatter if struck. It also is subject to cupping (concave distortion) if economy grades are used.

Vinyl is not readily adaptable for covering exposed wood trim, whereas aluminum is better suited for this purpose. Therefore, if you want vinyl siding and the coverage of all exterior wood trim, consider a combination of vinyl for the siding and aluminum for covering the wood trim, if color match is available. Or, if you prefer aluminum, use it for the entire job.

For the earnest traditionalist, synthetic siding and trim seldom match the nice profiles of real wood, especially moldings at the eaves and ornamental trim at windows and doors.

■ OTHER POPULAR SIDINGS

Among manufactured products are prefinished and textured simulated stucco board in plywood-size sheets. When used with wood battens, a traditional half-timber English or European look is created. Battens also may be prefinished to avoid meticulous painting or staining after installation.

Another system producing a stucco-like appearance uses acrylic plaster applied over foam board insulation, which in turn is installed over framing. Its great advantage is a super-insulated wall, but a disadvantage is vulnerability to impact from a thrown baseball or ladder carelessly leaned against the wall. To the eye, this system is virtually indistinguishable from traditional cement stucco.

Several manufacturers make "thin brick," which can be cemented to weatherproof plywood or mineral board sheathing. This treatment is not recommended where exterior exposure is severe, such as around a prefabricated chimney. It may, however, be used where it has good protection for durability, such as under a porch roof. Its advantage is a light weight where conventional brick is impractical.

Several proprietary brands of light-weight simulated stone that use cement plaster molded, tinted, textured and patterned to resemble real stone also are available.

■ = C H A P T E R 1 0 = ■

Roofs, Roofing and Chimneys

A dominant characteristic of any house style is the roof form or shape, be it a gable, hipped, single-slope (shed) or flat.

■ ROOF FORM

Pitched roofs are supported in two ways, either stick-built using rafters individually installed, or trusses that generally are factory-built and delivered to the building site. Stick-built roofs have the flexibility to accommodate many designs, while trusses are more economical for large spans where internal wall support is not desired. If trusses are installed, the usefulness of the attic is reduced, since the braces of the trusses interfere with full use of that space.

Examples of roof forms are illustrated in Figure 10.1 The stick-built construction method generally is necessary when dormers are used. Roof pitch is the ratio of vertical to horizontal dimensions. The horizontal dimension is customarily 12 inches.

FIGURE 10.1 ■ Pitched Roof Construction

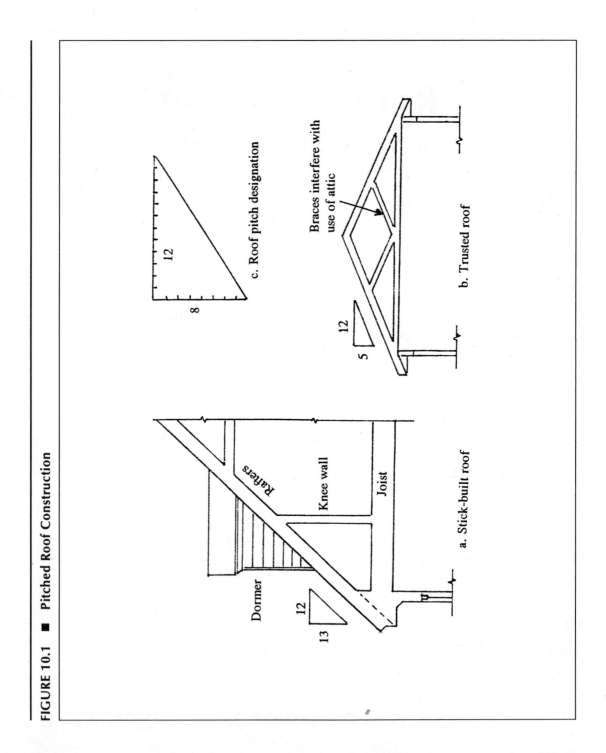

■ ROOF STYLE

Each architectural style of a house has a distinctive roof configuration; house style dictates not only pitch, but shape, type of roofing material, and the use of dormers or clerestory windows. Traditional roof shapes including the gable, generally with two balanced slopes, the gambrel and the hipped with four sides (all four with the same pitch) are illustrated in Figure 10.2. Shed roofs with one or more long slopes are a feature of many contemporary designs, as are flat roofs.

■ ROOFING MATERIALS

Roofing materials are in part determined by roof pitch and house style. Some roofing materials are more appropriate to certain house styles and may have practical limitations depending on roof pitch, as shown in the chart. For example, most shingle types cannot be used on very low-pitched roofs.

Recommended Slopes For Different Types Of Roofs

Roofing Type	Slope
Built-up, single membrane and flat-locked seam metal	1/2:12
Clay tile, metal shingles, standing metal-seam or corrugated and crimped metal	3:12 and greater
Asphalt, fiberglass, wood, slate, concrete shingles or wood shakes	4:12* and greater

*May be decreased to 2:12 if double-layer underlayment is used.

Color Selection

If your roof is complex with many dormers and valleys and varying planes, a dark colored shingle will tend to pull it together.

Check the other houses on the street. If all use more or less the same color, you may want to select a different one to break the monotony, but do coordinate the color with your house siding and trim.

A light color will reflect heat and thus is more desirable in climates where air-conditioning is the greatest user of energy. In colder climates,

FIGURE 10.2 ■ Roof Styles

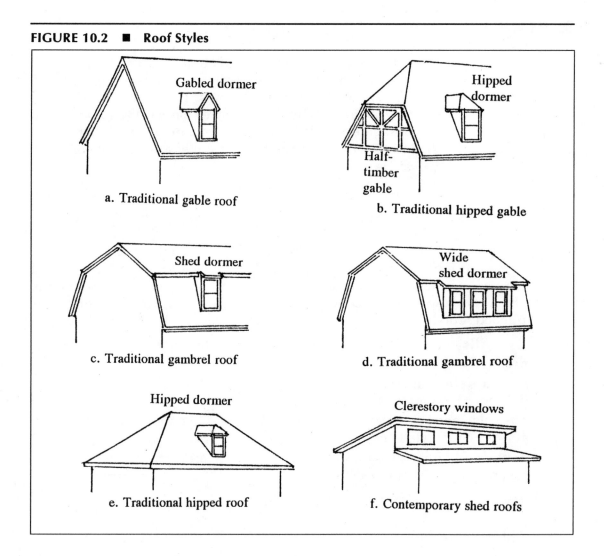

a. Traditional gable roof

b. Traditional hipped gable

c. Traditional gambrel roof

d. Traditional gambrel roof

e. Traditional hipped roof

f. Contemporary shed roofs

since black absorbs heat from the sun, a darker color may be the better choice.

If you live in a mildew-prone area, avoid light-colored shingles, since mildew and algae, which form black ugly stains, are virtually impossible to prevent or remove. Some brands of shingles have factory-applied inhibitors to avoid problems.

Shingles

Most eighteenth-century colonial and earlier houses had wood shingles or shingle-like clay tile roofs. Wood shingles and shakes are still a popular choice. Some traditional roofs had slate shingles. Modern asphalt and fiberglass shingles can approximate various traditional appearances at considerably lower cost; they are the most popular and most economical selection for roofing material in homes in the United States. As indicated in the earlier chart, they should not normally be used on roofs with a pitch of less than 4:12 (4 inches vertical rise for each horizontal 12 inches). At flatter angles, seepage of water, especially in high winds, may occur under the shingles. If installed over a properly applied two-ply underlayment (saturated felt), shingles may be used on roofs with a pitch of only 2:12.

Most shingles carry a manufacturer's warranty for material only, ranging from 15 years to 35 years at proportional increase in cost.

When selecting factory-colored shingles of any type, choose from actual samples, not from pictures, which can be deceiving.

Asphalt Asphalt shingles are made by saturating plies of "felt" paper. Made by many different manufacturers, they are finished with colored mineral granules in several textures. They vary in weight from 220 pounds per square (the common unit of measure for roofs is a square that equals 100 square feet of roof area) to 340 pounds. The heavier shingle is more expensive, but has greater texture and longer life.

Fiberglass Fiberglass shingles (single-layered) are similar in appearance to asphalt shingles, except fiberglass plies are used instead of felt. They are more resistant to fire and may reduce the premium for your homeowner's insurance.

Architectural Grade These shingles are thicker, heavier and project deeper shadows, which appear more dramatic than the single-layer type. Some designs resemble cedar shakes or slate.

Aluminum These shingles are very light in weight and generally have an embossed shake texture. They have a long life, although they are vulnerable to wind and impact damage.

Wood   Wood shingles are available in several species, with cedar being the most popular. In wood, the term *shingle* indicates that the material has been sawn, whereas the term *shake* means the material has been split. A shake is usually thicker and has a much more rustic appearance. The labor to install and the cost of the material can be four to five times that of standard asphalt or fiberglass shingles. Several companies manufacture large panels of wood shingles, which because of their size, require less installation labor.

Clay and Cement Tile   These types of shingles are very popular for their durability but are relatively expensive. They also are fragile and break easily if struck by a heavy object, such as a tree limb. Both are very heavy, weighing from 800 to 1,600 pounds per square foot. If your roof framing is designed for wood or asphalt shingles, have it checked by an architect or engineer before making the change to clay tile or cement shingles. Clay tiles may be used on Spanish traditional designs. Cement shingles also are made to imitate traditional wood shingles.

Synthetic Mineral   This type of shingle is a manufactured product that resembles a slate or wood shingle. No longer made with asbestos, synthetic mineral shingles are fireproof and durable, and usually do not require heavy roof framing. They are more expensive than wood shingles but generally less expensive than clay and cement tile or slate.

Slate   This is about the most durable material for roofing and is appropriate for many traditional designs; it also is one of the most expensive roofing materials. If this is your choice, be certain that the structural design of the framing can support a slate roof, which can weigh 700 pounds and over per square. Synthetic slate-like materials also are available at lesser cost.

Sheet Metal

Many different types of metal can be used as roofing materials: copper, terne and terne-coated stainless steel. Sheet metal roofing usually is installed in a standing seam, as illustrated in Figure 10.3. Metal roof sheeting should have no exposed penetration by nails or similar objects through the sheeting. Instead, concealed hold-down cleats are formed into the standing seams. The roof shape can be almost any pitched type.

FIGURE 10.3 ■ Standing Seam

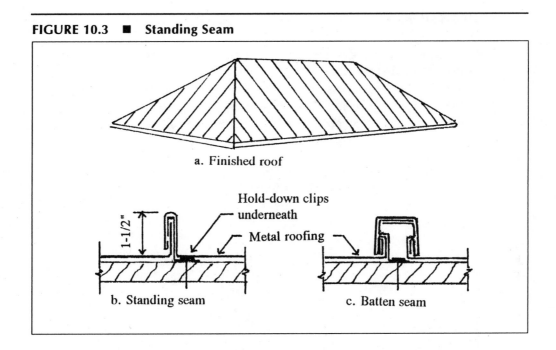

a. Finished roof

Hold-down clips
underneath

Metal roofing

1-1/2"

b. Standing seam　　　　　c. Batten seam

Copper Copper is available in shingles and sheeting and can be a striking choice, particularly on a contemporary home. In time, untreated copper turns to a salmon color and eventually to a beautiful green patina. A copper roof is very expensive, but can last up to 100 years.

Terne This kind of sheeting has been used in America since the late 1700s, and can last as long as 50 years with proper maintenance. It is therefore appropriate for use on many nineteenth-century traditional as well as contemporary designs. Modern terne consists of a lead-tin coating over a copper bearing steel base, and is moderately expensive. Typically, terne must be brush-painted with a linseed oil primer when installed and repainted every eight to ten years. It takes and holds paint well.

Terne-Coated Stainless Steel These sheets consist of stainless steel coated with terne alloy. It does not have to be painted, but it can be if its normal gray color is not desired. Terne-coated stainless steel is very long lasting and also is appropriate for many nineteenth-century traditional and contemporary designs. Because of its high cost, it is rarely used in residential construction.

■ BUILT-UP ROOFS

Built-up roofs are applied normally on houses of contemporary design with flat or nearly flat roofs.

Built-up roof construction is illustrated in Figure 10.4. It consists of several alternating layers of fiberglass or paper roofing felt with a coat of tar or pitch in between and a finish coat with gravel ballast on top.

FIGURE 10.4 ■ Built-Up Roof Construction

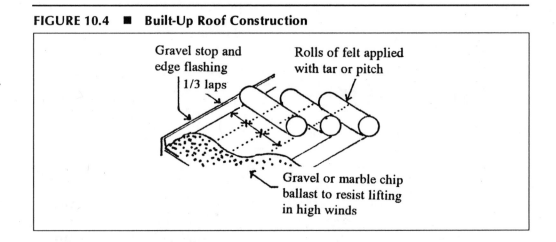

Gravel stop and edge flashing 1/3 laps

Rolls of felt applied with tar or pitch

Gravel or marble chip ballast to resist lifting in high winds

---

A newer flat-roof system uses a single synthetic rubber-like membrane which expands and contracts with the roof as the temperature changes. A number of brands are available, each with proprietary qualities and methods of attachment. Select a high-quality one that is resistant to degradation by harmful components of the sun's rays. Most roofers are familiar with these products.

For residences, avoid a built-up roof with no slope at all unless your plans specifically call for the collection of water on the roof for heating or cooling purposes. Under these circumstances, the roof must be specifically designed to hold the water. Flat (no-slope) roof joists made of wood tend to sag and cause water to pond; leaks may develop as a result.

■ CHIMNEYS

Chimneys are important character-defining features and are needed in most houses with operating fireplaces. Traditional chimneys are built of brick or stone masonry and require substantial foundations to support their heavy mass. Although construction is relatively expensive, the traditional masonry fireplace and chimney are still popular for traditional house designs.

In recent years, prefabricated fireplaces and flues have become widely used, due to their lower cost and energy efficiency when equipped with heat circulators and outdoor sources of combustion air. (For more information see Appendix F.) Most prefabricated fireplaces do not require special and costly foundations but instead rest on wood floor framing. The flue is enclosed in a wood frame which can be covered with wood or stucco. This structure usually will not be appropriate for a traditional-style house. If the fuel efficiency is important, however, the prefabricated fireplace can be installed within a masonry chimney system; the extra cost, of course, will be substantial.

The traditional masonry chimney that is external to the house wall is the most visually striking type of chimney, but also the most expensive. In many house designs, the chimney can be inside the house wall, requiring that the exposed part be only above the roof with cost savings on the brick work. This approach is suitable to many traditional style houses. For examples of chimney styles, see Figure 10.5.

In some contemporary house designs the exposed chimney is actually a metal-encased flue. This low-cost solution may be entirely appropriate.

FIGURE 10.5 ■ Chimneys

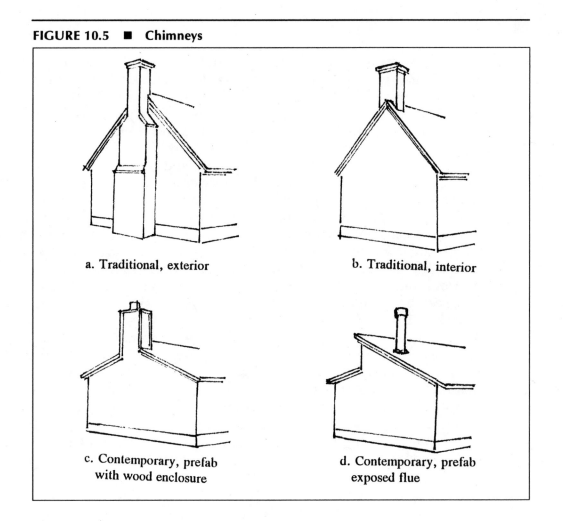

a. Traditional, exterior

b. Traditional, interior

c. Contemporary, prefab
with wood enclosure

d. Contemporary, prefab
exposed flue

Decks, Patios and Porches

These features not only should be convenient to use, but their effect on exterior appearance of the house must be thoughtfully planned and designed to relate to the house style. This planning should not be left to chance.

For most house styles, these features can be a part of the overall design. For example, on a traditional house, a deck should be located where it is not visible from the front of the house or it should be screened by landscaping or a fence. If the lot is small, a deck generally will be at the rear.

Contemporary house design usually offers greater flexibility in placing a porch, deck or garage in the overall design.

■ DECKS

Decks can be entirely exposed or partially roofed. They are a less costly outdoor extension of living space than a porch and may be nearly as useful, provided that climate and insects are not a problem. Even narrow decks can enhance the appearance and appeal of adjacent rooms including bedrooms and dining areas. If the deck level is at or near the house floor level, it is safer and easy to carry out food.

FIGURE 11.1 ■ Typical Deck Styles

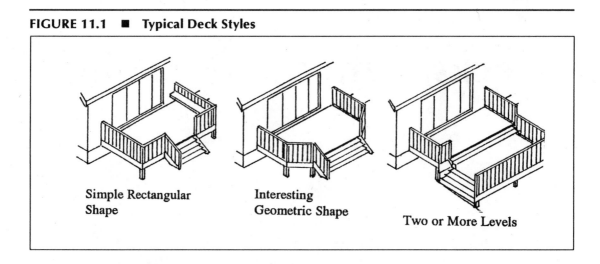

Simple Rectangular
Shape

Interesting
Geometric Shape

Two or More Levels

The size of the deck should be determined by its expected use. Usually a deck is the same size as a family room. The preferred location for a deck is where it can be private. An imaginative deck design may include many levels with steps and built-in seats. Deep decks tend to cut off views from windows especially if bounded by closed railings or designs with narrow openings. Note that of all the decks illustrated in Figure 11.1, the two-level deck on the right provides a better view from inside the house.

Most building codes require safety railings at least 36 inches above the deck where the deck is more than 30 inches above the ground.

Decks usually are supported at the house side by attaching them to the building and at the outer side on wood, steel posts or masonry piers. The best wooden materials for decks are naturally rot-resistant species (heart redwood, cypress) or pressure-treated wood. For drainage, deck planks should be placed about one-quarter-inch apart.

■ PATIOS OR TERRACES

The patio or terrace offers enhancements to outdoor livability similar to those of the deck. While decks can be built easily over irregular terrain, the patio is more economical and practical on flat ground. Patios are appropriate for nearly any style of house.

FIGURE 11.2 ■ Typical Patio

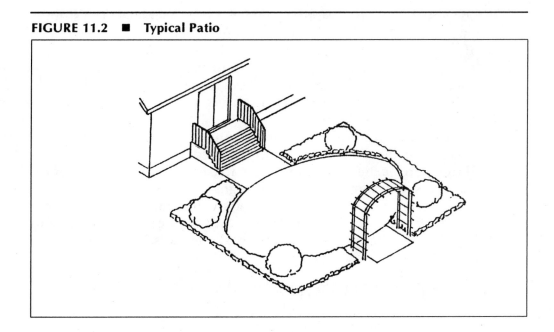

The patio can be simple or elaborate and really is a part of the garden or yard. It may be paved with brick, stone or even simple concrete, although a textured surface, such as exposed aggregate, is more appealing. A patio can be open along the sides or bounded by landscaping, fence, wall or trellises. It also may contain flower beds or a water feature such as a fountain.

Where a house floor is built over crawl space, some three or four steps down generally are needed, as shown in Figure 11.2. This is less advantageous than a floor-level deck from the standpoint of carrying out food, and can be a hazard.

Advantages of a patio compared to a deck include compatibility with the architecture of the house and attractive transition into the adjacent yard. Unlike a deck, a patio may be quite appropriate as an entrance courtyard at the front of a traditional house.

■ PORCHES

There are two types of porches: those used for sitting, which may be open around the sides; and those used primarily for weather protection at the entrances, with emphasis on decorative character. The sitting porch is appealing and useful if climate permits a reasonable period of use. Where flying insects are a problem, the sitting porch should be screened. It should be convenient to some part of the living area, such as next to a dining, family or living room, where it then becomes an extension of the interior when weather is pleasant and may even be used when it is raining.

Porches on traditional houses range from the primarily ornamental design for the front entrance to a roofed wing of the house. A veranda (large porch extending completely across one or more sides of the house) also is used in some traditional designs.

The roof of a porch will forever shade windows in rooms beneath it; for this reason, such rooms have other windows or skylights to permit direct daylight especially on heavily shaded lots.

■ WEATHER PROTECTION AT ENTRANCE DOORS

For many homes, the primary entrance door opens directly to the outside. It is always desirable to offer some sort of weather protection at entrance doors, including secondary doorways (patio doors, back door and so on). A porch roof may provide protection, or the doorway may be set into the house.

Alternatively, to control roof runoff over the doorway, gutters should be installed or a diverter may be positioned on the roof to direct water away from the steps. Examples of weather-protected doorways are shown in Figure 11.3.

FIGURE 11.3 ■ Weather-Protected Entrances

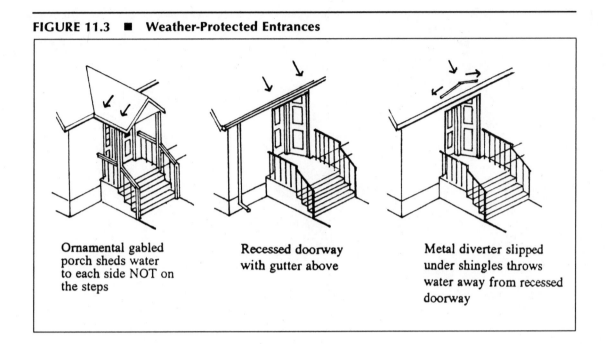

Ornamental gabled
porch sheds water
to each side NOT on
the steps

Recessed doorway
with gutter above

Metal diverter slipped
under shingles throws
water away from recessed
doorway

Garages and Carports

A garage or carport provides protection to the car and useful space for other purposes. Either carport or garage should be planned for storage of the numerous items commonly associated with the car (snow tires, anti-freeze, auto polish and the like), lawn and garden tools, hoses, fertilizers, left-over paint from the original paint job (protect from freezing), lawn chairs, bicycles and, perhaps, space for an extra freezer. A craftsperson may need a work bench and a project area if no other workshop is provided in the house.

Garages and carports are most convenient with direct entry into the house through the kitchen, family room or a mud room.

Garages or carports may be one-car or two-car size, or larger, and have a concrete slab floor. Gravel or asphalt paving also may be used. Gravel has the advantage of being inexpensive and does not readily show drips and stains from a car.

A garage also may be treated as a wing of a traditional house, incorporated within the body of the house or simply a detached separate structure. If the garage is near the front and if the lot is large enough, doors should open to the side rather than toward the front, thus minimizing the usually unattractive contents.

The choice between a carport and garage in part may be dictated by style of the house, climate and cost. If of equal size, a carport generally is less expensive. A carport usually has no doors, but they may be included if screening of the interior is important. Alternatives for storage include a separate storage shed or space under the house if available. A typical carport is shown in Figure 12.1.

FIGURE 12.1 ■ Typical Carport

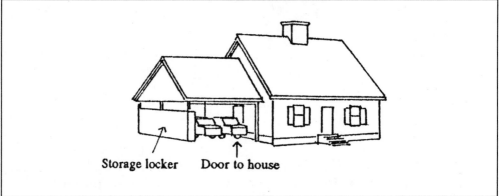

Storage locker   Door to house

In some house designs, a carport may be a *porte cochere* (covered way at the entrance), shown in Figure 12.2.

FIGURE 12.2 ■ Porte Cochere

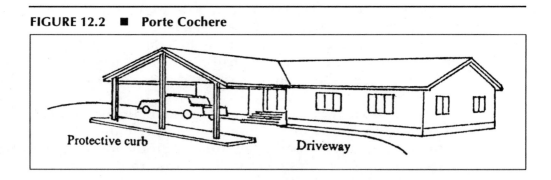

Protective curb   Driveway

A garage generally is more useful than a carport. It provides more secure storage for cars and greater protection from blowing dirt and leaves; it also may contain the indoor components of the HVAC (heating, ventilation and air-conditioning) system. Garage doors can be kept closed to conceal the sometimes unattractive, cluttered interior. Some subdivision covenants may require side-facing doors, which also may be your preference. Since double garages are nearly square, you may have a choice as to the side on which the doors are located.

Other possibilities include a detached garage or one connected by a breezeway. When a garage is connected by a breezeway, most zoning ordinances consider the garage to be a part of the house. Regulations for placing a detached garage usually are more lenient and permit the garage to be located closer to the property line, but they provide no protection for entering the house from the car.

The minimum size for a one-car garage or carport is 10 feet by 20 feet. To provide storage room, however, the dimensions should be increased at least two feet in width, length, or both.

The comfortable size for a two cars is 22 feet square, but 22 feet long by 24 feet wide is better to provide better storage including space for lawn equipment and a work bench.

A single garage door opening width is eight feet minimum, but nine feet is better. A double garage door minimum width is 16 feet; 18 feet is better. For traditional designs, two separate nine-foot doors are more appropriate. Garage door height typically is seven feet, but eight-foot doors are available if you wish to accommodate a van. Most garage doors are overhead-type in four horizontal sections. These are available in flush and paneled styles of wood, fiberglass or metal.

Garage doors may be equipped with automatic door closers, which are a great convenience to the home dweller who arrives home at night or during a rain or snow storm. For a two-car garage, get a second transmitter for the second car. For a two-car garage with separate doors, each door can have a different frequency to separately operate the door mechanisms. Also, both cars can be provided with a door closer to operate either door. Most door operators are equipped with a light that automatically goes on at the start of each cycle and remains on for several minutes. In some equipment, timing of the light is adjustable.

Garages usually are not heated, but can be where climate conditions make this desirable or when the garage is to be used as a workshop. Heating should be entirely separate from the house system using, for example, overhead electric quartz-tube heaters, a separate, through-the-wall small heat pump or some other form of thermostatically controlled heat source. It generally is undesirable to duct heat from the central heating system to the garage even if it can be shut off when not needed, since this upsets the heat balance in the house, and supply dampers cutting off heat to the garage are notoriously leaky. Also, air blown into a garage should not be recirculated into the house.

If the garage is to be heated, it should be insulated to the same standards as the house, including the slab perimeter.

Fumes from a car stored in a garage below a room in the house may be objectionable, particularly for a bedroom. Building codes require fireproofing between a garage and habitable space for safety.

It is desirable to have the garage floor lower than the house floor for several reasons. Where the house floor is over crawl space, usually about three feet above the ground level, this will almost always occur. It is generally impractical to raise the garage floor on a thick bed of fill. The garage slab, however, should be four to six inches higher than the outside grade for dryness with a slight pitch of the floor toward the garage door for drainage of water and melting snow brought in by the car. A three- to four-foot sloped apron outside the door will minimize water leakage under the door from blowing rain, and provide a ramp to ground level.

For a slab-on-grade house, it also is better to depress the garage floor several inches below the house floor to prevent unwanted seepage from the garage area into the house. All garage slabs should have a moisture barrier (usually plastic sheeting) beneath to minimize dampness from underlying earth.

■ ═ C H A P T E R   1 3 ═ ■

Basements

The decision of whether or not to provide a basement should be based on your answers to two questions:

1. Do you need the space?
2. Do the site and other physical conditions permit satisfactory, economical basement construction?

If a basement is built crack-free, adequately damp-proofed and provided with good subdrainage, it is an economical way of gaining usable and valuable floor space.

On sloping lots, since some of the foundation walls will be high to compensate for different elevations of the lot, a basement instead of crawl space is an inexpensive way to gain additional inside space.

Be aware, however, that in areas with high ground water or a lot with poor drainage, basements tend to be dank and odorous even with good waterproofing. This is due in part to basement humidity, poor ventilation and minimal sunlight. To every extent possible, basements should have windows to permit daylight and sunlight. Mechanical ventilation or a dehumidifier should be provided if window area is minimal.

Any crawl space, including that next to a basement, also should have good ventilation. The basic idea is to surround the basement with a dry area except where the walls must have earth behind them.

Basements generally do not greatly change the appearance of a house unless they have low windows, or if the main floor is raised substantially, as is the case with the traditional English basement designs.

In summary, once you have decided on the style of your house, consider how its lines relate to the lot and where rooms should best be located. Stick to your chosen style with its inherent features, especially on the front or where style is most important. Avoid tampering with roof lines and configuration. Make the best use of private areas and provide screening by plants and fences where needed. Give special attention to surface drainage. Consider auxiliary features such as porches, decks and detached buildings as an integral part of the overall exterior design.

PART THREE

Interior Home Design

House Style and Floor Plan

In planning a house, your initial goal is to achieve everything desired, but you will also encounter competing or conflicting requirements. It is important that you face these situations for the right reasons. For example, if the best privacy and views occur on the house's north side, the large glass areas needed will increase energy consumption. By deciding that views and large glass areas are most desirable, it is better in the long run to accept some unavoidable increase in energy consumption, minimized by using energy-efficient windows. Usually, one overriding factor stands out when conflicting considerations are weighed, but keep an open mind and be flexible in thinking, since ultimately you want the best overall final design.

In this and subsequent chapters, floor plans are the primary concern. They are usually drawn to a scale of 1/4" = 1', using conventional symbols for door swings, plumbing fixtures, built-in features such as kitchen cabinets, fireplaces, stairs and so forth. Most of these common symbols are illustrated in the figures of this chapter. They can be traced over for your use in planning.

■ FLOOR PLANS

The main entrance usually is at the front of the house, along with rooms not requiring much privacy, such as the living and dining rooms.

The best views should be reserved for the family room, kitchen or bedrooms where the indoor-outdoor relationship is important. Generally, the back of the house is the most private area and is best suited for a screened porch, deck or patio.

Bedrooms can be located along the side if far enough away from neighboring houses or if screened by planting. If the lot is quite narrow it may be better for privacy to limit windows to the front and back of the house.

Rooms least related to views of the lot are most baths, utility room, stairway, corridors or hallways and closets and other storage. While daylight is wanted in most of these spaces, view is unimportant. Where windows are impossible, such as in a hallway or stairway, consider installing skylights.

To take advantage of solar energy, it generally is preferable to have major glass areas on southerly sides. Bedrooms are more pleasant on the easterly side. The hot west sun is difficult to control by roof overhang, although shade trees and shrubs can be effective.

In the following examples, a comparison is made between one-story and two-story plans; similar thinking applies to split-level and split-foyer designs:

1. The one-story plan is more flexible and versatile, since no second floor dictates the size and shape of the house.

   In the two-story house, there must be two equal-sized arrangements between floors if the construction economy of the two-story is to be realized. However, if the first floor space must be larger than the second floor, wings can be added to the first floor, such as a garage or a bedroom.

2. One-story plans are less compact than equivalent-sized two-story plans, as shown in Figure 14.1. For good bedroom area privacy in a one-story plan, a hallway and a break in the sight line from the living area are needed. A wing can be used to accomplish the same thing.

   The two-story house is generally more compact, with shorter traffic routes than an equal-sized one-story house.

FIGURE 14.1 ■ Plans Compared

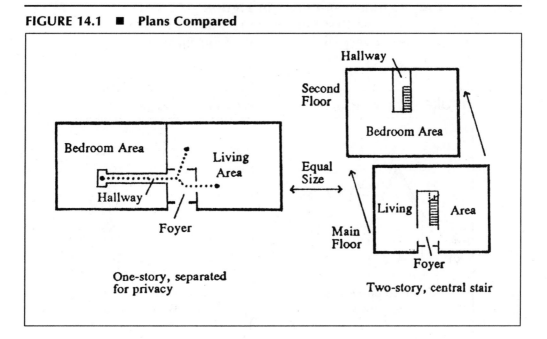

To summarize, the two-story house provides compactness, economy of construction and inherent privacy separation. The one-story house is more flexible, but results in longer traffic patterns and devotes more space to hallways, circulation through rooms, or both. On a square-foot basis, the one-story house also is more expensive to build.

If a family member has a mobility handicap, the one-story plan will be more practical. To adapt a two-story house, an elevator or lift along a stair can be provided, adding to the cost, or the incapacitated person must be restricted to a part of the house. A one-story generally is more suitable for elderly persons.

House Style and Floor Plans

The floor plans of traditional and contemporary style houses are not readily interchangeable. For instance, a good traditional story-and-a-half derives its stylistic character from its proportions, window and entrance door placement, steep roof, dormers and other stylistic features. The proportions cannot be changed without affecting appearance. For example, enlargement in the floor plan will change the proportions of the roof to the body of the house as shown in Figure 14.2. Note how the front-to-back dimension of the first floor is undesirably increased to the point that the roof becomes overpowering and stylistic character is weakened.

FIGURE 14.2 ■ How Style Changes Can Ruin Design

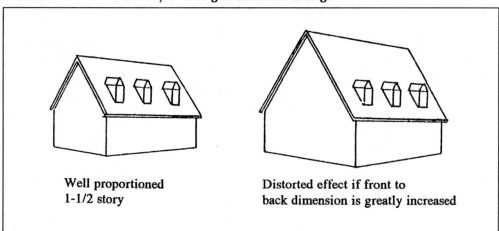

Well proportioned
1-1/2 story

Distorted effect if front to
back dimension is greatly increased

Traditional colonial character is difficult to attain in a one-story ranch-style house, and usually can be expressed only by a few decorative features, such as trim and window shutters. The important, dominant steeply pitched roof is missing. But if the roof is raised to a traditional colonial pitch just for effect, a lot of wasted space is produced in the attic. It is better to start with an appropriate colonial design.

The reader is cautioned against making changes to exterior form and proportions. Unless you have some architectural skills, it would be better to consult an architect who can help you find a better solution.

Fortunately, many traditional-style designs offer opportunities to satisfy a range of needs and appeals. For example, a two-story house may have abutting wings to increase main floor area without generating excessive upstairs space. One-story wings can be used for a great room, sun room, master bedroom, in-law apartment, utility area or garage. In some cases, topography may dictate a design with wings and still preserve traditional character. For examples, see Figure 14.3.

FIGURE 14.3 ■ Traditional Designs with Wings

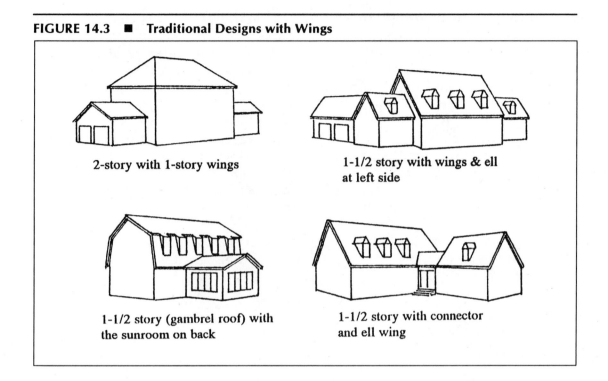

2-story with 1-story wings

1-1/2 story with wings & ell
at left side

1-1/2 story (gambrel roof) with
the sunroom on back

1-1/2 story with connector
and ell wing

In many instances, it is possible to preserve the traditional appearance on the front where the effect counts most, while making the back suited for views with large areas of glass, privacy, deck and patio. This degree of contemporary appearance is generally acceptable.

If a traditional design is wanted with rooms that open to a wide front porch or wraparound veranda, several period Southern styles can be considered, such as a Charleston style featuring two-story verandas on one side as shown in Chapter 8, in Figure 8.2. This design is ideal for a relatively narrow lot, where the front-to-back house dimension must be kept longer. It also permits capturing prevailing breezes or views toward a side. The traditional two-story formal Greek Revival style, also illustrated in Chapter 8's Figure 8.2, is another choice for a wide front porch.

Another characteristic of traditional designs is formality of the floor plan. For example, the Virginia colonial has an entrance hall from front to back flanked by separate rooms. Departing from this formality is possible by removing a wall or two for more open space if the structural changes are practical. Again, be cautious in making changes that affect the structure and seek help when necessary.

By their nature, contemporary house designs offer great flexibility. They can take advantage of, or respond easily to, unusual topography and views, and the house footprint can be closely adapted to fit the site if it has an odd shape. The contemporary lends itself to informality.

Contemporary designs also include flexibility in roof configuration, and the ease of adapting decks, porches, carports and garages to the design. For example, a design can be developed using shed roofs and clerestory windows to capture favorable sun orientation not possible in traditional designs as shown in Chapter 8's Figures 8.2 and 8.3, or a steep site mastered by placing the house on piers or pilings as shown in Figure 8.9.

In summary, select the house style that is most satisfying to you; work with its characteristics and attributes; and be sensitive to the lot and its requirements.

Arranging and Organizing Rooms

■ BASIC ROOM GROUPINGS

The house is comprised of three principal areas: living, private and utility including the garage (see Figure 15.1).

Living Areas

These areas are social places, where family and friends gather, talk and entertain, and are associated with recreation and the preparation and serving of food.

Rooms in these areas include the foyer, living room, dining room, kitchen, Florida room, family room and a guest bath or powder room. They are generally characterized by a higher level of architectural treatment featuring fine woodwork and floors, cornices, chair rails and wood paneling, and provide ample space for good furniture placement. Built-in features, such as bookshelves and stereo cabinets, may take the place of furniture. Other special features include fireplaces and space dividers. A screened porch or a deck may be included as an extension of living space.

Traffic patterns to and between these rooms should be convenient and not pass through private areas.

FIGURE 15.1 ■ **Areas of the Typical House**

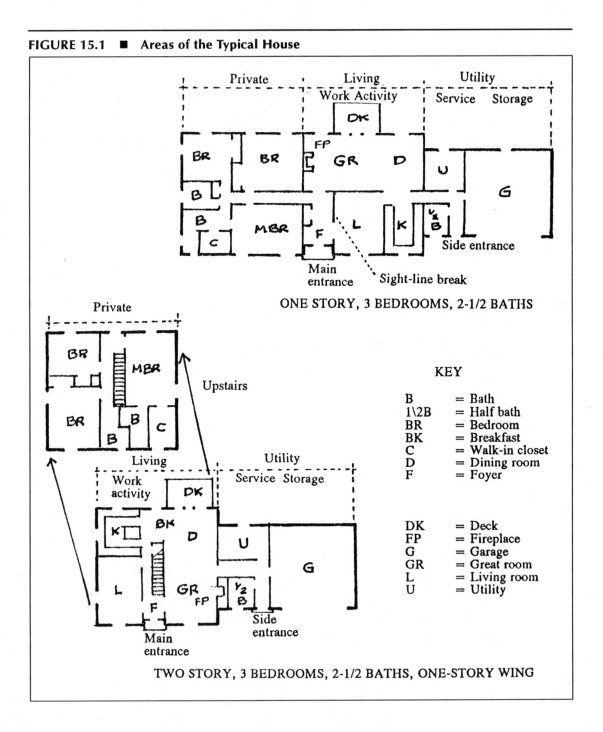

ONE STORY, 3 BEDROOMS, 2-1/2 BATHS

KEY

B	= Bath
1\2B	= Half bath
BR	= Bedroom
BK	= Breakfast
C	= Walk-in closet
D	= Dining room
F	= Foyer
DK	= Deck
FP	= Fireplace
G	= Garage
GR	= Great room
L	= Living room
U	= Utility

TWO STORY, 3 BEDROOMS, 2-1/2 BATHS, ONE-STORY WING

Private Areas

These areas include bedrooms, dressing areas, baths, exercise rooms and sometimes the study or home office. Also included are associated closets and storage. Some planners include the laundry and the sewing room, since most of the soiled linen and clothes come from bedrooms and baths. Bedrooms generally are private rooms that can be closed off. They usually do not require a high degree of decor but still should be appealing.

Bedroom areas should be separated from living areas and preferably no bedroom should directly connect to a room in the living area without a break in sight line. In addition, the route between a bedroom and an associated bathroom should be within the private area without exposure to living areas. In a one-story house, this can be provided by designing a bedroom section or wing. In a two-story house, the second floor can be planned exclusively for bedrooms, baths and related use such as a sewing room.

Utility Areas

Rooms in these areas include the laundry; out-of-season clothing storage; general storage; the heating; ventilating and air-conditioning equipment; the garage, workshop, plant room; and so forth. These uses are more strictly functional and some may be included in other rooms. Heating and air-conditioning may not be required in some of these rooms, which may be semi-finished or unfinished.

■ EXCEPTIONS AND LIMITATIONS

Exceptions to the basic room groupings may include a home office near the family room or a children's recreation room away from other living areas due to noise and playing stereo equipment. However, a mix of the basic categories should be carefully thought through to avoid mistakes and not to harm resale value. For example, placing an indoor swimming pool in the middle of the circulation area or locating a dining room too far from the kitchen are real drawbacks.

There are other limitations to consider. If an open space plan is preferred, remember that informality of the house also means lack of noise and sound control, less control over cooking odors and, at times, too much togetherness. These disadvantages may be alleviated if there are other rooms for family members or a later wing may be added for this purpose. Also remember that planning should take into account anticipated changes of family life.

Room Size and Shape

As suggested earlier, you should create your own list of rooms and spaces needed based on the priorities of your family's needs now and for the foreseeable future. After preparing this list, you are ready to consider qualities of individual rooms or areas as to size, shape and traffic patterns (circulation).

■ SIZE

One of the best ways to determine room size is to study rooms you like, either in your present house or elsewhere. Room size basically is determined by the furniture and its placement, and the traffic within or through the room.

Bigger is not necessarily better; a sparsely furnished room looks over-sized for its use. On the other hand, a room should not be loaded with furniture to the point where it is overcrowded. In most rooms, furniture generally is placed against a wall, except footstools, coffee tables and the like. If you have special or outsized furniture pieces, such as a piano, give particular consideration to their requirements as far as placement and clearance.

Usually the height of furniture pieces is not crucial except for an oversize family heirloom such as a tester bed or a tall wardrobe cabinet. For planning purposes, Figure 16.1 shows representative sizes of residential furniture. (The scale of these drawings is ¼" = 1'0", which means that a length of one quarter inch on the plan equals one foot and no inches of the actual house when built. This scale is used in drawing most floor plans.)

Room size is the chief, but not the only, factor to consider for a satisfactory room. More furniture placement problems result from poor shape and awkward proportion of the room, and difficult location of doors and windows resulting in lack of wall space, than from undersizing or oversizing of the room.

■ SHAPE

Rectangular rooms generally are easier to furnish, since most furniture is shaped to fit into rectangular patterns. The cost to build rectangular rooms with conventional construction is usually less than nonrectangular rooms. For illustrations of typical room shapes, see Figure 16.2.

If done selectively, however, rooms with acute or obtuse angles can be interesting and their shape may lend special emphasis and dramatic interest to the house. For example, a house plan may be angled to fit the topography, with one or more rooms having angled walls. A hexagonal living room can be a stunning feature.

Rectangular rooms should be proportioned from square up to a ratio of about one by one and a half—for example, 12 feet by 12 feet to 12 feet by 18 feet, and adequate for the intended furniture. Square rooms often are more pleasant and intimate if not too large. In large open space plans, some furniture may be free-standing.

Consider the normal circulation within the room, and any traffic that may pass through the room. Where possible, limit through traffic except in dedicated traffic spaces such as the foyer or hallway.

A room is more appealing if it has a focal point. This may be as simple as a picture or picture grouping, or an architectural feature such as a fireplace, built-in bookshelves and cabinets or a well-placed window with a daytime view. Special pieces of furniture also may be focal points, such as a piano, antique highboy or a dining room table.

FIGURE 16.1 ■ **Typical Furniture Sizes**

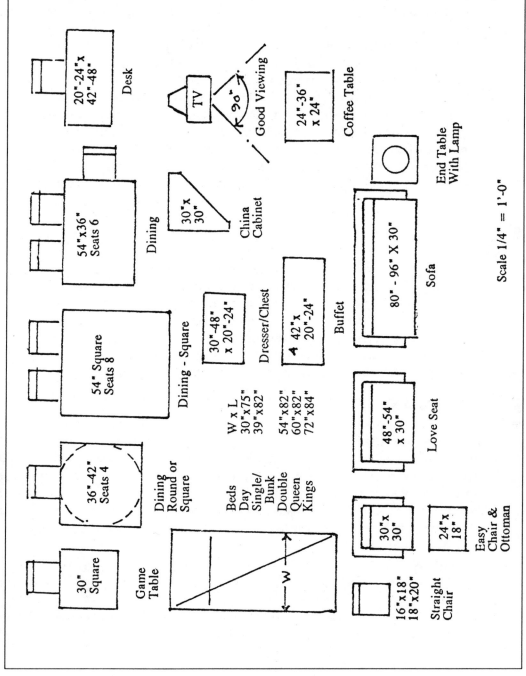

A rectangular room can be too long for its width, creating aesthetic and functional problems. For example, with the long dimension more than one and three-fourths or two times the width, the room tends to lack a focus when furniture is placed against the walls.

A long, narrow room, however, may be favored if divided into separate use areas such as dining at one end and sitting at the other, as shown at the upper right in Figure 16.2. The long proportions of the area create a dramatic effect and give a sense of space. This arrangement provides a large area for entertaining, but functions almost as two separate rooms. The use of a space divider (such as a large doorway, partial partitions, fireplace or drapes) differentiates between functional areas yet still preserves the large spatial feeling without making the area seem too large.

■ OPEN SPACE AREAS

The previous example illustrates the concept of open space areas rather than individual rooms and has become very popular in recent years. Other areas where open space may be desirable are kitchen-dining (with no formal dining room), kitchen-dining-family area and so on. The combination of functions promotes livability and social mixing. It also may result in space saving and make the house more economical to build.

■ ALCOVES AND ELLS

A rectangular room also can be made attractive and interesting by using alcoves (small recessed sections) and Ls (L-shaped areas). Such features make rooms less formal and also help to separate functional areas into intimate areas. Thus, the dining area may be an ell of the living room, or an alcove may be attractive and create an intimate area near a fireplace or a window bay. For examples, see Figure 16.3.

FIGURE 16.2 ■ **Room Shapes**

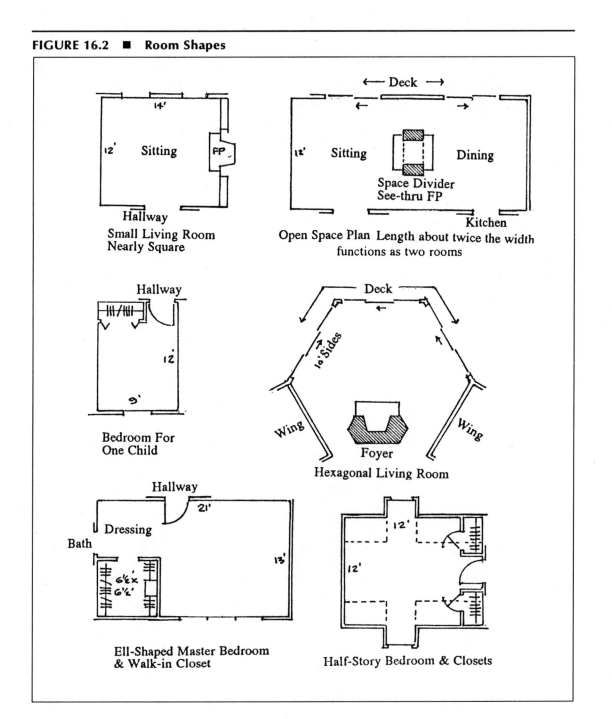

■ PLACING FURNITURE

Preplan the furniture you intend to place in each room, measuring the size of each piece and the clearances required for pulling drawers, opening table leaves, doors and so on. Study rooms of your friends' and neighbors' homes that you like and compare them to your own needs and furniture.

FIGURE 16.3 ■ Alcoves and Ells

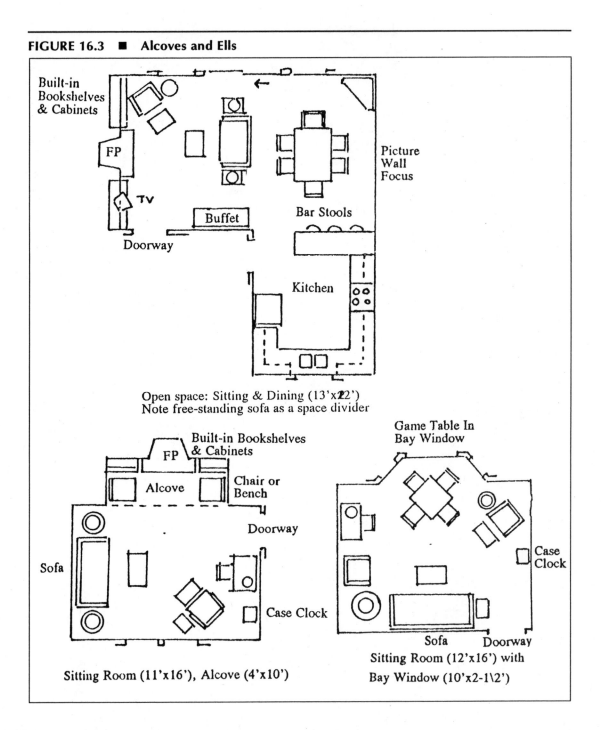

Open space: Sitting & Dining (13'x22')
Note free-standing sofa as a space divider

Sitting Room (11'x16'), Alcove (4'x10')

Sitting Room (12'x16') with
Bay Window (10'x2-1\2')

Room Windows and Doors

Generally, the longer side of a room should be along an exterior wall with windows for good daylight and pleasant view. If windows are on the short side of a deep room, the opposite end tends to be dark.

If a room has full-height windows or exterior glass doors, and wall space is limited, make the room deep enough to accommodate free-standing arrangements of chairs, tables and sofas (away from the windows) as shown in Chapter 16, at the top of Figure 16.3.

Rooms take on different focus or orientation from day to night. Even with a nice view or a lighted garden, the main area of attention at night shifts to activity or conversation within the room.

■ DOORS

Doorway locations affect placement of furniture and circulation within the room. While furniture may be put in front of windows, it is necessary to provide clearance at door swings and adequate unobstructed traffic space near doorways. Some spaces, such as foyers, may not require much wall space. See Appendix A for more detailed information on doors.

For smaller rooms, entering doorways should be placed near a corner in order to provide the longest unbroken wall space for furniture. In larger, more formal rooms, doorways may be centered to create a more symmetrical effect. Representative door locations and potential problems are illustrated in Figure 17.1.

For mobility-impaired family members, doorways should be planned to accommodate wheelchairs. Generally, these doorways should be at least two feet, ten inches wide. Maneuvering space should be provided on either side including the path of the door swing.

■ WINDOWS

Window planning is based in part on house style and in part on interior requirements. Planning also should include how windows operate and how they can receive curtains or drapes. For a detailed discussion of windows, see Appendix A.

Most houses built today have window areas that exceed building code minimum requirements of 8 or 10 percent of floor space. (Half of the required window area must be ventilated.) Placed to avoid relatively dark or poorly lit rooms where windows are shaded by roof overhang or trees, or where view is important, these window areas usually exceed the building codes substantially.

Windows should be located to provide good distribution of daylight. In a small room, this location is the center of the window wall. Depending on the style of the house, larger rooms may have two or more windows separated by wall space. Avoid a single window near a corner, except where placement is relatively unimportant in a small room such as a bathroom or where cross-ventilation is more important. For illustrations of suggested window placements, see Figure 17.2. Rooms with windows on two or more sides are bright and cheerful such as the hexagonal room, pictured in Chapter 16's Figure 16.2, and the bedroom pictured at the lower right of the same figure.

Window arrangement will affect the placement of furniture and should recognize the expected room activity. If daytime arrangement is satisfactory, then nighttime use generally is also.

FIGURE 17.1 ■ Location of Doors

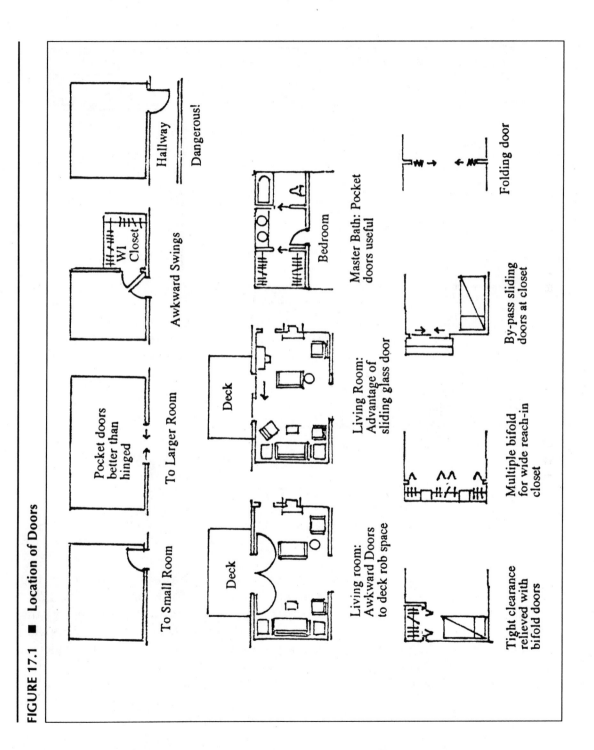

To Small Room

Pocket doors better than hinged

To Larger Room

W I Closet
Awkward Swings

Hallway
Dangerous!

Deck
Living room: Awkward Doors to deck rob space

Deck
Living Room: Advantage of sliding glass door

Bedroom
Master Bath: Pocket doors useful

Folding door

Tight clearance relieved with bifold doors

Multiple bifold for wide reach-in closet

By-pass sliding doors at closet

FIGURE 17.2 ■ Window Placements

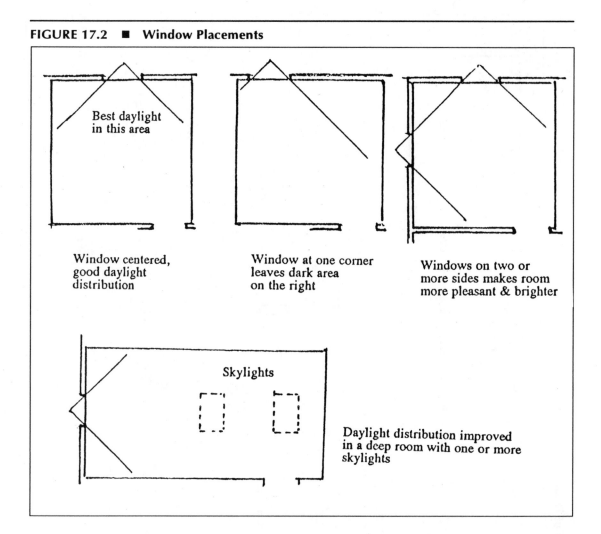

Window centered, good daylight distribution

Window at one corner leaves dark area on the right

Windows on two or more sides makes room more pleasant & brighter

Skylights

Daylight distribution improved in a deep room with one or more skylights

In a living or sitting room, it is nice to have a chair or sitting arrangement near a window to enjoy daytime view and provide good daylight for reading. The same may apply to a family room where visual connection to a deck, patio or yard is important. Most homeowners also appreciate good daylight in a kitchen and a view from the breakfast dinette. Bathrooms are nicer with daylight and natural ventilation although view is not usually important. Foyers and interior hallways preferably should have daylight unless you accept having electric lights on constantly. The alternative to a windowless room is skylights if the roof is immediately above. In rooms where the attic is above the ceiling, skylights also can be installed with a light well through the attic. Skylights also can be used to illuminate the dark end of a deep room.

To avoid blocking daylight, furniture placed in front of windows should be lower than the sill. Open furniture may be acceptable in front of a window. Remember that upholstered furniture, drapes and curtains will fade when exposed to sunlight for long periods.

Since furniture typically is placed along a wall, wall space is very valuable. Too many doors and windows in a room reduce the options for furniture placement. An open space plan is more suitable for placing furniture away from the wall (free-standing) with less reliance on wall space, but room size must be adequate. Common examples of free-standing furniture are dining room tables, a seating group in front of a sliding glass door to a deck, a fireplace in the middle of a large room and a gaming table with all-around seating. Be sure to provide a circulation path around free-standing furniture. For suggested placements of free-standing furniture, see Figures 17.1 and 17.3, as well as Chapter 16's Figure 16.3.

FIGURE 17.3 ■ Wall-Placed and Free-Standing Furniture

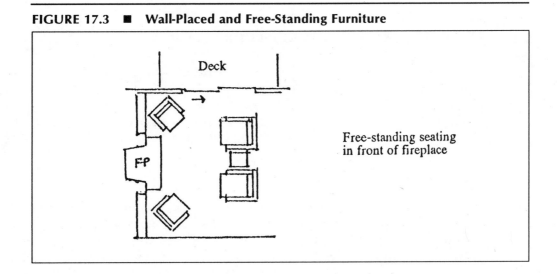

Free-standing seating
in front of fireplace

Operation and cleaning of different types of residential windows usually is not a problem; however, having to reach over furniture can be bothersome.

Most windows can be provided with a blind, shade, curtain or drape for daylight regulation and nighttime privacy. Roll shades and venetian blinds are common for double-hung windows. They also can be used on casement and awning windows mounted on the room side of the window screen. Some brands of dual glazed (double-paned) casements and awning windows permit mounting venetian blinds between the panes. Sliders and sliding glass doors do not lend themselves to horizontal blinds or shades but vertical ribbon or slat-type shades with traverse movement are satisfactory.

Curtains and drapes should be mounted so that when fully opened the stacking of the curtains clears the window glass (see Figure 17.4). Plan for curtain or drape-stacking space at least one foot or more wider than the window. The required amount will be based on the material and how it is pleated. Also, when using thermal (insulated) glass remember that control of daylight, privacy or thermal losses still make some type of window covering desirable.

FIGURE 17.4 ■ **Stacking Space for Drapes or Curtains**

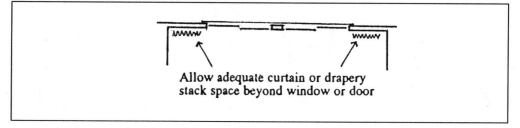

Allow adequate curtain or drapery
stack space beyond window or door

In standard construction, the window top or head is six feet, eight inches above the floor. Window widths vary according to the type of window. The height of the windowsill should be determined by view, furniture and house style. Tall windows often are preferred where view is important. Short windows are better in bedrooms and elsewhere if a desk or other furniture would block the view or ventilation. Most windows of a given type can be put together into multiples side by side, and awning and hopper types can be stacked vertically or combined with fixed panels. Again, take into account windows suitable for the house style. Awning-type windows would be inappropriate in a traditional-style design where double-hung windows are customary.

Room Ceilings

■ CONVENTIONAL

In house-planning, keep in mind that the eight-foot ceiling is standard, since studs and wall finish materials are presized to this height. Lower ceiling heights generally do not result in savings, since standard materials will be cut and wasted. Most residential building codes require a minimum ceiling height of seven feet, six inches for at least 50 percent of required minimum room areas and not less than five feet in the other 50 percent. Typical required minimum room areas are as follows: general living, 150 square feet; other habitable rooms, 70 square feet; and kitchens, 50 square feet. Most people generally want rooms larger than this. Check your local code.

■ HIGH CEILINGS

A height greater than eight feet (conventional height) is sometimes desired for better room proportions, particularly in very large rooms. A nine-foot ceiling height will cost at least 15 percent more than an eight-foot ceiling for the area affected, due to added wall height and the increased loads on HVAC systems.

■ CATHEDRAL CEILINGS

A cathedral ceiling achieves a feeling of spaciousness that works well in some plans, particularly contemporary. The ceiling joists are eliminated and the ceiling becomes the bottom side of the roof rafters. Insulation is installed between the rafters, and the bottom side of the rafters can be finished by installing plaster, drywall or paneling. An exposed rafter effect also is possible but usually is added as ornamentation with lumber about three-and-a-half inches thick and or synthetic beams of similar size spaced 36 to 48 inches apart.

■ DOUBLE-HEIGHT CEILINGS

Another alternative for dramatic effect is a ceiling height of two floors enhanced by a balcony or second floor overlook (see right side of Figure 18.1). Again, allow for extra cost and added HVAC load.

These special features make a house distinctive and will generally increase its value, although they also will increase construction and energy costs. For some houses, particularly large ones, it would be a mistake not to capitalize on ceiling design opportunities in at least some of the rooms.

FIGURE 18.1 ■ Cathedral and Double-Height Ceilings

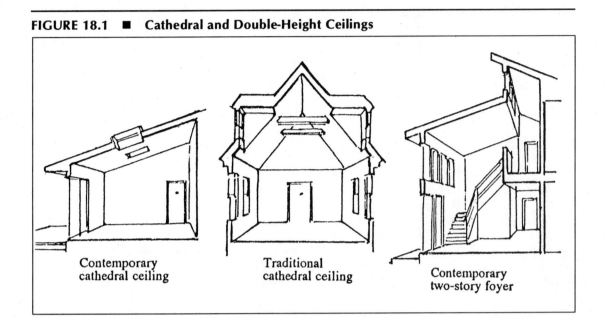

Contemporary
cathedral ceiling

Traditional
cathedral ceiling

Contemporary
two-story foyer

Fireplaces and Stoves

■ FIREPLACES

The words *hearth* and *home* are almost synonymous, and the fireplace is still important even if it is not the principal source of heating. Many people would not be without a fireplace, enjoying the cheerfulness of a fire on a crisp winter day or evening, or its beauty in either a traditional or contemporary house. Moreover, in open-space houses, one or more wood burning or gas fireplaces may be used as backup heating, or as the only heat in cases of power failure.

The most popular rooms for the fireplace are the family room, recreation room, great room, living room and master bedroom.

The two basic types of fireplaces in use today are the traditional all-masonry and its close cousin with a manufactured steel firebox, the all-prefabricated fireplace with associated prefabricated flue. See Appendix F for a discussion of energy-efficient fireplaces.

Functionally, most types of fireplaces are interchangeable, but there are aesthetic differences, particularly involving the visible part of the chimney on the exterior. The all-masonry and the masonry/steel box combination both have exterior masonry chimneys, but the all-prefabricated type has a prefabricated flue generally enclosed by light-weight material such as wood or stucco as it emerges through the roof or is run on the outside of the house. In some contemporary house designs, the prefabricated flue pipe itself may be fully exposed.

Advantages of the masonry fireplace with manufactured steel firebox compared to the all-masonry type are energy efficiency and somewhat lower construction cost. Both require heavy foundations at ground level and massive masonry construction, which are expensive. The energy-efficient all-prefabricated fireplace, however, can be installed on wood framing and may be placed on any floor without the massive masonry foundations required for the other types.

All fireplaces and chimneys require code-approved construction, including the flues and adherence to minimum clearances from combustible materials in the room such as the mantel and flooring. Prefabricated fireplaces are available in a limited number of sizes and three configurations: standard front opening, see-through, and open corner (see Figure 19.1). Masonry fireplaces also can be built in a range of custom sizes to suit a given application.

FIGURE 19.1 ■ Fireplace Configurations

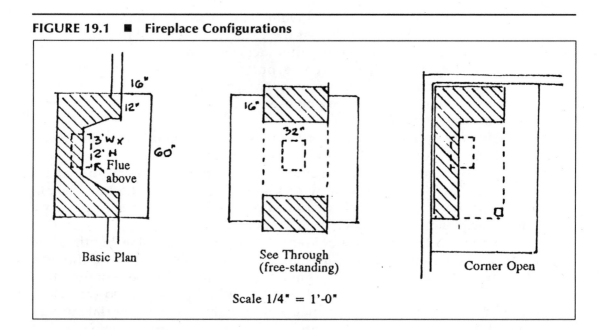

Basic Plan

See Through
(free-standing)

Corner Open

Scale 1/4" = 1'-0"

Gas log fireplaces may be the choice where firewood is scarce or if a homeowner objects to handling firewood and removing ashes. Also, gas fireplaces burn cleaner, since no ash is produced.

A popular front-opening fireplace is three feet wide by two or two-and-a-half feet high. Most codes require the hearth (front projection at the base) to be at least 16 inches deep and extend 12 inches on each side of the opening when the opening is six square feet or larger. The hearth may be at floor level or raised (popular in contemporary houses). Prefabricated units are installed over the subfloor, which puts the bottom of the firebox about six inches above the floor.

In planning locations for a fireplace at an exterior wall, there are two choices: the chimney and fireplace outside or inside the wall. With the first choice, if the fireplace projects outside, no space is lost to the room, and with the second, the room size is reduced by the space needed for the fireplace and corresponding space for the chimney above. With the fireplace and chimney outside of the wall, the cost is greater than if they were inside since the components usually must be enclosed.

In planning locations in interior walls, make sure that there is clearance for the vertical route for the chimney. This is critical in a two-story house, and will affect the second floor plan.

A fireplace generally does a better job of heating if it is placed near the center of the wall or at the room corner, as shown in Figure 19.2. Do not crowd furniture too close to the front of a fireplace; placement of the furniture should be six feet or farther away from it.

For the best traditional appearance, the all-masonry or masonry/steel box should be selected. For contemporary designs, the prefabricated unit with its nonmasonry chimney can be appropriate.

■ STOVES

Wood stoves can be used as primary heat or back-up heat sources. Many models and sizes are available. Critical considerations are clearances to wall or combustible materials (furniture and woodwork), and most codes require the use of protective fireproof panels on the wall behind the stove and floor pads of noncombustible floor material. Stove placement will affect furniture arrangement, and the useful room area will be reduced. Masonry or prefabricated flues are required.

Compared to wood stoves, gas-burning stoves like gas fireplaces are cleaner burning, with no residue (such as wood ashes), have a continuous supply of fuel from either an outdoor tank or a line to the house from a public supply and can be vented to the outside by a simple flue from the back of the stove directly through the exterior wall.

Kerosene stoves also can be considered, but their fumes may be objectionable.

FIGURE 19.2 ■ Fireplace Arrangements

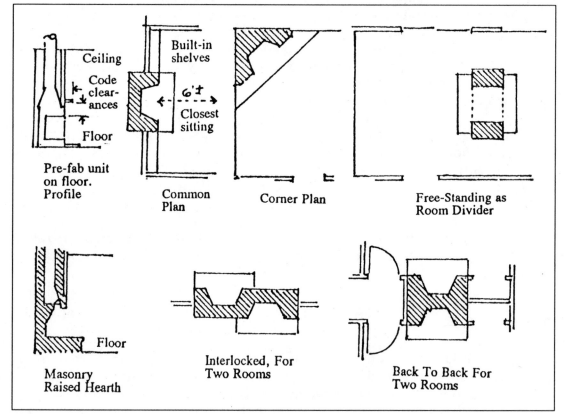

Foyers and Living Areas

■ ENTRANCE FOYER

A foyer or entrance vestibule is desirable for receiving guests as well as unexpected callers. It should have a convenient guest closet. Make sure that the entrance door swing does not block circulation to other parts of the house, including the stairway if it is located in the foyer area of a two-story house. A front entrance that opens directly into a formal room should be avoided, since during wet weather it brings tracks and wet coats into the living room. Typical foyers are illustrated in Figure 20.1.

Adjacent bedroom and living areas should have cutoff sight lines to preserve privacy.

Daylight generally is desired in a foyer and can be provided by door glass sidelights or a transom above. If security of a door next to a sidelight is a concern, an interior deadbolt requiring a key can be installed.

■ LIVING ROOM

The living room, used primarily for sitting and social conversation, also may be used for a piano or tailored to other compatible functions, including entertainment such as card playing and watching TV. Several living room arrangements are shown in Figure 20.2.

A living room should be at least 12 feet wide. For one conversational grouping, the living room should be at least 12 feet by 12 feet. For two conversational groupings, it should be at least 12 feet by 16 feet.

FIGURE 20.1 ■ Typical Foyers

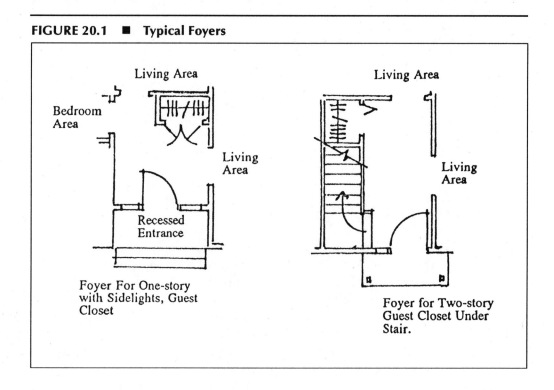

Foyer For One-story with Sidelights, Guest Closet

Foyer for Two-story Guest Closet Under Stair.

Basic seating arrangements are at right angles, or across from each other or a combination of the two. The dimension across the conversational group area (from person to person) should not exceed eight to ten feet. As distance increases, the sense of contact is lost and the grouping becomes too formal and unsocial.

In many homes, the living room may connect directly to the dining room or other compatible rooms such as a family room. In any case, it usually is preferable to avoid making the living room dead-end with only a single entrance. Circulation and attraction to dead-end rooms intended for entertainment is poor, and dead-end rooms receive little use unless a special effort is made to distribute guests.

FIGURE 20.2 ■ Typical Living Rooms

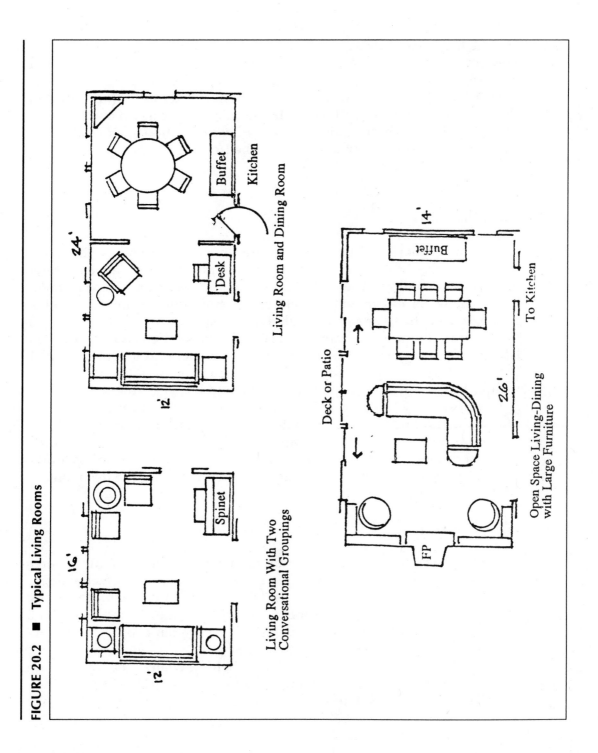

Living Room With Two
Conversational Groupings

Living Room and Dining Room

Open Space Living–Dining
with Large Furniture

The living room as a formal parlor is waning in popularity. For many families, it represents seldom-used space, considering today's living patterns. A favorite instead is a large family room or "great" room.

Family living pattern will govern your choice. Resale of the house generally is not diminished if it has no living room, especially if another room or space is available for quiet sitting and conversation such as a library, study or private sitting area in a master bedroom suite. For larger houses, a living room is a plus.

■ FAMILY ROOM

A family room should provide features that a family enjoys. To some, a fireplace is desirable, as is the place for the family television set, stereo sound system or both. The wiring for stereo and television can be installed before the walls and ceilings are closed in, thus avoiding unsightly wires trailing across the floor and through doorways.

A family room with dining area is sometimes called a *great room*. The label comes from the traditional room at the center of the house in which family and friends gathered to enjoy the comfort of a fireplace in the winter. The idea is just as appealing today and has year-round popularity as well. It should have a central location and be close to the kitchen. Its informality and use permit through traffic. A great room can be used for entertaining at most stages of family life, although with teenagers their habits and interests may be in conflict with those of other members of the family. For this age group, a separate recreation room may be desirable.

■ DINING ROOM

Your choices are a separate dining room (traditional) or a dining area as part of a larger space. A dining room should be at least 12 feet wide; 13 feet is better if furniture, such as a sideboard and hutch, is placed along both side walls. A 12 foot by 12 foot room will provide enough space for a dining room table seating six. For seating eight to ten people, the dining room should be at least 12 feet by 16 feet.

Allow sufficient space for circulation behind chairs when guests are seated at the table. Clear space around the table should be 3 to 3½ feet. Such clearance is important for access by guests and service to the table.

Also, most families need a sideboard or buffet, and some may wish a corner cupboard or cabinet for china. Other furniture generally will not be needed and vacant wall space is useful for placing unused dinning room chairs.

The doorway to the kitchen should be conveniently located and without obstacles to traffic (see Figure 20.3).

A dining room should have daylight, although an outside view is of secondary importance since the focus of attention is the table, eating and conversation. A dining room chandelier centered over the table is an attractive ornamental feature, although the quality of light from a chandelier generally is somewhat harsh; recessed ceiling lights may be preferred. If a chandelier is large, ensure that it is mounted high enough so as not to interfere with guest circulation around the table. For effect, candlelight on the table adds charm to the grouping.

FIGURE 20.3 ■ Typical Dining Rooms

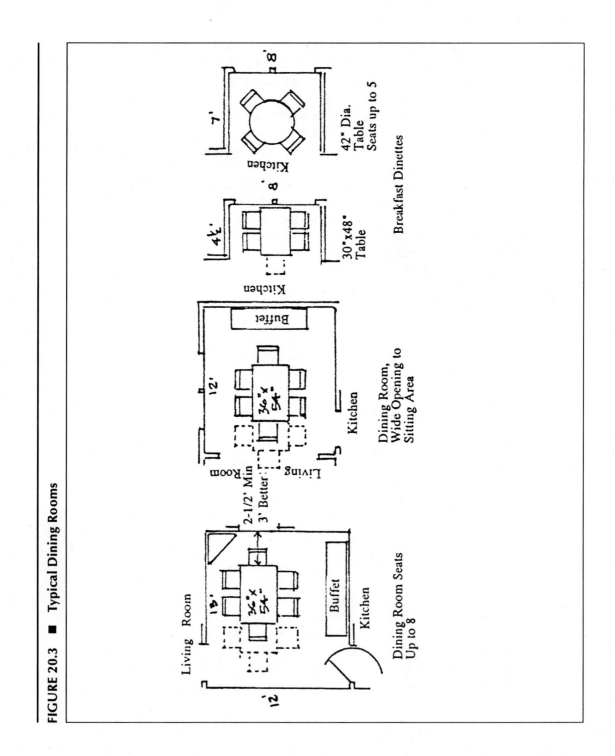

Kitchens

In many ways the kitchen is the most important room in the house and a great deal of thought and planning should go into it to create a convenient, efficient and attractive layout to facilitate food preparation. Usually a work triangle is planned between the three principal work areas: the sink, refrigerator and the stove, with the sink being the central point. Typically, where one person performs most of the kitchen activities, the combined distance between these three points should not exceed a total distance of 18 to 20 feet to ensure proximity and convenience among work areas and to eliminate unnecessary walking. Even if the kitchen is very large, the work triangle should be held to this size.

Several popular kitchen shapes are the U-shape, the L-shape, an L-shape with an island, a one-sided linear type and the aisle-type (with work areas facing each other). For illustrations of typical kitchen layouts, see Figure 21.1. Whatever the arrangement, an important consideration is to avoid a major traffic route through the work triangle. This minimizes accidents and frayed tempers. If a major route must pass through the kitchen, provide adequate space for traffic to pass without interfering with the person or persons preparing food.

A U-shaped kitchen will need about a six-foot distance between the faces of the opposite cabinets. In an island kitchen, the space between island and other cabinets should be three feet, and four feet is better. If two people habitually are at work, five feet of space is needed. Islands work well in an L-shaped kitchen and also may be practical in a U-shaped kitchen if it is large enough. An island on rollers could be convenient if more working space is needed at special times—preparation for parties, for instance. For a layout of an island the work triangle should not go around or behind the island.

FIGURE 21.1 ■ Basic Kitchen Layouts

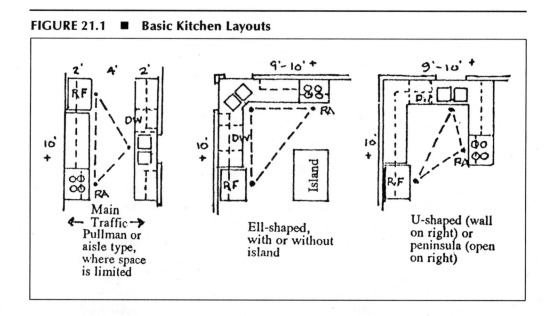

The sink is the busiest work center and generally should be near the middle of the kitchen. Location at a window usually is most enjoyable, although an island or peninsula location may be advantageous in some layouts. Two bowl sinks are more useful than a single bowl, and three bowl sinks also are available but require more space.

In many homes, it is convenient and desirable to have a breakfast or snack bar in the kitchen or just adjacent, sometimes built into a kitchen counter or as a separate area or alcove. Some favor a built-in snack space with a booth, while others prefer the flexibility of table and chairs; however, they do require more space than a booth, but they can be moved when necessary. For examples of kitchen eating space, see Figure 21.2.

FIGURE 21.2 ■ Kitchen Eating Space

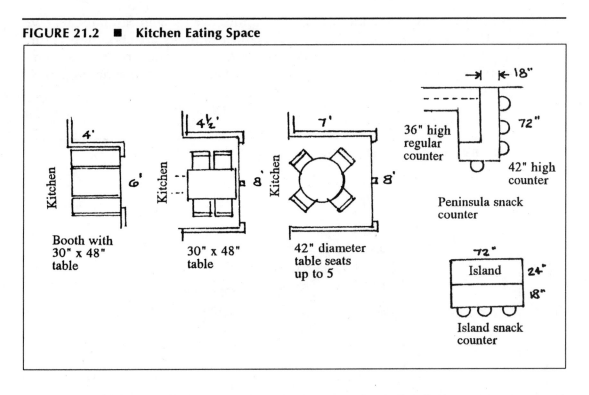

Kitchens should be well lighted and well ventilated, especially in open-space plans. Lighting should be relatively free of shadows, especially in the primary work areas. Where daylight is limited to a single window, most homeowners prefer that it be located above the sink. Range and ovens should be provided with exhaust fans to remove cooking odors and steam, preferably ducted to the outside. Building codes may require this. Some surface cook tops are down-vented (with the duct extending downward through base cabinet), which is particularly useful at island locations. Most exhaust fans are quite noisy, which should be remembered in open-space plans. The conventional cook top and range has a hood two feet above. Better-quality hoods provide for different rates of air movement. The slow speeds are relatively quiet.

Cabinets typically are of two types: base cabinets beneath the countertop and wall-mounted cabinets. Wall cabinets cannot be mounted in front of windows. To provide a lot of useful cabinet storage, it is important to have adequate wall space. A cabinet can be hung over a peninsula counter; however, a cabinet usually is not hung over an island, since it awkwardly blocks the kitchen space. A microwave oven can have its own shelf above the counter work space. Typical cabinets are shown in Figure 21.3. Open shelves may be provided for cookbooks and ornamental items if cooking vapors are not close by. Cooking vapors can cause damage from grease or steam.

FIGURE 21.3 ■ Typical Cabinet Layout

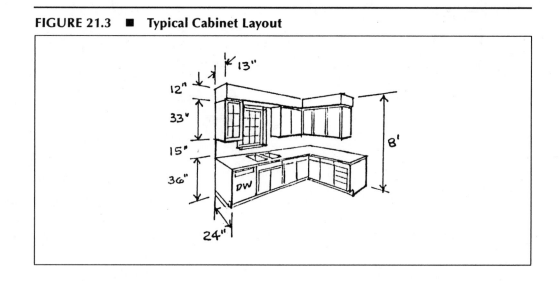

Most kitchen cabinet dealers provide advice on kitchen planning at no charge if you buy their cabinets. Some sell manufactured brands, others do made-to-order work and most offer a combination of the two for custom service. In any case, do your own planning in advance as to general layout, appliances and special features. Lead time between order and arrival of cabinets may be four to six weeks, or more.

Standard kitchen counters are 36 inches high by 24 inches deep. Inside corners are difficult to use efficiently, but units are available with rotating shelves to capture otherwise lost corner space. Conventional kitchen appliances, except refrigerators, are designed to fit standard base cabinets (under-the-counter dishwasher and oven). Most refrigerators are about 28 inches deep overall, and hence project forward of the base cabinets. Several appliance makers offer 24-inch-deep refrigerators for a built-in appearance, but at a sacrifice to interior depth.

Drawers are generally desired directly beneath the countertop for flatware, tea towels, kitchen utensils and miscellaneous storage. Space beneath the drawers usually is fitted with a shelf for pots, pans and other large items such as portable appliances (toaster, mixer and blender). Pull-out trays on drawer slides may be more convenient than conventional drawers but are more expensive.

Wall and base cabinets may contain vertical compartments for baking sheets and serving trays. In the base cabinet near the sink, a trash receptacle is handy.

Corner wall cabinets that rest on the counter and provide room for storage of small appliances also are available.

Many ready-made wall cabinets are 33 inches high. When placed over a standard 36-inch-high counter, the bottom of the wall cabinet is 15 inches above the counter and allows a space of 12 inches from the top of the wall cabinet to a standard 8-foot ceiling. Wall cabinets with less height are available for installation over sinks, ranges and refrigerators, as shown in Figure 21.3.

You may prefer to leave the space above the wall cabinets open to the ceiling so that decorative things may be put there or you may have this space boxed in as part of the wall for easier cleaning, as shown in Figure 21.4. Oversized wall cabinets above the 7-foot line also are available, or can be custom-made to fill the gap to the ceiling. Although difficult to use routinely, this high space may be used for long-term storage.

FIGURE 21.4 ■ Wall-Hung Kitchen Cabinets

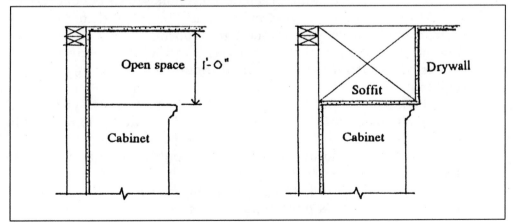

Ensure that cabinet doors are hinged for easy access to the interior. Where a cabinet is hung over a peninsula, the doors may open on both sides, a convenience for access to table china.

Custom-made wall cabinets are available with heights from 15 inches above the countertop to full-height floor to ceiling.

If you have selected factory-made cabinets, however, you may not have any choice in wall cabinet height, since most are made only at the size that requires a one-foot open space or one-foot soffit down from the ceiling.

The decision with regard to the soffit for kitchen cabinets should be made before the completion of the framing so that the carpenters can install the framing needed to hang the drywall and secure the wall cabinets if enclosed soffits are your choice.

Make sure you have cabinets and drawers or shelves where you most need them:

- Cabinets beside the stove for pots and pans
- Tall slots for cookie sheets, muffin tins and other oversized utensils
- Drawers for cooking utensils and hot pads
- Drawers convenient to the dishwasher and eating areas for tableware

You should be able to empty the dishwasher into nearby cabinets above it. Everyday china and glassware storage should be the most convenient.

For extra dishes, glasses, bowls and other utensils, a more remote cabinet is usually satisfactory, but ensure that these shelves are deep enough to accommodate various items.

For more information on cabinet selection, see Appendix D.

All finishes used in a kitchen should be durable and easy to clean. Kitchen spills are not uncommon and flooring should be easily cleanable and slip-resistant such as vinyl and ceramic tile. Carpeting and wood floors, while attractive, are more difficult to keep clean, especially with children.

The kitchen should have a convenient route for carrying groceries in and trash out. If possible, the route should be directly to the parking area or the garage with as few level changes as possible.

Avoid kitchen locations that require routes through the kitchen work area to reach other living areas.

Added service and storage space may be needed for entertaining. For example, a butler's pantry adjacent to the kitchen and dining area, equipped with counter sink, a second dishwasher, an ice-maker or second refrigerator is very handy. This pantry should be large enough to permit two-way traffic between kitchen and dining room and provide efficient counter workspace. Cabinets may be there for china, glass and silver storage. A separate dry storage closet or pantry may be useful for storing canned and bottled foods, paper goods and portable appliances. This will be described in more detail later.

A wet bar also may be put in other places than in the kitchen area, such as the family room, recreation room, Florida room or other rooms used frequently for entertainment. For convenience, a wet bar should have a small ice-maker–refrigerator under the counter. Upper cabinets should be provided for glassware and base cabinets for beverage storage. If plumbing is not easily installed and the bar is used relatively little, a dry bar may be satisfactory.

A wine cellar or closet could be near the dining room or in a basement. Manufactured wine storage cabinets are available with self-contained refrigeration to preserve proper temperature. Large custom designs can be built-in, such as walk-in cellars. Modest wine storage can be provided in a kitchen cabinet with suitable bins for bottle storage.

FIGURE 21.5 ■ Typical Appliance Sizes

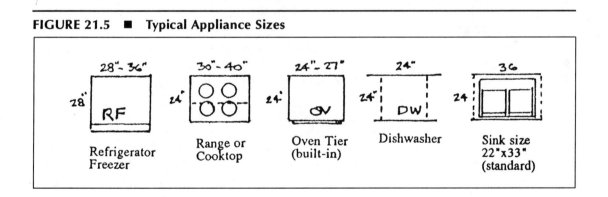

■ APPLIANCES

Costs of appliances reflect their features and quality. Midprice appliances often are the best value. Typical sizes are shown in Figure 21.5. A refrigerator with ice-maker is important. The ice-maker requires tubing connected to a water supply. Refrigerator choices include side-by-side refrigerator-freezer or top-and-bottom arrangement. The latter is more energy-efficient; the former is more convenient, but will not accept some large items such as turkeys for freezing because of its narrow width.

For most families, an additional full-size freezer may be needed.

Ranges are available in basic models with the oven beneath the cooking top. Other models have an oven above the cooking top. A separate cooking top also is popular with remote wall ovens. Some ovens include microwave and browning features. A self-cleaning oven is recommended. A separate microwave oven may be hung under a wall cabinet or built into the wall cabinet system. Most ranges and ovens are available in either gas or electric models. Ranges should be vented with exhaust to the outdoors. Some codes prohibit recirculating vents. Downdraft vents are built into many cooktops, permitting installation in an island and thus do not require overhead venting.

Some appliances such as the dishwasher and refrigerator can be given custom decorator fronts to blend with the kitchen decor.

The dishwasher is most convenient if located next to the sink. The hot water supply and waste pipes are already adjacent. A wall cabinet near the dishwasher for the storage of dishes just washed is most convenient.

A garbage grinder or disposal may be desired unless you are inclined to compost organic food scraps for garden use. Usually the disposal is mounted under the drain of the sink bowl. The switch to operate it may be installed in the wall near the sink.

A trash compactor that compresses paper and other bulky items is useful in locations with limited trash pickup. It can be installed in a base cabinet. A conventional waste can or receptacle is handier.

■ OTHER KITCHEN AMENITIES

A pantry is very useful to provide more storage space. A reach-in pantry can be built into the cabinets. Some are elaborate with shelves at the back, an inner hinged shelf section and shallow shelves on the backs of the doors. A walk-in pantry takes more space but may be preferred if you are accustomed to, or desire, a large storage area. A pantry also provides for storage of infrequently used small appliances, mops and brooms as well as canned goods and dry food products. Typical pantries are shown in Figure 21.6.

FIGURE 21.6 ■ Pantries

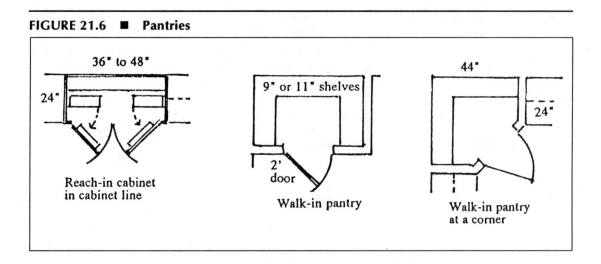

A broom closet can be built into the cabinet line for cleaning paraphernalia and can be sized to accommodate a trash can and recycled materials.

A desk in or near the kitchen is convenient for keeping appliance literature and to take care of household business correspondence. Shelves or a cabinet above the desk can be used for cookbooks. The desk also is a good location for the kitchen telephone. An example of a kitchen desk is shown in Figure 21.7.

FIGURE 21.7 ■ Desk with File Drawers

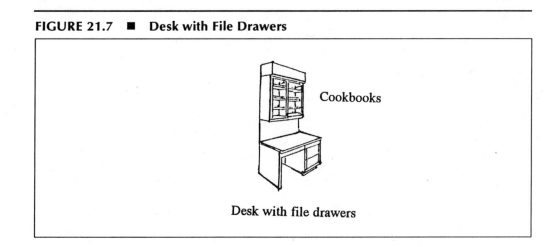

Even the nongourmet kitchen can be an efficient yet attractive area. Here one's interest can be expressed with a display of artwork or house plants. Take advantage of the opportunities, since the kitchen is the focus of so much time and activity. A complete but modest layout reflecting some of the features mentioned is shown in Figure 21.8.

FIGURE 21.8 ■ Complete Moderate-Sized Kitchen

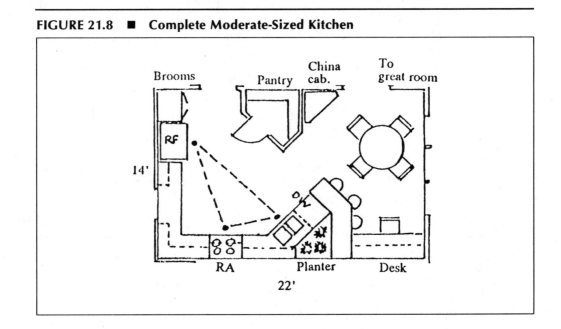

Activity and Utility Rooms

■ FLORIDA ROOM

A glassed-in or enclosed porch, commonly called a Florida room, is increasingly popular. Such rooms also may have skylights, and their essential character is lots of daylight and a sense of being in the garden or permitting good visual contact with the out-of-doors while still part of the house living space. For an example of a Florida room, see Figure 22.1.

Passive solar heating, discussed further in Appendix G, is important for most Florida rooms, especially if room orientation is southerly. The Florida room offers the sense of outdoor space, yet, with proper design, it may be made comfortable. In most moderate to colder climates, a Florida room requires additional heating due to the large thermal losses through the extensive glass even using insulated or triple glass and low E glass. Insulating draw draperies also may be needed for comfort. Air-conditioning will be needed in localities that are very warm, since summer heat buildup in the room can be extreme. Use of ceiling paddle fans will help the distribution of air and make the room more comfortable.

FIGURE 22.1 ■ Florida Room

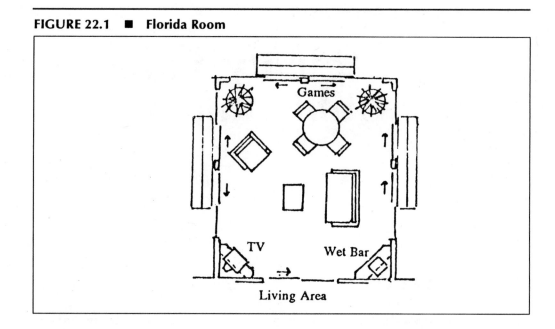

■ RECREATION ROOM

Once consigned to the basement or over the garage, the recreation room may be made more convenient or merged with the family room. Many people still, however, want to locate a recreation room somewhat remotely depending on use. This is particularly true with teenagers who have their own stereos, or even with smaller children whose floor games and toys may escape routine tidying up. Family habits and interests will dictate decisions for such rooms. Installing insulation in ceilings, walls and floors will reduce noise transmission to adjacent rooms and to those above and below.

■ OTHER ACTIVITY AREAS

A larger house plan may include rooms for special activities. The size of these rooms will depend on their function, furniture requirements and location, based on how the activity relates to adjacent rooms.

Library and Home Office

A library may be in or near the private area, since seclusion and noise control are important. A library should have good daylight for reading. Wall space should be generous regardless of whether shelves are built in or provided by furniture.

A home office also may be desired. If business visitors are to be received, it should be independent of the house circulation to avoid intrusions. A separate door to the outside remote from the main house entrance will provide better privacy for the family.

Another special room might be one for a computer and its associated equipment although it could be located in a home office or other room.

Exercise and Spa Rooms

An indoor spa (hot tub) is best located where control of excessive room humidity can be separated from the rest of the house. It is generally better to isolate it from the house HVAC system and provide a quiet large capacity exhaust fan. The weight of a water-filled tub usually is so heavy that it should be ground supported in a basement or in a one-story addition with slab-on-grade construction or, if crawl-space construction, with extra wood floor support. If the spa room has lots of glass (like a solarium) it is difficult to prevent fogging during cold weather without excellent air circulation. Most codes require that a spa have its own water heater system, which must be isolated from the domestic house hot water. Check the particulars on an outside spa you select. Some homeowners install a spa on an open deck.

You may wish to locate an exercise room in or near the spa or bedroom area. A bathroom nearby completes the arrangement.

Hobby Rooms

An indoor plant room or greenhouse is great for those who love indoor plants. The best location for a greenhouse room is on the southerly side of the house with good winter sunlight (not blocked by other parts of the house or evergreen shrubs and trees). If the room is independent from the house HVAC system (which is recommended), the high summer heat build-up can be exhausted without interfering with house comfort. It is possible to skillfully plan and build a greenhouse room that serves as a winter passive solar storage area, and use a transfer fan with a damper control to move heat from the greenhouse into other parts of the house when needed. A number of manufactured greenhouse designs are available for residential application.

A darkroom for the photo enthusiast will require total light control and ventilation and can usually be served by the house HVAC system.

A workshop will require clean air and good ventilation and it should be separated from the house HVAC system to avoid circulating paint and other odors, and sawdust.

A sewing room may be near the laundry or in the bedroom area. Good daylight is desirable.

■ UTILITY AREAS

Mud Room

Families with younger children and those who enjoy and spend a great deal of time in the yard may want a mud room with half-bath near a back, side or garage door. Space should be adequate to remove coats and boots. A small closet or wall hooks for coats are desirable. The mud room may be close to or a part of the laundry, as illustrated in Figure 22.2.

Laundry

The laundry can be located in the kitchen in a small house plan, but often is in a separate utility room, the garage or, since most of the household laundry is generated within the bedroom area, near the bedrooms.

Wherever located, a separate room is preferred, since machine noise and chemical odor can be objectionable. In a larger house, it is preferable not to have laundry equipment in the kitchen. The laundry should have a soaking tub plus space for storage of laundry supplies. The laundry room also can be a convenient place to store, mops, brooms, a vacuum cleaner and other household cleaning supplies.

There are two conventional arrangements for washer and dryer: side by side and stacked (dryer above). Machines are specifically designed for each arrangement and usually are not interchangeable. The stacked arrangement requires less floor space, but there are fewer models to

FIGURE 22.2 ■ Mud Room and Half-Bath

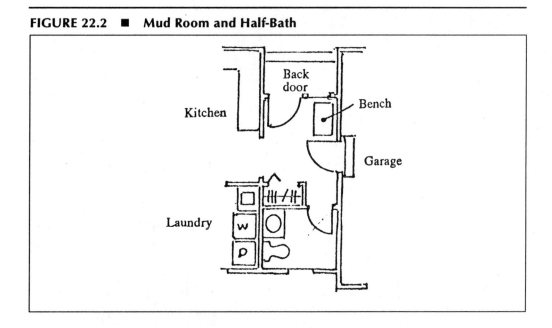

choose from. Many stacking models have smaller capacity. Side-by-side models are compatible with standard kitchen base cabinets, although they project several inches into the traffic aisle to accommodate hook-up hoses, cables and dryer vents.

Dryers are available in both gas and electric models. They should be vented to the outside to rid the house of moisture and lint.

Washers and dryers are available in white or color-tint finishes. Machine operating features vary widely, as do prices. Midprice machines are generally a best buy if special features are infrequently used.

If the laundry is in the garage, the washer should be installed adjacent to a house wall to protect pipes from freezing, and the dryer should be accessible to an outside wall for easy venting, but near the washer. If interior location is necessary, it may be possible to vent downward under the floor and then horizontally to the outside. Vents should not dump into an attic or crawl space, as this solution is prohibited by most building codes.

Coordinate the door swing on the dryer so that the clothes can go directly into the dryer from the washer. Most washers are top-loading with a 15-inch clearance above to a wall cabinet, which is usually adequate. Confirm this before installing the cabinet.

FIGURE 22.3 ■ Laundry Equipment and Layouts

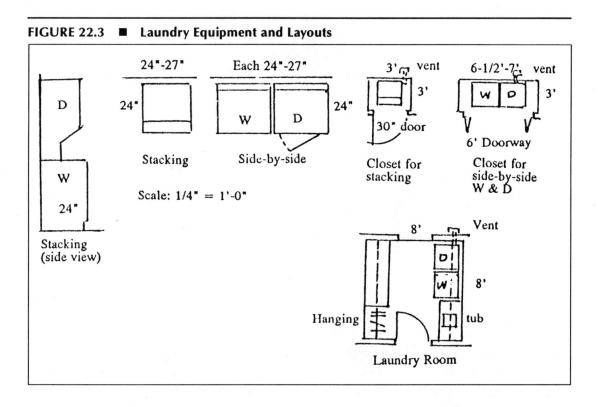

In a large house, you could have more than one laundry. For example, the main laundry may be located in the bedroom area and a smaller one in the kitchen area, or vice versa. The convenience of such arrangements may greatly outweigh any added cost for space and equipment. The small laundry may be in a closet using stacked washer-dryer.

To minimize damage from possible water leakage, provide under the washer a drip pan connected to a drain.

Bedrooms and Closets

A three-bedroom house generally has widest appeal. A two-bedroom house may suit a retired couple, with the second bedroom used for guests or a sick room. A four-bedroom house is increasingly common for large families and families with older children. For a family with an infant, a small bedroom next to the master bedroom can serve first as a nursery and later as a sitting room, den or office for parents.

Since bedrooms and baths are for personal use, they should be located for privacy and quiet with respect to other parts of the house and placement relative to the lot. A bedroom near a noisy street is not pleasant. Avoid placing an outdoor HVAC unit near the bedroom window. Typically, bedrooms and baths are grouped together except for special privacy needs situations, such as a remote master bedroom suite or an in-law suite.

As mentioned before, there should be no direct sight line between the living area and the bedroom areas. In a one-story house, this can usually be arranged with a foyer and offset walls between living and bedroom areas. In a two-story house, floor separation solves the problem.

Bedrooms should have good daylight, ventilation and a view. Baths should be convenient and the bedroom-to-bath traffic should not be directly visible from living areas. Bedroom closets should be within or open into bedrooms, or an adjacent closet-dressing area should be provided. Beds are normally placed with the headboard at a wall for easy housekeeping. For typical bedroom arrangements, see Figure 23.1.

The master bedroom, with fully private bath and often associated dressing area, is first class. Other bedrooms need not be large, but children's bedrooms should be planned to accommodate two children each if only for resale value. If space in a children's bedroom is tight, consider the use of bunk beds. Bedroom layouts should be large enough at least for a nightstand near the bed (two for a master bedroom) and a dresser or chest. A child's bedroom should have a chair and desk, and possibly a hobby or play area. Children's closets, although smaller than adults' closets, may use the same types of hanging and shelf arrangements. For small children, install hanging rods at lower levels, then raise them later as children grow.

Even though table lamps are used in bedrooms, an overhead ceiling light is practical in all bedrooms and better for overall light, particularly when cleaning.

In a master bedroom, you may want a sitting area large enough for a chaise or easy chair and a table. A television in the bedroom should be placed for viewing from both the bed and the sitting area. Also include several straight chairs. Ensure that bed size, especially king or queen, fits the space available. If necessary to economize on bedroom size, consider built-in drawers, shelves and bins in the closet to substitute for dressers.

Bedrooms require much less open space than do rooms in living areas, even with furniture as large as a bed, since room occupancy is limited to one or two persons. For typical bedroom sizes, see Figure 23.1. A small bedroom for a single bed, exclusive of closet space, can be about nine feet by eleven feet plus a closet, and a middle-sized bedroom for a double bed about 11 feet by 13 feet plus a closet. A bedroom for a king-size bed plus dresser, chests and chairs should be at least 13 feet, six inches by 15 feet.

■ CLOSETS

The longer one lives in a house the more it is wished that closets were bigger and more numerous. Plan the size and number of your closets as generously as possible.

FIGURE 23.1   ■   Typical Bedroom Sizes and Arrangements

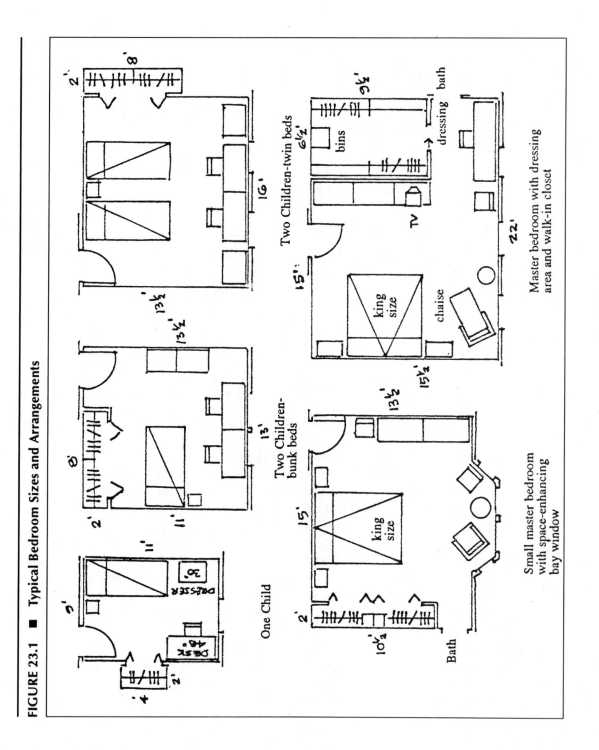

Closets are of two basic types: walk-in and reach-in (see Figure 23.2). A reach-in closet need be only two feet deep. Added depth is wasteful, since one is limited by arm reach. Doors, often bifold, to a reach-in closet should be as wide as practical for easy access to all of the stored clothing. Walk-in closets require more floor area for the same hanging space but the single door provides more wall area in the bedroom.

FIGURE 23.2 ■ Walk-in and Reach-in Closets

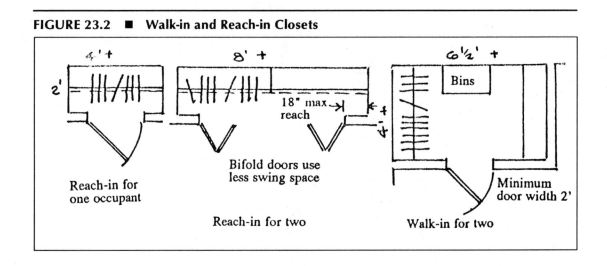

To get more efficiency from either type of closet, use dual high and low rods in part of the closet where folded trousers, shirts, blouses, skirts and jackets may be hung. Also install shelves above the hanging rods. If bedroom space is restricted and chest of drawers space is limited, use built-in shelves, bins or drawers in the closets.

In addition to bedroom closets, at least one general linen closet in the bedroom area, and linen closets in each bath are usually needed. A separate seasonal closet may be useful for clothes storage and can be lined with cedar to help guard against moths.

Locate a coat closet at or near the front door with perhaps another one near the back or side door. Alternatively, near the back door, exposed hanging pegs may be provided for often-used outerwear.

A table linen closet may be helpful near the dining area where silverware also may be stored and locked. Install round horizontal poles under the shelves for hanging tablecloths. Other special storage may include a place for children's toys and games, a gun collection, cleaning equipment and so forth. An attic often may be useful for storage, but uncontrolled temperature and dust from attic ventilation can reduce its usefulness. A basement also can be used for storage provided dampness and mustiness are controlled.

Bathrooms

Bathrooms in today's homes are expected to be attractive as well as functional. In some cases, a homeowner may invest in high-grade ornamental fixtures as well as expensive finishes such as tile and marble commensurate with the overall quality of the house, especially in the master bedroom area or a guest powder room. At the same time, secondary baths may be more modest such as those used by children, or a convenience half-bath for family use.

Where economy is important, group two bathrooms together to reduce the cost of installing expensive plumbing. Minimize piping by grouping fixtures together, or by arranging bathrooms back-to-back or near other plumbing such as for the kitchen or laundry.

Avoid locating the plumbing next to or above the living and dining rooms where the noise of a flushing toilet would be objectionable. If this is impractical, the noise still can be muffled by using insulation in the wall or ceiling framing.

Where possible, locate a bathroom along an outside wall for daylight and natural ventilation, which most people find more pleasant than a completely interior location. An alternative for a windowless bath is a ventable skylight if the roof is directly above. If a bath works out best at an interior location, an exhaust fan will be needed and is required by most codes. It should be ducted to the outside and not dumped into an attic or under the house. An exhaust fan also may be desirable near a shower where moisture clouds are a problem. In localities where winters are cold, it also is preferable to provide occupant-controlled auxiliary heat from a wall-mounted electric heater, ceiling mounted radiant heat lamp or a combination heater and exhaust fan.

To respect modesty in a home, try to position bathroom fixtures so that the toilet is least visible through the open bathroom door or the open door itself interrupts a direct view of the toilet.

One or more medicine cabinets with mirrored fronts are desirable directly above or near washbasins. Double or triple cabinets with opposite swinging doors can provide simultaneous views of the front and back of the head. The use of a large mirror on the wall of a small bathroom makes the room seem twice as large, which is nice in a guest powder room as well as other bathrooms.

Bathroom finishes should be easy to clean, especially near toilets, showers and tubs. Ceramic tile for both floor and walls is a good choice, although more economical vinyl flooring and washable wall covering are satisfactory finishes. Prefabricated plastic wall panels also are available for use around a tub/shower or shower cabinet. If the bath is compartmentalized, carpeting may be used in dressing areas where wash basins are located.

Baths should have a self-contained closet or cabinet for bath linens and other supplies too large for a medicine cabinet, or else a linen closet nearby. Where built-in-the-counter basins are used, the base cabinet also can serve this function. Open shelves provide room to display decorative items to make the bathroom seem more a part of the house. Baths also should have conveniently placed towel bars and other accessories that may be keyed to decor.

Bathroom size will be determined in part by the occupancy and in part by the size of fixtures desired and suitable access to them. A shared bath such as the master bath, or one located between two bedrooms should be generous in size with adequate traffic space to avoid bumping into each other.

■ THE HALF-BATH OR POWDER ROOM

This consists of a lavatory or a washbasin with a wall mirror or medicine cabinet, and a toilet, as shown in Figure 24.1. The minimum size half-bath has a wall-mounted washbasin. The larger, more luxurious half-bath has the bowl in a counter above a vanity cabinet where bathroom supplies can be kept, or a free-standing bowl mounted on a pedestal.

FIGURE 24.1　■　The Half-Bath

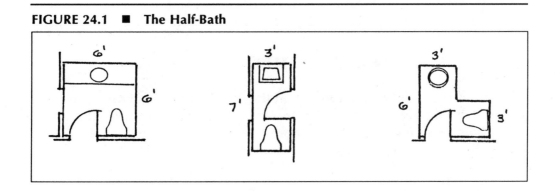

Half-baths are placed for the use of visitors, for cleanup when returning to the house from yard work as well as for the convenience of family members. For visitors, locate one near the front hall or foyer, or the family room. A half-bath for family use is usually located near the kitchen or laundry or close to the back door or the door to the garage.

A powder room should be located so that its door is hidden from social areas such as living and dining rooms. Suitable locations include the foyer, or just inside the bedroom area adjacent to the foyer.

■ THE SMALL BATHROOM

This consists of a tub or shower, a wall-mounted washbasin and a toilet, as shown in Figure 24.2. At least one bathroom in the house should have a tub.

FIGURE 24.2 ■ The Small Bathroom

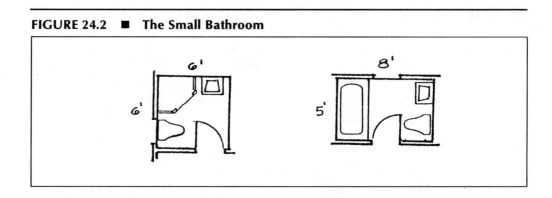

■ THE MEDIUM-SIZED BATHROOM

This offers more room than the small bathroom and is equipped with a tub-shower combination, toilet and a cabinet-mounted washbasin, as shown in Figure 24.3. It is more comfortable and can be satisfactory for the bathroom for the master bedroom in a small house.

FIGURE 24.3 ■ Medium-Sized Bathroom

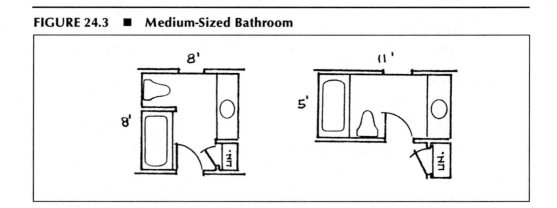

■ THE LARGE BATHROOM

This is equipped with a toilet, cabinet-mounted double washbasins and separate tub and shower. It is large enough for two people to share at the same time. The toilet may be placed behind a half or full-height wall screen for privacy, or in an alcove.

FIGURE 24.4 ■ The Large Bathroom

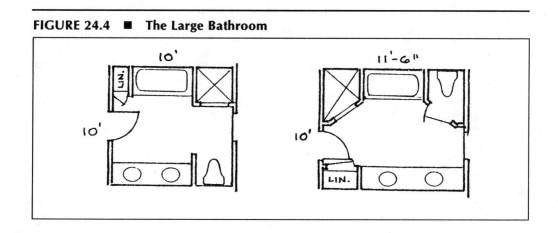

■ THE SHARED BATHROOM

FIGURE 24.5 ■ The Shared Bathroom

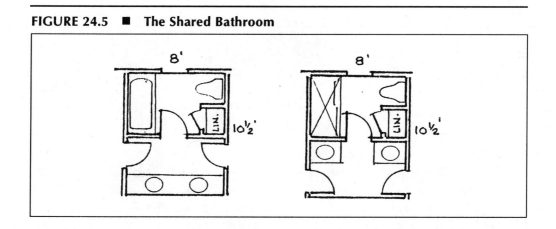

Where two bedrooms share the same bathroom, an alternative arrangement between the two bedrooms that provides more privacy is shown in the two designs of Figure 24.5. Although the space required is about the same as for two bathrooms, the scheme is more economical, since fewer fixtures are involved. Privacy for the bathing and toilet area is attained by separate compartments. Separate washbasins are recommended.

■ THE GRAND BATHROOM

This is even larger and more luxuriously equipped, with a separate tub and shower, two toilet alcoves and two separate cabinet-mounted washbasin alcoves. It also may have a whirlpool bath, a bidet, heated towel racks and any other equipment the owners desire, as illustrated in Figure 24.6.

FIGURE 24.6   ■   The Grand Bathroom

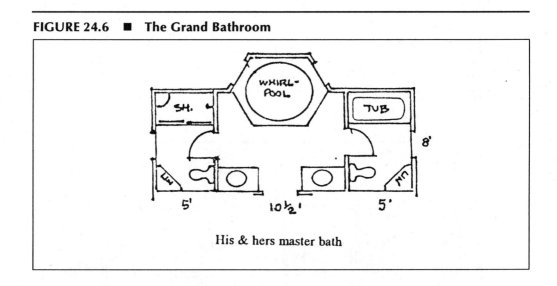

His & hers master bath

The bath for the master bedroom usually should be placed so that entry to it is only from the master bedroom. Baths serving more than two bedrooms should have an entry from a bedroom area hallway.

The effect on space planning is important, since the combined size of a luxury master bath plus closets may equal or exceed that of the master bedroom itself.

A bathroom for a mobility-impaired person should have special features, such as safety rails, grab bar, a special toilet (often higher) and special fittings. In addition, the lavatory should be designed with knee space for a wheelchair and the doorway should be two feet, ten inches wide, or wider.

Typical bathroom fixtures and their space requirements and the piping system are discussed in Appendix H.

Stairways, Traffic and Circulation

■ HALLWAYS AND PASSAGES

These necessary spaces are very important to the effective circulation pattern of the house.

Primarily, a hallway permits access to one or more rooms without going through others, preserves privacy or avoids interference with room activities. In a bedroom area, this purpose is greatly appreciated, but in the general living area, a hallway is needed less. In fact, in an open space living area, the purpose is to eliminate separation and enhance sociability unless an interfering constant parade of traffic results. For examples of corridors, see Figure 25.1.

A foyer is useful at the entrance to define the reception area as already mentioned so that all comers do not enter directly into the living area.

Wherever possible, hallways and other passages should have daylight to make it unnecessary to switch on lights. In a two-story plan, there should be a window near the head of the stair, if possible.

Hallways should be limited in size and excessive length and should be avoided for purposes of economy. When needed, hallways should be given some character and made attractive. Since a three-foot width is minimal, increasing this width to three feet, six inches, or four feet will make a hallway more pleasant and less crowded.

FIGURE 25.1 ■ Corridors with Interruptions

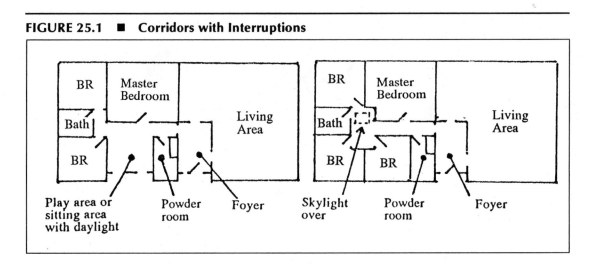

Furniture in a passage usually is not needed except in an entrance foyer. Where furniture is placed in a passage, width should be adequate to provide at least three feet of clear walking space.

A long corridor may appear lessened by recessing doorways into adjacent rooms. Such enlargements of the hall also are effective in giving a sense of space, and make bedroom entrances more private. In addition, see Appendix B for ideas in using wallpaper to improve the appearance of long hallways.

In plans where the roof is directly over the corridor, the use of one or more skylights for daylight will enhance the space and make it less necessary to use electric lighting in the daytime.

■ STAIRWAYS

In space planning, coordination between floors and allowance for proper stair dimensions is critical.

Most building codes require that stairs be at least three feet wide, treads nine inches minimum and risers (tread to tread height) not more than eight and one-quarter inches high. A house with a conventional eight-foot ceiling requires 13 risers (12 treads) floor to floor and a horizontal length of nine feet. A more comfortable stair uses seven and three-quarters–inch risers and ten-inch treads, for a total of 14 risers and a run of ten feet, ten inches. In addition, about three feet of clear landing space is needed at both the bottom and the top. Most codes require a handrail along at least one side of the stair. For examples of basic stair layouts, see Figure 25.2.

FIGURE 25.2　■　Basic Stair Layouts

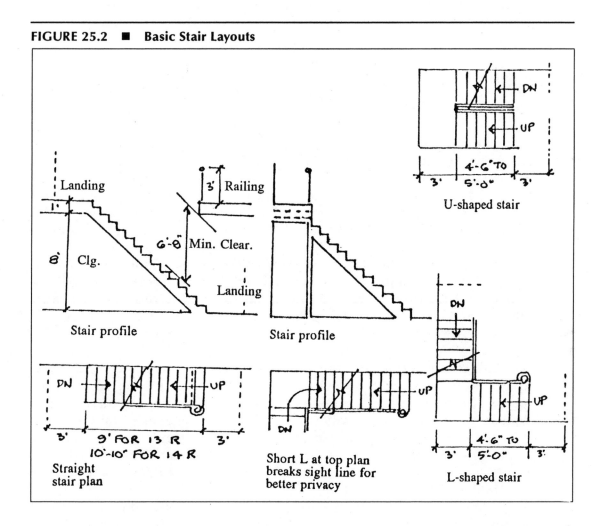

A straight stair is most economical and uses the least floor area. It is also the most convenient design for moving furniture up and down. The L- and U-shaped stairs take up more space due to intermediate platforms but may permit a better floor plan. For privacy at the second floor, L- and U-shaped stairs break the sight line better than a straight stair. The length of L- and U-runs need not be equal if better suited to a plan; for example, a straight run of 11 or 12 risers, then a turn followed by two more risers permits enough height under the short run for a doorway.

If the house has a basement, its stair is most economical if located directly below the main stair. If the basement stair is to be closed off with a door, the door should not open across the steps; instead, a landing on the stair side of the door should be provided. This safety feature is required by most codes. If such space is not available in the floor plan, an alternative is to open the door away from the stair but allow adequate and safe clearance for the door swing. If the house has no basement, the under-stair space can be used for a closet, a small powder room, or HVAC equipment.

Since a foyer is desirable to buffer the entrance from the living areas, it is also the logical place for the stair. This location varies according to the floor plan. In traditional-style houses, the stair is usually along one side of the foyer, as shown in Figure 25.3.

A large foyer with a wide opening to the second floor creates a dramatic effect for a stairway. If this design exposes bedroom doors to view from the first floor, it may be necessary to recess the bedroom and bathroom doors or install a connecting hallway for bedroom privacy. The large two-story space of the open stairway will increase the load on the HVAC system.

Stair treatment may be plain or it may have architectural character and distinction appropriate to the house style, be it traditional or contemporary. For example, in a colonial design, the stairway can have turned balusters (spindles), decorative newels (posts at the ends of railings) and molded handrails. In a contemporary house, the steps may be backless (open risers) to provide a striking see-through effect. This type of stair may cause an uneasy feeling in some people, so carefully consider before you build your own.

Dramatic stair shapes are available such as the half and quarter circle. While relatively expensive, they are quite beautiful and enhancing.

FIGURE 25.3 ■ Typical Stairway Locations

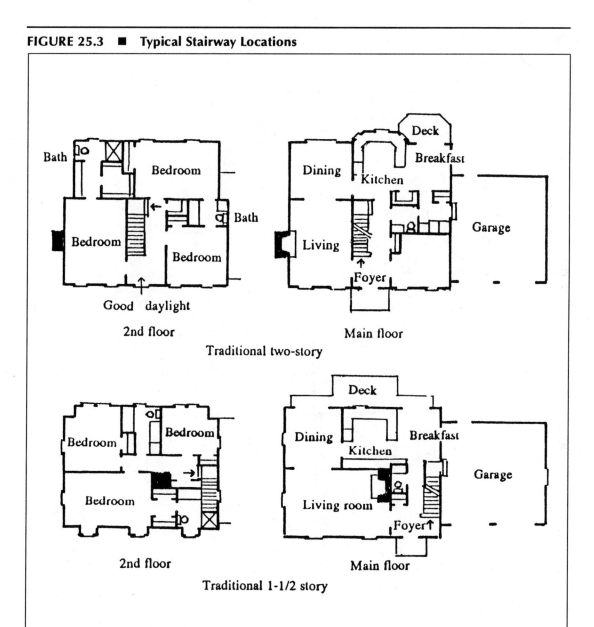

Good daylight

2nd floor   Main floor

Traditional two-story

2nd floor   Main floor

Traditional 1-1/2 story

FIGURE 25.3 ■ Typical Stairway Locations (Continued)

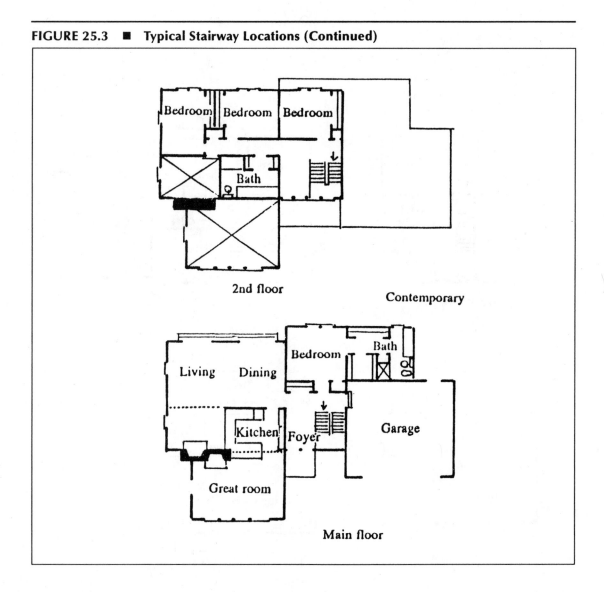

2nd floor

Contemporary

Main floor

■ TRAFFIC AND CIRCULATION

Keep traffic patterns as compact as possible. Avoid long corridors that consume space better used for living areas and add to the cost of construction. Where traffic passes through a room, provide a clear and direct route—straight, if possible—and avoid obstacles. Wherever possible, avoid unrelated traffic through a room or area unless it is essential to the plan. The test is, does the traffic interrupt the primary purpose or activity of the room? For example, it is better not to have all traffic pass through the kitchen to reach the family room as shown in Figure 25.4. In the kitchen, it is especially important to avoid crossing the work triangle. In rooms where guest circulation is desired, such as the living or dining rooms, avoid the dead-end. Make bedrooms dead-end where privacy is an important requirement.

In homes where wheelchair movement is expected, the principal traffic routes should be wide enough to accommodate convenient safe passage and maneuvering. Doorways should be at least two feet, ten inches wide (three feet is better). Hinged doors are generally preferred over sliding doors, especially those with floor tracks. Avoid step-down rooms such as a sunken living room. In a two-story house, a main floor room for a handicapped bedroom with adjacent adapted bathroom should solve the problem. An alternate solution is to install a stairway lift, or if space permits, a home elevator to the second floor. Then adapt a bedroom and bath there as necessary.

■ SUMMARY

In Part III of *The Home Design Guide*, we have discussed what goes into a good floor plan. We have described the relationship and organization of various areas, particulars of rooms and house circulation. With your notes and diagrams, you now have the essentials of creating successful floor plans, or of evaluating a set of stock plans, if this is your preference.

Remember that competing requirements are to be expected—it's a matter of how you evaluate them and your emphasis of importance. However, guard against compromising the important basics. Here is a checklist to review when planning your house:

1. Determine suitability of floor plan type (one-story, story-and-a-half or two-story, including wings) and house style (one of the traditionals or a contemporary).
2. Plan the location of rooms best suited to the lot for privacy, views, neighboring houses and the street.
3. Determine best room sizes, shapes and furniture layouts.

4. Plan for the best circulation and traffic pattern. In story-and-a-half and two-story designs, coordinate upper and lower stairway levels.
5. Determine your desire for and plan for features such as fireplaces, nonstandard ceiling heights, cathedral ceilings, skylights, porches and decks.

Once satisfied that you have addressed these matters, you can proceed to refinements and particulars such as product selection and architectural details, discussed further in the appendixes that follow.

FIGURE 25.4 ■ Problem Circulation

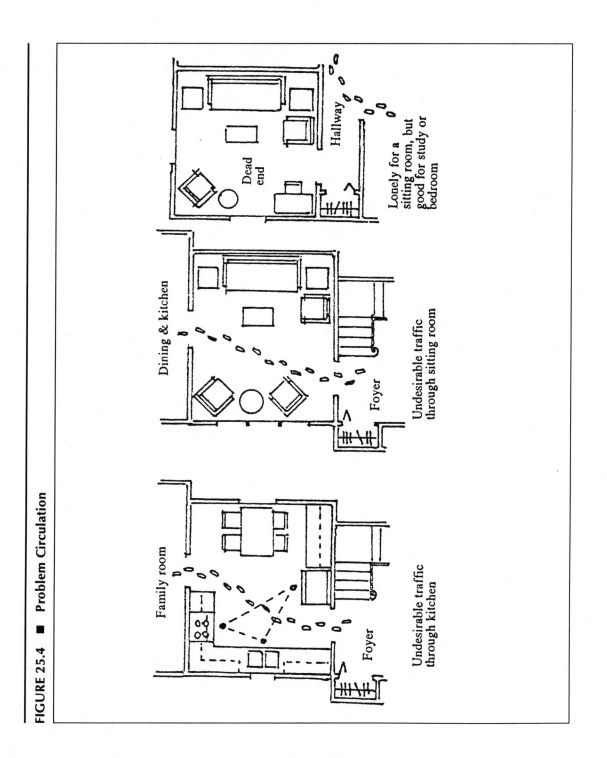

Windows and Doors

In these days of high energy costs, the selection of windows and doors assumes much more importance than it did a few years ago. In addition to selecting windows appropriate to the style of your house, you should consider insulating and anti–air infiltration properties, ease of operation, maintenance, ease of cleaning and price to fit your pocketbook, and in just about that order of priority. Do not use cheap windows that will erode initial savings and will lead to increases in heating and cooling costs, maintenance and lessened comfort.

The most widely used residential window types are shown in Figure A.1.

■ DOUBLE-HUNG WINDOWS

The most widely used of all window types is the double hung with two sashes within the frame. One or both sashes can be moved up and down. Double hungs are appropriately used in both traditional and some contemporary house designs. The traditional application is illustrated in Figure A.2.

The small window panes in historic designs create an attractive scale and effect that large one-piece glass cannot achieve. Modern double hungs are equipped with invisible sash balances so that sashes are easily moved up and down and then remain in an open position for ventilation.

FIGURE A.1 ■ Types of Windows

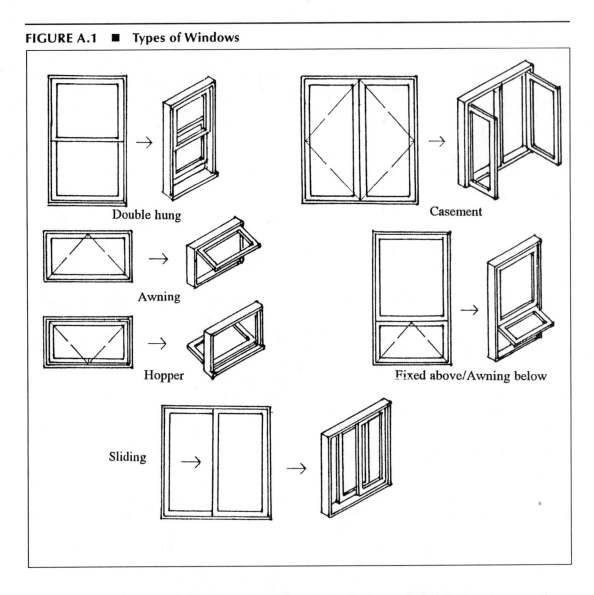

In some brands of windows featuring dual or triple glazing (two or three panes or layers of glass), grids can be applied between the glass panes or one side of the glass to imitate the appearance of small historical panes. However, for authenticity, individual single glass panes inserted into wood dividers (muntins) achieve the best appearance.

FIGURE A.2 ■ **Double-Hung Windows**

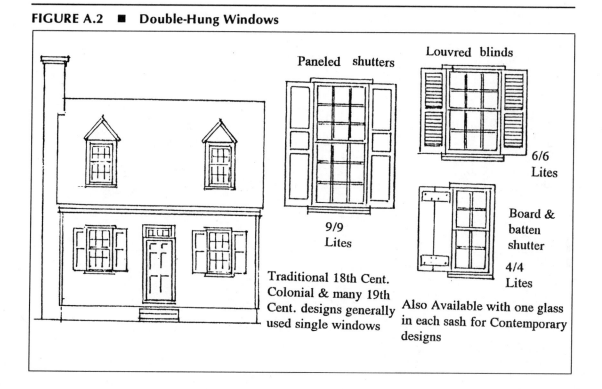

Paneled shutters

Louvred blinds

9/9
Lites

6/6
Lites

Board &
batten
shutter

4/4
Lites

Traditional 18th Cent.
Colonial & many 19th
Cent. designs generally
used single windows

Also Available with one glass
in each sash for Contemporary
designs

■ CASEMENT WINDOWS

These are the second most widely used residential window type.

Historically, casements with small panes held in place by lead strips, often in a diamond pattern, were in use well before the double hung style. One-glass versions are now often used in contemporary house designs (see Figure A.3).

Modern out-opening casements are tight fitting when closed and usually are operated by a crank mechanism. They are available in several common widths and varying heights and can be installed in multiples (two or three together).

■ AWNING WINDOWS

This type of window earns its name from its similarity to an awning. It is like a casement, except that its hinged edge is horizontal along the top. This window is popular with designers of contemporary-style houses and offers some weather protection when left open in a rain, since water drains off the out-opening sash. It is usually crank operated and available in various widths and heights.

FIGURE A.3 ■ **Casement Windows**

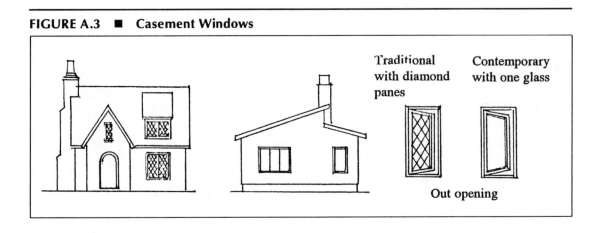

Traditional with diamond panes

Contemporary with one glass

Out opening

FIGURE A.4 ■ **Awning Windows**

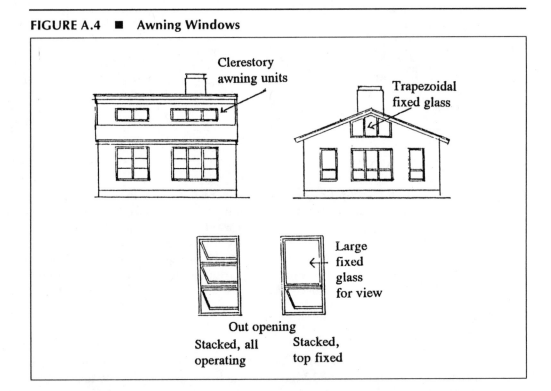

Clerestory awning units

Trapezoidal fixed glass

Large fixed glass for view

Out opening

Stacked, all operating

Stacked, top fixed

For maximum ventilation, stacking of the operating units is desirable. Where view is important, a tall fixed glass (without a visual bar) is installed above an operating sash. A band of awning windows can be used in a horizontal clerestory as shown in Figure A.4.

■ HOPPER WINDOWS

This window, illustrated in Figure A.5, looks like an awning window when closed, but it is in-opening and hinged along its bottom edge. When opened, it interferes with drapery curtains and for this reason hopper windows are little used in houses except as basement windows.

FIGURE A.5 ■ Hopper Windows

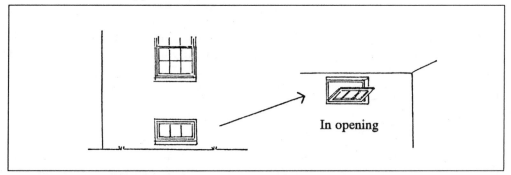

In opening

■ HORIZONTAL SLIDERS

These windows are a close cousin to sliding glass doors. They are available in several widths and heights. Like sliding glass doors, one panel operates and the other is fixed, as illustrated in Figure A.6. Some manufacturers make a three-part slider with one panel operable. This type of window is advantageous where a wide view is desired.

■ OTHER WINDOW VARIATIONS

Specialty windows can be used as accent features in both traditional and contemporary house styles. One of the most popular is the half-circle "add-on" above a conventional window or window grouping, as illustrated in Figure A.7. This arrangement generally requires ceiling heights taller than the standard eight feet.

Other special windows include those that are used independently due to the self-contained geometry, such as round, hexagon and octagon.

FIGURE A.6 ■ Horizontal Sliders

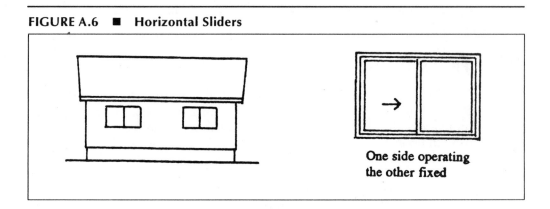

One side operating
the other fixed

Glass jalousies are another special type of window generally used around porches. They are vertical rows of horizontal glass slats linked together by a crank mechanism to permit maximum ventilation when opened. When jalousie windows are closed, the air circulation is still considerable; hence, this type of window is not energy efficient.

■ INSULATING GLASS

Single glass is traditional in windows and still is used where climate is mild. Otherwise where energy losses are considerable, insulating glass has advantages. This glass exists in two forms. One is a special double pane of glass separated by an air space with the glass edges welded together to form an airtight center space much like the liner for a thermos bottle. More common, today, however, are two sheets of glass held by mastic-sealed edges with air or inert gas in the space between. For areas of the country where winter air temperatures are frequently below 40° F, the selection of windows with insulating glass (or some type of storm panel) is well worth considering, especially in houses with a lot of glass area. You should save enough in fuel costs to more than make up for this expense in a few years, and have a more comfortable house in the meantime.

Those who live in very cold climates should consider using windows with triple glazing, that is, three layers of glass with two separate air pockets in between.

Glass itself is a very poor insulator and acts as a high heat loss area unless inert spaces are interposed to block the ready escape of heat. Even then, the insulating qualities of the double- and triple-insulated glass windows and doors will provide only one-eighth to one-fifth at best the insulating value of a two by four stud wall with three-and-a-half inches of insulating batt and a one-inch-thick polyurethane or polystyrene sheathing. One principle to keep in mind is to care-

FIGURE A.7 ■ Window Variations

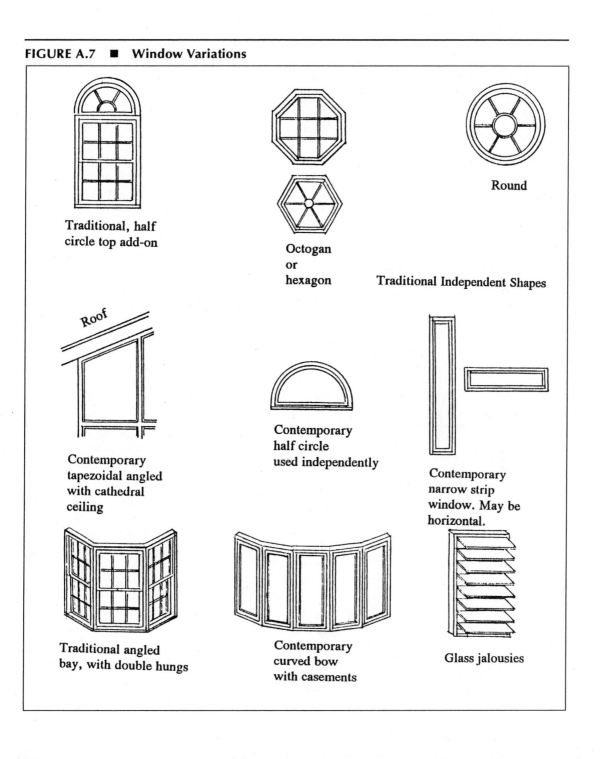

Traditional, half
circle top add-on

Octogan
or
hexagon

Round

Traditional Independent Shapes

Contemporary
tapezoidal angled
with cathedral
ceiling

Contemporary
half circle
used independently

Contemporary
narrow strip
window. May be
horizontal.

Traditional angled
bay, with double hungs

Contemporary
curved bow
with casements

Glass jalousies

fully plan the amount of window area in a house such as limiting the large glass areas for view. Also, plan to take maximum advantage of the winter sun to provide daytime heat, which can be a definite asset. See Appendix G, Solar Heating, for more information.

■ TYPES OF GLASS

Tempered Safety Glass

This glass should be used in doors, glass panels adjacent to doors and other areas where it is likely that people, especially children, might fall against the glass and break it. Most codes require the use of tempered or other types of safety glass in wall areas that are within four feet of a door. When broken, tempered glass crumbles into more or less harmless granules.

Once tempered glass is made, it cannot be cut, so be certain that your measurements are correct before ordering. Allow about one-eighth of an inch on each side of the frame for expansion. Standard sizes cost less and usually are readily available from stock.

Annealed Float Glass

Formerly called plate glass, this glass is used in most house windows. If it breaks, the pieces usually are very sharp. The untreated version of this glass is largely being replaced by Low E glass. Annealed glass can be cut on the job for special fitting.

Tinted Glass

This glass, usually annealed float, is designed to reduce the passage of solar heat. It is particularly useful in areas such as the seashore where solar glare is objectionable and in the Southeast, Southwest and similar environments. Tinting may be factory-applied or field-installed film. Film applications may blister in time.

Reflective Glass

This serves a similar function to tinted glass but is more effective. It reduces solar heat passage to about 50 percent of that of annealed float glass, whereas tinted glass only offers a 25 percent reduction. This type of glass is designed primarily for commercial buildings with large window areas to reduce heat loss to the outdoors in the winter and to reduce heat gain in the summer. From the outside, the windows look like mirrors and from the inside it is like looking out on a cloudy day, which most homeowners will not want.

Low E Glass

This glass is used in dual-glazed windows. It has a low emissivity (low E) coating on the inside to reduce heat loss in the winter and heat gain in the summer. It is an excellent glass for houses but does cut down on daylight transmission.

The type of glass alone does not guarantee an energy-efficient window. The edge seal of the glass and the type and effectiveness of the seal along the edges of the window sash also are important to prevent excessive energy transmission. Typically, even seemingly tight windows allow air infiltration, which causes energy loss and drafts. Also, metal window frames without a thermal break lessen efficiency. When investigating windows, look for the overall energy efficiency rating. Other fabrication characteristics are described below.

■ WINDOW FRAMES

Windows may be selected with the following choices of frames: wood; wood clad with vinyl or aluminum; aluminum; or steel.

Wood

Usually excellent quality woods are used for window frames. Wood frames must be stained or painted; thus the maintenance cost is higher than other choices. Color of the finish depends upon the selection of the paint or stain. Because wood is a relatively good insulator, wood frames and sash are generally desirable.

Wood Clad with Vinyl

This is a very fine type of window frame, with a long life and the thermal advantage of wood. The wood frame is completely encased in a thick layer of tough prefinished vinyl. Since no painting or staining is required, the maintenance on this window is very low and the wood provides good thermal qualities. The choice of color usually is limited to white, brown or bronze.

Wood Clad with Aluminum

This is another fine choice with almost no maintenance, and about as efficient as vinyl clad. In this case, the wood frame is encased in a layer of aluminum, which is coated with baked-on factory applied paint. Choice of color usually is limited to white, brown or bronze.

Aluminum

Aluminum-framed windows are available in natural mill finish and several selections of anodized coloring. This is a long-life material and is inexpensive compared to most others. Aluminum is an excellent conductor of heat, though, and conducts energy losses from within the house through the frame or sashes. Aluminum windows may cause excessive moisture condensation on the interior portion of the frame under conditions of very cold outside temperature when indoor humidity is high. For this reason, if you buy aluminum-framed windows, be sure to select a brand that has a thermal break using an insulating material to separate the exterior and interior sections of the metal frame.

Steel

Steel-framed windows are inexpensive and sometimes are used in basements. They have the same disadvantages as the aluminum-framed window without the thermal break and, in addition, they must be kept painted to prevent rusting.

■ SCREENS

In localities where insects are a problem, screens should be included in the window specifications for those portions of the window that will be opened. The nylon screen material is popular, as are coated copper and aluminum. In some atmospheres, nylon as well as metal screening may be attacked and deteriorate. Inquire locally about which materials hold up best.

Screen doors should be provided for those entryways that will be frequently open during the warmer months.

■ STORM WINDOWS

When properly installed, storm windows provide additional insulation and present another barrier to air infiltration. They generally are used with double-hung windows and installed on the outside. They are difficult to operate, however, so it usually is preferable to use more energy-efficient windows with dual or triple glazing and better design and construction rather than storm windows. In special situations for existing double-hung windows, several systems are available that use interior acrylic storm panels and screens, which serve the same purpose as and are more aesthetically pleasing than the exterior storm window.

■ SKYLIGHTS

Skylights are special types of windows that are mounted in the roof. They are particularly popular in contemporary styles and are useful at interior locations and for taking advantage of passive solar heating. A fixed skylight commonly used in house construction is shown in Figure A.8. Ventilating skylights also are popular where overhead venting is desirable, such as in a Florida room or interior bathroom.

FIGURE A.8 ■ Skylight

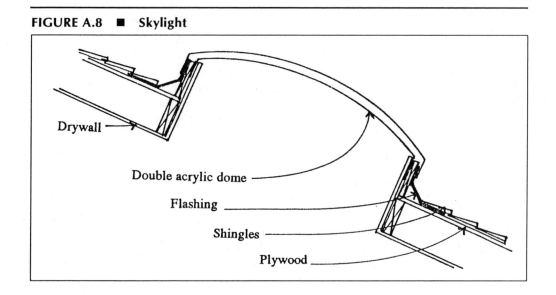

Basic skylight materials include translucent acrylic or other transparent plastic, and glass. Plastic types usually are in the shape of a dome, and glass types usually are flat. Two layers with inert airspace between are preferred for insulation against heat loss through the roof. A type that is mounted on a rim curb projecting above the roof is recommended for home building, since it is less troublesome and provides greater assurance against leakage.

■ DOORS

Residential doors are made differently for exterior and interior use. Those made for interior use generally cannot be substituted at exterior locations, since they will not withstand weather. However, many equivalent patterns are available in both types.

Exterior Doors

Like windows, exterior doors should be energy-efficient in this era of high energy costs. They should be weather-stripped tightly to minimize air infiltration along the edges and insulated against the loss of heat through the material, yet still provide for easy closing and opening. Today, door selection is much more than just appearance and style.

While a house may have only a few entrance doors, their appearance and surrounding doorway treatment is important in relating to the architectural style and creating a nice sense of reception to the house. Typically, the primary entrance door is three feet wide and six feet, eight inches high, the minimum size according to most building codes. Secondary entrance doors can be two feet, six inches or two feet, eight inches wide. Seven-foot-high doors also are available but are used more in commercial buildings. Typically, hinged doors should be installed to open inward. This permits better weather stripping.

For traditional houses, the door pattern should imitate the appropriate design of the house style represented. The most common pattern is the colonial six-panel with raised panels having beveled edges, shown in Figure A.9.

FIGURE A.9 ■ Traditional Door Patterns

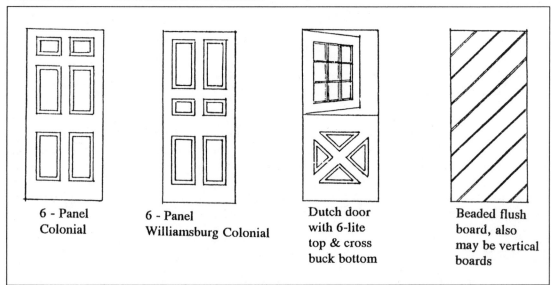

6 - Panel
Colonial

6 - Panel
Williamsburg Colonial

Dutch door
with 6-lite
top & cross
buck bottom

Beaded flush
board, also
may be vertical
boards

Traditional entrances also may include double doors, a transom above the door, sidelights on one or both sides, and doorways embellished with appropriate period trim, as illustrated in Figure A.10.

FIGURE A.10 ■ Traditional Entrances

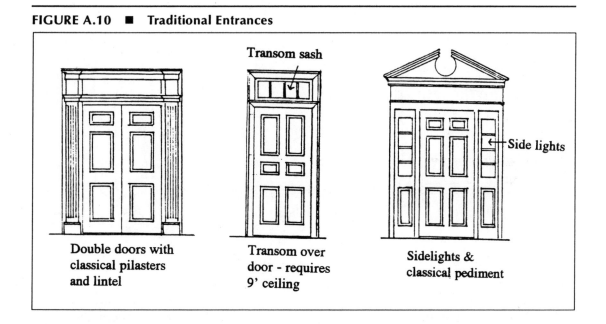

Double doors with classical pilasters and lintel

Transom over door - requires 9' ceiling

Sidelights & classical pediment

Types of Exterior Doors Basically, there are two types of exterior doors—hinged and patio or sliding doors.

Hinged doors, as their name applies, operate with hinges applied to one side and operate inward. Locking for security is easy.

Patio doors operate by sliding. Most patio doors consist of one or more sliding and stationary glass panels with widths of two feet, six inches or more per panel. Three-foot panel widths are the most common. Their frames are available in the same choices as the windows discussed earlier and with single, dual or triple glazing. Patio doors usually are supplied with a locking device, and a drop bar can be added to prevent movement of the operating panel.

A variation of the patio door uses a swinging rather than a sliding panel hinged to the fixed panel. The appearance is similar to double French doors. If swinging door units are selected be sure that there is adequate clearance inside the room for opening the door. The sliding and fixed panels generally have narrow edges that minimize the amount of openness, unlike hinged doors. All glass units, sliding, fixed and hinged, may be fitted with grids to suggest small panes as shown in Figure A.11.

FIGURE A.11 ■ Patio Doors

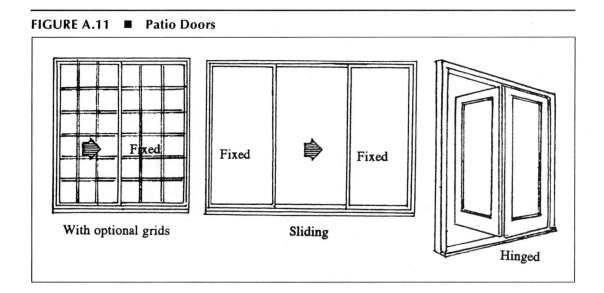

Exterior Door Materials   Exterior hinged doors are available in wood, molded plastic, steel, fiberglass and various glass door types. Patio doors are made of aluminum or wood frames with large glass panes.

Exterior doors typically are one-and-three-quarters-inches thick and heavy, as they should be, and can be selected in standard widths. Interior doors should not be substituted, since they are not made with moisture-resistant glue.

There are two types of flush doors, those with solid-core particle board or similar filler between the two outer surfaces and those with solid-lumber core between the two outer faces. The latter is a stronger door but more expensive. The door faces may be ornamented with moldings and cutouts made for glass if desired.

Most paneled residential wood exterior doors are made of high-grade pine or fir. The advantage of traditional wood doors is the beauty of their panels. Woods also can be selected to show off their grain in a wide array of choices for natural or stained finishes. The chief disadvantage of wood doors is that the inexpensive ones may warp, crack or shrink, and cause sealing problems. Higher quality doors can provide better insulation and weather stripping. Both paneled and flush doors may be made with various sizes and shapes of glass inserts. An advantage of wood doors is that they may be trimmed to accommodate wall settling (which slightly changes the size of the door opening).

Molded doors have an advantage over wood doors in that they are less likely to warp, crack or shrink, but are available only in limited patterns. They usually cannot be stained, although some brands have an embossed grain character that can be seen through paint. Often they are prehung with installed frame, hinges and door trim. They are difficult to trim in the event of wall settling.

Steel doors are made with a steel outer shell filled with insulating material. They are usually prehung with their own frame, jamb and hinges, and are either already assembled or precut for easy assembly on the job. The steel door provides an excellent seal against air infiltration, is well insulated, is more difficult to force open and is not affected by moisture. Its principal disadvantage is that it must be painted. In most steel doors, the panel pattern is shallow and not as handsome as that in the wood door. Plastic decorating panels are available for application to the face of the door providing considerable variation in design.

Some steel door systems are made with magnetized weather stripping (similar to that used on modern refrigerators), which clamps to the door when closed and forms an excellent seal. This stripping, as well as that used in other than steel doors, must not be painted or the magnetism will be lost.

Fiberglass doors are made from a molded fiber skin, often with an etched wood grain appearance, wrapped around an insulating urethane core and wood trim. When stained or painted, the fiberglass door looks very much like wood, but it has none of the warping and splitting problems of wood doors. The fiberglass can be trimmed like ordinary wood doors. Design patterns are limited.

Although sealing to minimize air infiltration is just as important as it is with windows and other exterior doors, by the nature of their design it is difficult to properly seal patio doors against air infiltration. Even with high-quality doors, the wear and tear caused by the door movement across the sealing material is prone to eventually cause leaks. Sliding doors are usually fitted with sliding screens.

Sliding doors are advantageous where large glass areas are desired for view and where furniture placement or traffic clearance would be difficult with hinged doors. Where outside ventilation is important, units should be equipped with screens.

If large amounts of light and sunshine are desired, sliding units can be used in multiples or combined with double swinging doors in a similar manner to French doors. (See Appendix G for more information on solar heating.) If appropriate for the house architecture and where passage is not needed, units can be fixed to eliminate the air infiltration problem. In recent years, some manufacturers have introduced folding glass doors designed for exterior use. These doors operate with one or more sections that are hinged and others that slide along a track.

Interior Doors

There usually is no requirement involving insulation and air infiltration with interior doors, except doors to a garage or other non-air-conditioned and unheated space. Hence, interior doors are not normally weather stripped. If the house heating system depends upon the free flow of air to a central air return, interior doors should be undercut at least one-half inch or more above the finished floor or carpet to permit air flow. This does not apply in those rooms with both air supply and return outlets. Several locations where insulated or heavy interior doors may be desired are where sound control is important, such as a recreation room or perhaps a bedroom.

Types of Interior Doors There are five basic types of interior doors: hinged, pocket, bifold, sliding and folding.

Hinged doors are by far the most convenient for regular traffic areas. Ordinarily, hinged doors open into the room or space served. They are easily latched or locked. Variations include double doors at a wide doorway and two-way swing or double-acting (swings either way). Two-way swinging doors are useful between the kitchen and dining area for two-way traffic such as for carrying food and other items. Two important principles to remember about hinged doors: Allow for the arc of swing and the stand open positions. For a double-acting door—to avoid conflicts in traffic—use a door with glass or provide a small opening (usually glass covered) in the door to allow users to see the other side before opening it.

Hinged doors also are available in a prehung form. A prehung door is one that is supplied already hinged to its frame. However, the choice of prehung doors is limited. Prehung doors are supplied with part of the casing installed and part precut but not installed, and you must select the type of door casing for the entire house before you order the doors. Casing selections also are limited to several of the most popular designs. The installed cost of prehung doors often is less due to savings in labor.

Sliding doors are useful where traffic is infrequent or where hinged door swing clearance is awkward or unavailable. An example is bypassing doors at a reach-in closet, but note that only one-half of the closet is open at any one time.

A *pocket door* is a variation of the sliding door that when opened disappears into the wall. The pocket door, illustrated in Figure A.12, is used where there is no space for a hinged door to swing or stand. This often occurs where several doorways are close by. Double pocket doors are useful at a wide opening between two rooms requiring occasional separation, such as between the living and dining rooms.

A pocket door requires careful installation since it must fit within wall framing that is generally 2×4 studs. On occasion, the pocket door can cause problems if not skillfully installed or the door itself later warps. In order to

FIGURE A.12 ■ Pocket Door

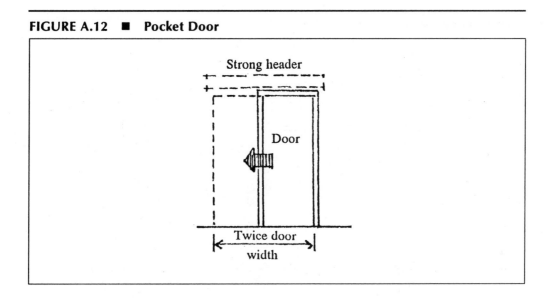

provide the pocket, a pre-built pocket frame is recommended. It should be of a high quality with adequate header above to guard against distortion and warpage. This warpage can interfere with the operation of the pocket door. To minimize the probability of warpage, an alternative is to use 2×6 studs to accommodate a stronger frame around the pocket. The pocket door, which is available in most designs to fit house decor, is illustrated in Figure A.12.

The bifold door is made of two or more narrow hinged sections. For small openings, it usually consists of two sections hinged together to cover the opening, as illustrated in Figure A.13.

FIGURE A.13 ■ Bifold Doors

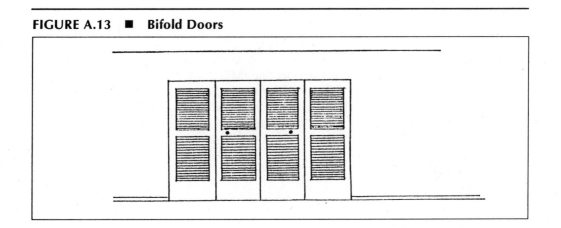

FIGURE A.14 ■ Closet Doors

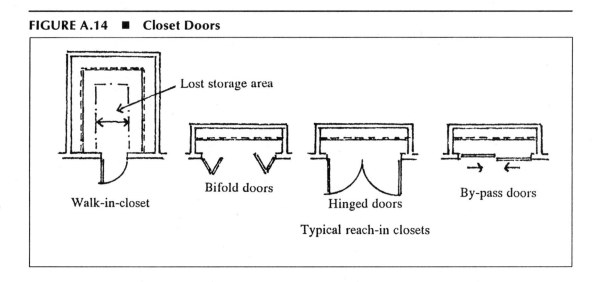

Lost storage area

Walk-in-closet

Bifold doors

Hinged doors

By-pass doors

Typical reach-in closets

For large openings, a double set of four panels are used, or even more for very wide openings. These doors are designed to be operated from one side only and, consequently, are best suited for closets. Standard bifold widths are two feet; two feet, six inches; and three feet (two panels each). They are most useful in providing wide openings to shallow closets making the most use of the square footage available. Door patterns are available to fit decor of most houses.

Figure A.14 illustrates various arrangements for closet doors. Note that the single hinged door requires the least amount of room wall space.

A *folding door* is most useful in those cases in which there is little room to swing a regular door. They move like accordion bellows and are usually made of vertical slats or fabric that gather together when the door is opened. Their use is most popular at wide doorways, although they can be used at almost any doorway. Their disadvantage is that they take up space in the doorway when fully opened. Folding doors can be used singly or in pairs at a wide opening for a balanced appearance as shown in Figure A.15. Latching and locking hardware is available. Some fabric doors are semi-soundproof.

Wood doors are available in various styles such as paneled, flush or louvered. They are usually one-and-three-eighths-inch thick. The flush doors may be solid (heavy) or hollow and made with finished surfaces, such as birch, luan, mahogany, pine and hardboard. Hardboard cannot be stained but will take paint well. Hinged and sliding types are generally one-and-three-eighths-inch thick and six feet, eight inches high. Standard widths are from 12 inches to 3 feet in two-inch increments.

FIGURE A.15 ■ Folding Doors

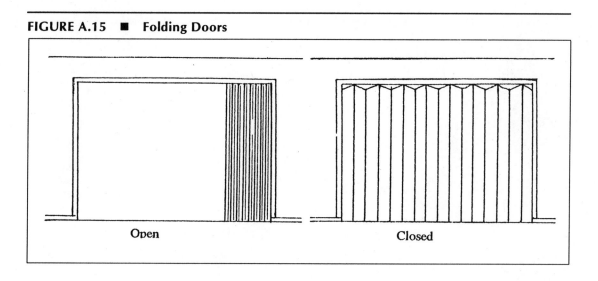

The paneled and louvered doors usually are a species of quality kiln-dried western pine.

Louvered doors are available as full louvered, top and bottom louvered or partially louvered with either the top or bottom paneled. They are particularly useful in those locations where the free flow of air is desired, such as in closets. They may be required for rooms needing ventilation that contain mechanical equipment, hot water heaters and heating equipment.

Molded doors of wood fibers are available primarily in the paneled form. They are less expensive than paneled wood doors but will not take staining. They are hollow or foam filled, except along the edges and at points where the door hardware is to be applied, and will not readily accept coat hooks or towel racks. An advantage is they will not warp or split as wood doors occasionally do.

Interior Finishes

Interior finishes are the surface treatments of walls and ceilings and the underlying materials on which they are applied. Examples include job-applied paint or wallpaper on gypsum board, and paint or stain on wood paneling and various prefinished materials such as plywood paneling. In today's homes, both job-applied surface finishes and prefinished materials are used widely, depending upon the desired effect as well as economy.

Some interior finishes are more appropriate for traditional designs and others are better for contemporary ones. For example, prefinished plywood better suits the character of a contemporary design; however, plaster or plaster-like materials can be used appropriately in both styles. Your best guide is to use finish materials and surface finishes that carry through the effect of the house style.

■ PLASTER

Little used in houses today because of expense, plaster provides a hard white finish that can be left unpainted or, if you prefer, it readily accepts paint, wallpaper or other applied coverings. Plaster holds pictures and other wall decorations well if the proper hangers are used.

Compared to other wall finishes discussed in this chapter, it is costly in labor, since several wet coats must be applied and the final coat is hand-troweled.

Conventional plastered walls and ceilings are dense and relatively soundproof.

■ DRYWALL

The most widely used wall finish is drywall (also called sheet rock and gypsum board). It is a highly versatile material, quickly installed and relatively inexpensive.

Drywall must be given a surface finish, such as paint or wallpaper, because its unfinished appearance (tape joints and fasteners) is not uniform.

For those rooms such as baths, kitchens and laundries, a special moisture-resistant drywall, called "green board" because of the green color of the face paper, should be used. It is finished in the same manner as standard drywall paneling and also is suitable for thin-set ceramic tile. For dense, more soundproof walls, two layers of drywall can be installed.

Some building codes require a fire-resistant drywall panel of a half-inch or five-eighths-inch thickness on walls and ceilings where there is a potential fire hazard, such as attached garages and furnace rooms, where the spaces are adjacent to habitable rooms. Even if not required by the local code, a fire wall is recommended for the safety gained at very little additional cost.

■ CLOSET AND GARAGE FINISHES

Where economy is essential in the application of drywall, only one coat of the joint compound instead of the usual three can be applied in closets and garages. This will result in some savings but will show a poorer looking finish.

■ PLASTER VENEER

This plaster system provides a very hard finish, which is much less susceptible to damage than drywall, with greater strength than the drywall, and a plaster-like appearance. It consists of the application of two thin coats of plaster over specially manufactured "blue board" drywall. Its wet coats are very thin, and since they dry quickly, it can be applied in a matter of several days compared to the much longer time to complete conventional plaster.

Plaster veneer offers an excellent choice for interior wall finishes. In selecting this system, it is very important to ensure that the contractor has the experience and skills to do the job properly. Neither conventional plaster nor plaster veneer should be attempted by amateurs.

■ PREFINISHED PANELING

There is a wide range in the choices of prefinished natural wood paneling and prefinished wallboard to give wood-like effect or the effect of wall paper. Prefinished paneling has the advantage of low maintenance, but little flexibility in changing the decorating scheme of a room several years later.

Thin sheets (of a five thirty-seconds– or one-eighths–inch thickness) of plywood or wallboard paneling should be installed over a base of finished or unfinished drywall to give better soundproofing. They require matching trim material for inside corners, outside corners and crown molding at the juncture of the paneling and the ceiling. The base used at the juncture of the paneling and the floor also may be matching trim or it can be the same baseboard used elsewhere in the house and finished on the job.

■ PANELING FOR SPECIAL APPLICATIONS

In bathrooms and especially around tubs and showers, factory wallboard, acrylic and other plastic panels intended for the purpose can provide cost savings. These panels are prefinished and necessary accessories, such as corner or joint moldings, are available. Where fire resistance is important but appearance is secondary, mineral board can be used adjacent to a furnace or stove. Check your local building code.

In kitchens, it may be desirable to apply decorative panels to the fronts of the refrigerator and other appliances. Generally this is done by the kitchen cabinet-maker.

■ THIN-SET BRICK

This thin veneer of brick or brick-like material can be cemented to drywall or another suitable surface such as hardboard or plywood to achieve the appearance of brick. Most of these materials are decorative and should not be used where heat and moisture exposure is very high.

■ INTERIOR WOOD TRIM

Wood trim gives the interior of the house a finished appearance around doors and windows, and for baseboards, chair rails and room cornices. Selection and installation is important, since these trim items are constantly in view and thus contribute to the character and quality of the house (or lack of it, if done poorly). Trim profiles or design that are appropriate to the house style should be selected.

The various types of interior trim and the application for a colonial-style house are illustrated in Figure B.2. If moldings are to receive a clear or stain finish, use an unjointed grade of wood. If the trim is to be painted, finger-jointed material is less expensive. This material is factory-joined from short pieces.

Room Cornice

This trim is applied at the juncture of the ceiling and the walls in the form of a crown and other moldings. Components are made in several sizes with the somewhat larger ones being used with higher than standard ceilings (more than eight feet in height). A room cornice can be one piece or made up of two or more pieces of trim to give a more ornate appearance. Synthetic moldings also are available to replicate the appearance of elaborate traditional cornices.

Casing

This molding is applied around the doors and windows to cover the juncture of the door or window frame and wall finish. It is available in several sizes and styles with the ranch style often being used in contemporary houses, and is shown in Figure B.1. While one-piece casings are used most widely on account of cost, a more authentic appearance for traditional houses can be obtained with two pieces, as shown in Figure B.2.

FIGURE B.1   ■   Prefinished Paneling and Trim

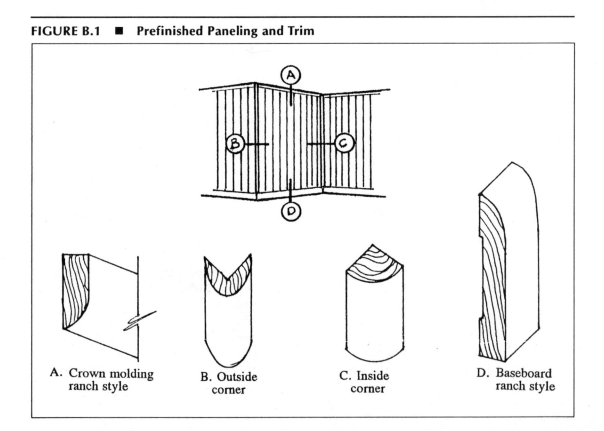

A. Crown molding   B. Outside   C. Inside   D. Baseboard
   ranch style   corner   corner   ranch style

FIGURE B.2 ■ Typical Traditional Wood Trim

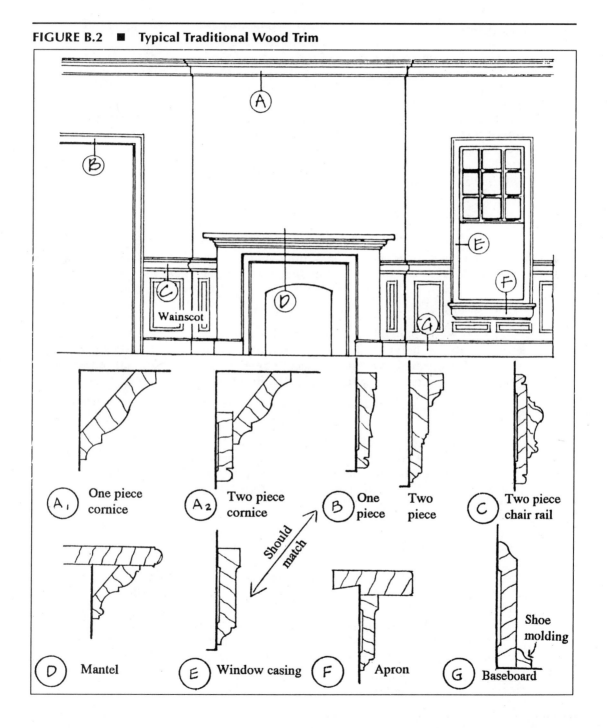

In addition to casing, the window also requires a stool with an apron beneath, or the window may be trimmed with the picture-frame technique where the same casing is used on all four edges of the window frame.

Baseboard

This provides enhancing trim and protection between the floor and the wall finish. Its upper edge is usually molded above a flat surface below. Where ranch-style casing is used, the base is generally ranch-style also.

The wall is finished far enough down to the floor so that no unfinished wall will show above the baseboard.

Chair Railing

This decorative trim is installed about 32 inches above the finished floor. It can be one-piece or two-piece. It is functional as well as aesthetic, since it protects the wall surface from damage when furniture is placed near the wall.

Wainscoting

This is wood paneling or sometimes boards with tongue-and-groove or other similar material, between the baseboard and the chair rail. Usually, the chair rail and base are applied over the wainscot edges. In some traditional rooms with a fireplace, the wainscot may fully cover the fireplace wall from floor to ceiling.

Shoe Molding

This trim is applied between the floor and the baseboard. It is very flexible and can snugly fit both the floor and the baseboard to compensate for any irregularities of the structure, which are always present even in the best of wood construction. Shoe molding frequently is not used if the floor is carpeted from wall to wall.

■ CERAMIC-TILED WALLS

Ceramic tile often is used on the walls of baths in the form of wainscoting (to a height of about 38 inches to 48 inches) and fully on the walls and ceilings of showers or on walls over tubs or tub/shower combinations. It also is popular in kitchens as the back splash above countertops. Where water exposure is severe, such as in showers and above tubs, ceramic tile should be installed "mud-set" on a cement bed. Thin-set tile usually is satisfactory elsewhere and is a less expensive installation.

■ INTERIOR PAINTING AND STAINING

Paint is the most widely used finish in homes for trim, walls and ceilings, although stains or natural finishes are used often in dens and family rooms to enhance the natural wood effect. The choice of finishes (including wallpaper) is largely a matter of personal preference, yet it should complement the style of the house where drywall is used. Select a flat or satin finish paint for walls and ceilings, except in baths and kitchens, where an enamel paint should be used, either gloss or semigloss, for easier cleaning. The enamel paint also gives better protection to the drywall or plaster. For walls and ceilings, paint may be sprayed, brushed or rolled on. Spraying usually is less expensive if done before the flooring is installed, particularly where walls and ceiling are to be the same color. Rolled surfaces generally have a stippled effect; where surfaces meet at right angles, brushing is usually required, such as at corners or along wood trim. Brushing is the most labor-intensive but provides the maximum control for delicacy and avoiding overrun.

For natural appearance it may be desirable to apply penetrating stains, depending on the type of wood and the desired effect. Apply one or two coats of a clear sealer over the stain for easier cleaning. Generally, stain or natural finishes do not show soil or damage as readily as paint finishes do.

Since bare wood is subject to discoloration from light and soil by hand and both are difficult to remedy, it should be painted with an enamel paint or stained. Apply a good-quality primer and then compatible top coats of alkyd (modern equivalent of oil based paint) or acrylic latex. Usually a minimum of two top coats is required.

In selecting colors for the interior consider the following:

- Dark colors make a room seem smaller but give a more dramatic appearance. Too many dark colors, however, may make a room seem depressing.
- To create a more buoyant room, use white or pastels.
- A white or light-colored ceiling gives the impression of height, whereas a dark color appears to lower the ceiling.
- Neutral colors are a better setting for vivid colors of furniture fabric or carpeting. For coordination of paint colors and furnishings, consider the services of an interior decorator unless you feel confident with your ability to make the proper selection.

Plan your paint finishes carefully. If you are inclined to redecorate often remember that high-gloss enamels do not take overpainting easily and must be deglossed to avoid peeling and cracking

Imitative paint finishes (faux finishes) are popular to simulate the appearance of materials such as marble or costly ornamental woods. Other ornamental painting includes stenciling for interesting effects at relatively low cost.

■ WALLPAPER AND WALLCOVERING

Many patterns and textures of wall coverings are available, some in printed patterns and others made of embossed vinyl to resemble leather, grass cloth, other fabrics and metallics. Selections suitable for both traditional and modern house designs are available in wallpaper and vinyl.

If you select wallpaper or wallcovering on some of your walls, here are some tips:

- For baths or kitchens, choose a vinyl or vinyl-coated wallcovering that can be scrubbed.
- Behind the kitchen stove, use a decorative laminate (melamine), ceramic tile or fabric-backed vinyl covering. These are the easiest to clean. Avoid unprotected natural wood and any other material that absorbs grease or spatter.
- Using stripable wallpaper will facilitate its removal if you redecorate in the future.
- If you want to make the room seem taller, select a vertical stripe for the wallpaper pattern.
- If you want to make the room seem larger, select a pattern with small figures and light colors with relatively large areas of clear space.
- Wallpaper can be used to expand (widen) the appearance of a narrow hallway by applying wallpaper borders at the top of each long wall and a matching full wallpaper at each end of the hallway.
- Where walls are to be painted, decorative wallpaper borders can be used for accent as an inexpensive treatment. Repetitive stenciled patterns also can be used for this effect.
- Leftover wallpaper can be cut to the proper size and used to cover switch plates, or line drawers or cabinet shelves. Keep remnants of all of your remaining wallpaper; they can be used for later patching in the event of damage.

Some wallpapers are coated for water- or moisture-resistance. However, if the desired pattern is not available in the treated variety, you may be able to use a wallpaper sealer on it after it has been installed and the paste has dried. Since sealers can change the color of the wallpaper, test a sample before covering the entire wall.

For application to plaster or plaster veneer or untreated drywall, sizing should be applied before hanging the wallcovering. Without this sizing the paper may not adhere properly to the wall or ceiling. In addition without sizing, when repapering in the future the paper will be difficult to remove and the drywall or plaster may be damaged.

■ SPECIAL CEILING FINISHES

Other methods are popular for finishing ceilings or walls. One is to use a texturizing paint for stipple or a sandy effect. Another is for the drywall finisher to cover the entire ceiling with a coat of joint compound and then go over it with a broom or texturizing device, putting a swirling pattern into the still-wet compound. Have a sample prepared before deciding whether you like the effect.

■ ═ A P P E N D I X   C ═ ■

Flooring

■ WOOD

Wood flooring is available in strips, planks (wide strips) and tiles. Wood strip flooring ordinarily is installed on joisted construction, usually over felt paper and a plywood or oriented strand board subfloor beneath. When installing wood flooring on slab-on-grade construction, a special precaution is needed to minimize movement of dampness from the earth into the wood floor. Install wood sleepers over the slab covered by a vapor barrier such as asphalt saturated felt paper. The flooring is nailed to the wood sleepers.

Wood flooring is available in a number of woods including oak, teak, birch, beech, pecan and maple.

The most popular strip flooring is white or red oak. These hardwoods have excellent wearing qualities and hold long-lasting finishes. The standard types, with or without precision tongue-and-groove joints on their edges come in a width of two and a quarter inches to minimize shrinkage, and in random lengths. To achieve a more distinctive look, oak flooring also can be supplied in tongue-and-groove planks of random wider sizes with or without a V-groove between the planks. V-groove flooring minimizes surface irregularities caused by cupping or the tendency of wide boards to develop concave surfaces.

The best grain for any wood flooring is quarter-sawn to produce vertical grain, not plain or flat-sawn which cups (distortion) and shrinks to open up cracks. For an illustration, see Figure C.1.

If exposed cut-type nails are driven at joist lines (either two or three depending on the width of the particular plank) a colonial look can be obtained. It

FIGURE C.1 ■ Wood Grain for Flooring

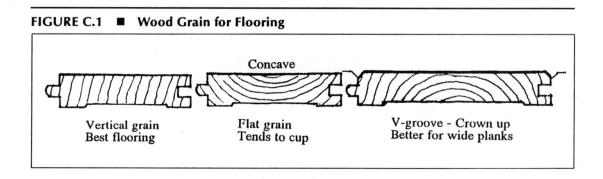

Vertical grain
Best flooring

Concave
Flat grain
Tends to cup

V-groove - Crown up
Better for wide planks

may be necessary to predrill nail holes to prevent splitting near the ends of the flooring. Another method of attachment uses counter-sunk screws covered by round wood plugs. While more expensive to install, the effect is quite attractive. See Figure C.2.

FIGURE C.2 ■ Random Width Wood Flooring with V-Groove and Exposed Nails

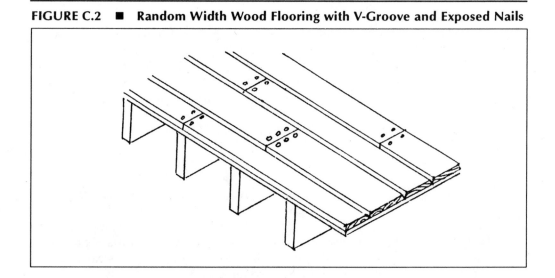

When visible nailing is done, it also is usual to blind-nail along the tongue side into each floor joist. For good anchorage, nails should be driven into the joist rather than into the subfloor, which has little holding ability, as shown in Figure C.2.

Fir and pine also can be used for flooring material in standard or random width. These are softer woods than oak and may show wear and heel marks before the oak does. However, both of these woods have a beautiful grain and take staining well. Pine is the historically traditional flooring for most colonial houses.

Parquet flooring, which usually consists of small pieces of wood combined into a square block, is another choice of wood flooring. For an illustration of parquet, see Figure C.3. Some parquet flooring is very thin. This type is installed with adhesive on an underlayment of particle board over the subfloor. Unfinished parquet requires careful sanding with fine paper to prevent scratches across the grain. Some parquet flooring is prefinished with slight V-grooves between blocks.

FIGURE C.3 ■ Parquet

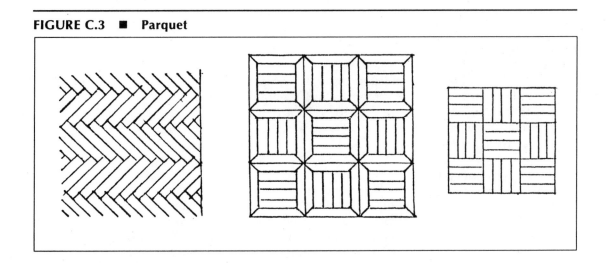

Prefinished Wood Flooring

There are many different kinds and styles of prefinished wood flooring, including strip and plank types. The factory-applied finishes are excellent and generally are long lasting. Follow the manufacturer's instructions for installing. Prefinished flooring is desirable in situations where time is critical or the mess of sanding may be a problem.

Wood Floor Finishing

The most widespread finishing system for wood floors consists of filling (if required by the type of wood), sanding and applying a top coating such as polyurethane or traditional varnish. If staining is desired, it is applied before the top finish. Varnish is little used today because of its tendency to yellow with age. Polyurethane is made with either a matte (soft shine) or hard shiny finish. Both do an excellent job; the choice is one of personal preference. Matte finish tends to show scratches and scuffing less than the shiny finish does. It also gives a more historic appearance. Almost any hard-top coat including polyurethane may show scratches, especially in high traffic areas, such as doorways, so for this reason a matte finish may be preferred.

Polyurethane requires no waxing and gives a pleasing look, but the finish will eventually have to be renewed.

Another type of floor finish uses commercial penetrating resins or sealers, which are soaked up by the wood. This finish does not cover the wood with a hard film. Its principal advantage is that to refinish the floor merely add additional penetrating resin without removing the original coating.

■ CARPETING

Wood and other hard surface floorings do not muffle footsteps and other sounds in a room or to a room below. Where this attribute is not desired, consider the use of area rugs and wall-to-wall carpeting. These also will give a softer and more comfortable feel to the feet and are nicer for crawling infants. Carpeting also adds insulation.

Construction

Virtually all residential carpets are tufted, which means that the carpet pile is formed by yarn loops inserted into a backing material. If the carpet is to be cut pile (the most popular) the tips of the loops are sheared off, resulting in a smooth finish. If the carpet is to be loop pile, the loops are not sheared.

Quality and Performance

The carpet should be warranted for stain and dirt resistance as well as protection against static and wear.

A carpet with a dense, thick pile wears longer, resists crushing and matting better and retains texture longer in heavy use than one with a thinner pile does. Compare density by bending two carpet samples as they would be bent over a stair tread. The higher density carpet will show more pile fiber and less backing material.

In general, the deeper and denser the pile, the better the carpet will perform. In carpets of equal density, the one with the higher or the heavier pile will perform best and last longer.

Cushion

Properly installed, a cushion or pad will add 17 percent to 50 percent to the carpet's useful life. A medium-thick pad is the best place to start. Thin pads can tear, wear or disintegrate too quickly. Ultra-thick pads can be too soft for comfortable walking and balance.

Styles

- Velvets are the most elegant; they give an ultra-smooth sweep of rich color.
- Saxsonies or lushes, while not as formal as velvet, are easier to live with.
- Textured saxsonies are the most casual-styled and rugged of pile carpets.
- In the level loop style, loops are easily visible and, depending on color and pattern, blend with most decors.
- Multilevel loops have a carved pattern and a more random effect.
- Cut-and-loop styles, or traceries, are a combination of cut pile and loop pile. They offer an infinite variety of effects.

Color Selection

- Light-colored carpets will make the room seem larger, particularly if the walls are white or a light tint of the carpet color. They also are the most versatile with room decor.
- In cold, snowy climates, red, yellow and brown carpets can warm up north-facing rooms.
- In warm climates, blue, green or violet carpets can be used to "cool off" south-facing rooms.
- Warm reds and oranges create an active atmosphere, which is great for family rooms.
- Cooler blues and greens generate a tranquil setting for bedrooms and other quiet areas.

Installation

Carpeting should be installed over an approved underlayment nailed to the subfloor with at least one layer of building paper in between. If the room has little moisture exposure, the underlayment can be five-eighths-inch-thick particle board, an inexpensive material. If the carpeting is installed in a bathroom or kitchen, however, the underlayment should be five-eighths-inch-thick plywood. This material is more expensive than the particle board, but usually will not be affected by normal amounts of moisture found in kitchens and baths. Particle board, on the other hand, tends to absorb moisture, swell and eventually disintegrate.

If carpet is to be installed over a concrete floor, first lay down a cover of high-density fiberboard (usually a half-inch thick), followed by the carpet padding, then the carpet. This system will provide a warmer, softer floor with better personal comfort.

■ RESILIENT TILE

Asphalt tile is little used in homes today due to its disadvantage of pitting and color bleeding from organic solvents and spilled grease. Because of their superior qualities, vinyl materials have generally replaced both asphalt tile and linoleum.

Vinyl tile and sheet material make a fine floor covering for baths, kitchens, sun rooms or any other room where easy maintenance and this appearance is desired. Sheet material with few or no seams is preferred in baths, kitchens and other rooms where water spillage may be a problem. The choices in pattern, color and quality are many, including simulated tile, brick, marble and even wood. Printed patterns tend to show wear in heavy traffic areas such as doorways. Embossed patterns, which have a three-dimension appearance, usually show less wear. Modern vinyl flooring is manufactured without the use of hazardous asbestos.

Joisted flooring should be installed over smooth plywood underlayment. Make sure that the joints between the sheets of plywood are flush. Most manufacturers will void their warranty if the vinyl flooring is installed over particle board. Over concrete the material usually is directly applied using an approved adhesive.

Other resilient floor materials are rubber tile and cork. Wall base in a room covered with resilient tile may be vinyl or rubber, or wood if it is to match the other base in the house.

■ CERAMIC TILE, EARTHSTONE, SLATE AND STONE

All of these materials make excellent flooring because of their hardness. They will show practically no wear and require little maintenance. For the best results, they should be laid in cement mortar, although the thin-set method with grouted joints is widely used in homes. The latter method is more compatible with joist floors and is more economical. Thinner versions of slate are available for thin-set installation but thicker stone usually requires mortar setting.

Slate and stone can be very heavy depending on size and thickness selected. For these heavier materials, the floor joists in the area should be doubled or installed 12 inches on centers to give more strength. A disadvantage of any hard flooring material is lack of comfort if one must walk or stand on it for a long period of time, such as in a kitchen.

■ BRICK

Brick with mortared or unmortared joints makes an excellent floor and can be laid over concrete or a wood subfloor. Use the special paver brick (thinner than regular brick) made for this purpose.

Remember that brick is a heavy material, so double the floor joists or install them 12 inches or closer on centers in that area.

Most brick is porous and should be sealed. Use a phenolic type of concrete sealer and apply at least two coats. If the brick has been installed with mortared joints, be sure that the material is completely dry before applying the sealer. Drying time can be as long as eight weeks. Workers should take special care to avoid mortar stains on the brick face, as they are difficult to remove.

Brick is usually very rough or textured compared to other flooring and does not clean very well with a mop. It gives an "outdoor" informal feeling when used inside.

■ CONCRETE

Concrete is usually considered to be just utilitarian, although interesting effects are possible. One is to cover the concrete with a colored monolithic topping such as terrazzo or to paint it, which is inexpensive. Another effect is to score it with simulated joints to achieve the appearance of tile or stone. For interior use, such as in a recreation room, the surface should be steel-troweled for smoothness.

Cabinets

■ CONSTRUCTION METHODS

Most cabinets are supplied in one of three ways: local custom-made, factory-made and custom-made in a factory.

Local Custom-Made

This type of cabinet is made in a local cabinet shop according to your exact plans. Depending on the cabinetmaker's capabilities, this method offers a wide selection of material, design and finish. These cabinets also may be the most expensive if unusual woods and special sizes and features are requested. However, this may be your best choice for the desired quality and effect. If possible, get bids from several cabinetmakers before making your final selection. Ask to see samples of their work.

Factory-Made

These cabinets are made according to the factory's standard specifications. Thus, your choices are more limited in the selection of design, material and finish, but there are variations among brands. Sizes are generally standardized in widths from 9 inches to 36 inches, which can be joined together to fill wider spaces. Cabinets are made up in advance and are stocked by the factory or by factory outlets. Costs range from very expensive with premium grades with more options to least expensive, depending on features and quality of construction by the individual manufacturer.

Custom Factory-Made

These cabinets are made at a centralized plant. Your cabinets are not built until your order has been received by the plant; then, they are customized according to options and finishes selected. You can expect a much greater choice in design, special features, size, material and finish than with most standard factory-made cabinets, and in some cases, custom sizes for spescial features. Prices usually will run from almost the same as locally custom-made to more than any medium and lower lines of the factory-made cabinets.

■ LOCAL SOURCES

Few home builders make cabinets. Locally, a kitchen and bathroom cabinet dealer usually offers a wide selection of cabinets and also the sale of major kitchen appliances. Ask whether this supplier has contacts with several standard factory lines as well as custom factory types. You also will probably find that the local dealer has in-house fabrication service or has connections with one or more local custom cabinet shops and therefore can supply the entire gamut of cabinet selection. Most dealers offer good advice as to the design of your kitchen, but will generally want a commitment from you before offering free design service. Some dealers are willing to offer their designs for a fee in the event you do not purchase their cabinets. You generally have the option of having the cabinet dealer work directly for you or as a subcontractor to the home builder. The former arrangement is less expensive but leaves you with the full responsibility, not the home builder.

The local custom cabinet shop can supply cabinets made in its shop, built to your specifications. Some of these shops also may be able to procure various types of factory cabinets.

The building supply store usually sells only standard types of the factory-made cabinets for the greatest economy, but your choices will be limited.

■ TYPES OF CABINETS

Wood

Unfinished wood cabinets can be bought least expensively. Most painters can do a good job of finishing these cabinets, either before or after installation. However, check their experience and have the painter prepare sample finishes for your approval. This will avoid possible disappointment.

Cabinets finished at the shop or factory are done in an environment that ensures an excellent application and curing of the finish for furniture-like quality. Natural finishes should complement the species of wood selected, such as cherry, walnut or oak. Birch and other woods may be stained to resemble furniture woods, and should be selected from actual sample panels. Paint or lacquer finishes also are available as shop or factory finishes.

Job finishes may be less predictable than factory or shop finishes, but may be the better choice if custom color or matching is necessary.

Another popular finish is plastic laminate applied to wood or particle board. The plastic laminate provides a flush surface appearance. In some cases, the laminate also is cemented to the inside as well as outside of the cabinet; in others, only the door (all sides) and the front of the cabinet are covered, with the interior being painted or coated with a clear sealer. The plastic laminate offers a wide variety of colors and patterns and is easily cleaned.

Front panels for refrigerators and other appliances can be made to match cabinet fronts, provided the appliance is made to accept this modification.

For traditional raised-paneled doors, wood construction is necessary and desirable. Traditional construction, where doors fit within the frame, are more expensive, due to the precision of work.

Tambour doors work like a rolltop desk and are popular for an "appliance garage," which fits under the wall cabinet and rests on the counter.

Cabinet hardware must be considered in terms of aesthetic appeal as well as function. Several hinge types are available, including spring-loaded or self-closing, and most of these are concealed or semi-concealed. Traditional hinges and pulls are available in reproduction designs and compatible metals such as brass and iron. Drawers in quality cabinets have side-mounted slides. Full extension slides permit full opening of the drawer without its falling on the floor (built-in stop). Other special cabinet hardware options include rotating shelves and track-mounted pullout shelves.

Metal

Several manufacturers offer high-quality (and high-priced) factory-made metal cabinets in a variety of finishes. These cabinets usually have premium features although, like other manufactured units, sizes are standardized.

■ COUNTERTOPS

The most widely used countertop is plastic laminate available in two basic choices: custom and postformed, illustrated in Figure D.1. The custom-made top has the advantage of greater flexibility to fit a custom or unusual shape. It has a seam between the back splash and the top that is somewhat difficult to keep clean. It also has a seam in front, which is exposed to wear and, like all laminate seams, may part when the cement fails. A well-made top with proper care, however, should last 20 years or longer. Plastic laminate can be scorched by a hot pan or cigarette.

FIGURE D.1 ■ Countertops

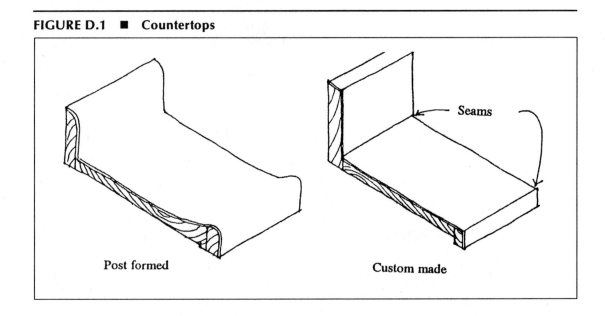

Post formed   Custom made

The postformed top is molded under high pressure by machinery especially designed for this process. The result is a rounded back joint with no seam that is easy to clean and a lip on the front, also without seam, that will prevent liquid spills from falling on the floor. The laminate used in the manufacture of this top is thinner than that used for the custom top so that it will bend and adhere properly to the base. Pattern and color selection of postformed tops are more limited than for custom-made tops. For any laminate-type top, the sink will be cut in by the cabinetmaker.

Other counter choices include ceramic tile, marble, stone and solid plastic materials. All of these are more expensive than plastic laminate tops. Marble and stone are used in premium designs and are the most costly. Wood-cutting tops also can be built into counters.

Solid plastic materials, such as Corian, and other proprietary materials, with or without integrated sinks, make excellent kitchen and vanity countertops. They are long-wearing, easy to install and go well with almost any cabinet. However, choice of color and pattern is limited.

Ceramic tile countertops enjoy popularity for their decorative appearance and the practicality of installing matching or coordinated back splashes. They are less often used than the plastic laminate, which offers a smoother top without the problem of cleaning the grouted joints. Ceramic tile is very hard and may increase breakage of china and glasses. There are many choices of color, texture and shape of tile available today to achieve a desired effect.

■ OTHER CABINETWORK

If your house plans contain other cabinetwork, such as bathroom vanities, built-in china cabinet, wet bar and bookcases, you may have this work done by the same source as your kitchen cabinets, especially if raised panel doors are required. Also, you may want to consider a TV or stereo cabinet in a living or family room.

For simpler built-ins, this work can be done on the job by the trim carpenters and finished by the painter. Job-built cabinet work generally is limited, since many finish carpenters do not have the equipment on the job for such work, except probably for bookcases.

Energy Efficiency, Insulation, Air Infiltration and Noise Control

A home requires follow-through planning to avoid undesirable energy losses. This planning includes the provision of insulation and related features, including well-fitting windows and doors. Even if energy availability and cost are not critical, the house will be more comfortable with appropriate energy-saving features.

In basic planning, first consider the size and number of windows and exterior doors. Together, these account for a major portion of energy loss, which occurs year-round. Next, consider the quality or performance of these components in terms of energy efficiency. This information is available from the dealer or manufacturer. While insulated glass windows are thermally superior to those with single glass, from a thermal standpoint, the overall amount of glass often is more significant when it comes to energy loss.

This point can be illustrated by showing what happens when window area is increased, and also when windows with better performance are substituted for those with single glass. The winter energy loss in a typical two story 2,100-square-foot insulated house with basement, having single glass windows, is illustrated in Figure E.1. In the example, if total window area is increased 50 percent, the increase in energy loss is about 15 percent. Note that the combined losses for

FIGURE E.1 ■ Effect of Increasing Window Area 50 Percent

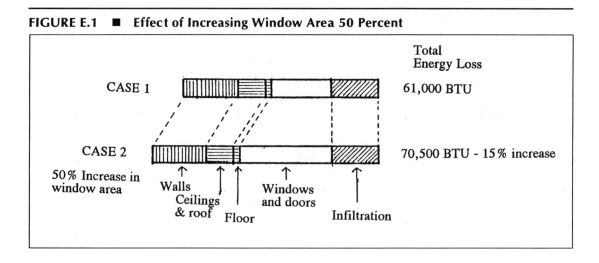

walls, ceiling and roof, floor and air infiltration remain essentially unchanged. Also note that, together, these account for the greater part of the house energy loss.

The same basic house is illustrated again in Figure E.2. This time, however, the window type has been changed to double insulating glass, to triple insulating glass, or high E double glass. Note that much more energy is saved by going from single glass to double glass than from double glass to triple glass or high E double glass. For your own house, ask for an energy comparison to determine whether the extra cost of the higher efficiency windows is worthwhile compared to the gain in efficiency. Note that the best windows available won't reduce the wall and ceiling losses.

No two houses are alike, so these comparisons should be regarded as examples only. Each house must be evaluated for its own characteristics of the five energy loss sources indicated. These calculations are usually done by the HVAC contractor, but you must decide such things as the type and amount of insulation, window area and type of glass.

■ INSULATION

Now, let's look at insulation and the principles of energy movement in a typical house. In addition, also read Appendix F.

Building insulation slows down or interrupts the passage or loss of heat through the walls, ceiling and roof, floors, windows and doors. A comparison of conductive qualities of several materials is shown in Figure E.3

FIGURE E.2 ■ Effect of Changing Windows

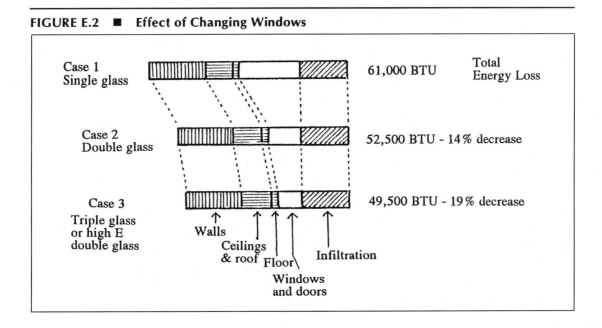

The less dense the material (i.e., the greater the inert air space in the material), the greater its insulating value. For example, in Figure 8.3 the two-inch-thick polyurethane has the same insulating capacity as the 137½-inch-thick concrete.

In house design, the living area (the area heated or air-conditioned) should be completely enclosed by the proper amount of insulation for the local environment. This process consists of insulating the exterior walls, ceilings and under the floor for both crawl space and concrete slab construction.

The ability of material to resist the passage of heat is expressed in terms of R (resistance). For example, a fiberglass batt six-inches thick has an R-value of 19. The same material in batts 12-inches thick has an R-value of 38. The greater the R, the greater the material's resistance to the passage of heat. Recommended R-values for areas in the U.S. are shown in Figure E.4.

When batt insulation is installed, it should fit the space provided and should not be compressed or part of its insulation value is lost. Thus a six-inch batt in a two-by-four stud wall will not produce an R-19 effect.

FIGURE E.3 ■ Thicknesses of Materials for Same Insulation

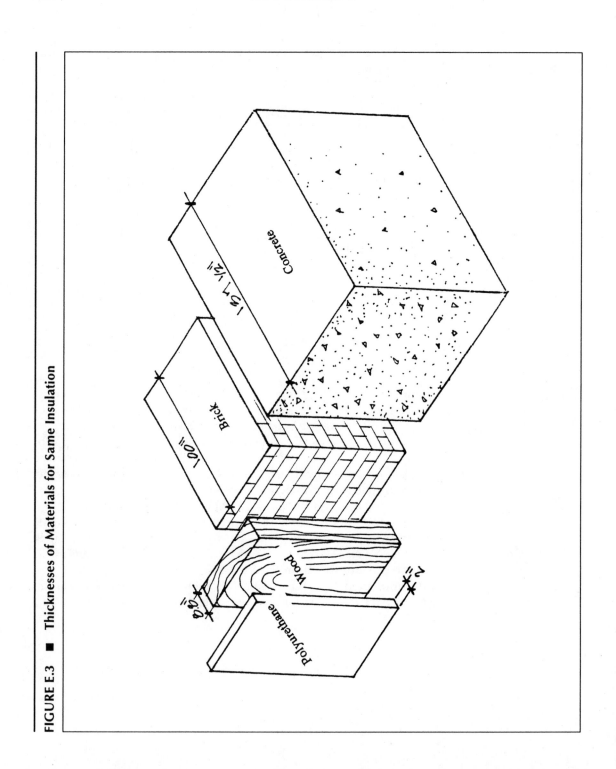

FIGURE E.4 ■ Recommended R-Values for Areas in the U.S.

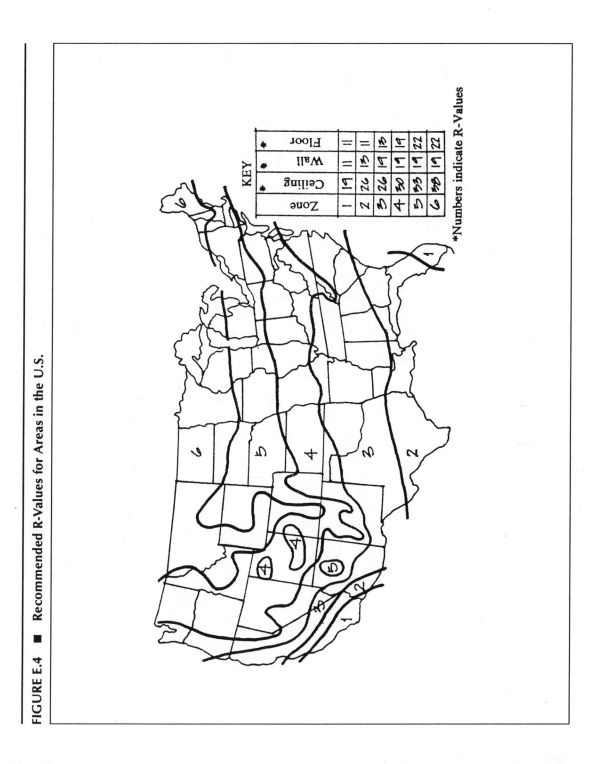

Zone	Ceiling	Wall	Floor
1	19	11	11
2	26	13	11
3	26	19	13
4	30	17	19
5	33	19	22
6	38	19	22

KEY

*Numbers indicate R-Values

■ VAPOR BARRIER

In addition to insulation, particularly in northern climates or where low winter temperature is commonplace, the living area also should be sealed with appropriate material applied to the inside of the studs and ceiling and floor joists to minimize the movement of moisture from the living area into the insulation. This can be accomplished by installing batt-type insulation with an integrated vapor barrier or batt-type insulation without the integrated barrier but adding an independent barrier such as polyethylene. Check local practices to determine its need. A vapor barrier is usually positioned on the heated area side.

The vapor barrier serves several purposes. First, insulation will lose some of its thermal resistance if it becomes damp and, second, if the moisture is retained inside the living space, the occupants will be more comfortable with less heat. And third, if condensation occurs within the construction, the moisture may lead to rot of wood materials such as the framing. In some localities with a high level of ground water and high humidity, this is a severe problem.

A vapor barrier generally is not needed for geographic areas that only require air-conditioning. In humid climates, one of the principal functions of air-conditioning is to remove moisture from the air as it circulates through the equipment. Here the moisture is condensed on the cooling coil and is drained away. This moisture removal makes the occupants of the conditioned space feel more comfortable.

■ AIR INFILTRATION

In the cases illustrated in Figures E.1 and E.2, the air infiltration is about the same. Infiltration is the leakage of heated or cooled air to the outdoors through such areas as cracks around windows, electrical outlets, lighting fixtures, fireplace, and kitchen and toilet exhaust fans. These losses can be reduced by using tighter fitting windows and doors, storm windows, house wrap, caulking and so on. Some controlled infiltration is desirable, however, to prevent accumulation of house odors and other unhealthy conditions such as spores and biological growth. For a tightly sealed house with a fireplace, a special air intake is needed for proper combustion and to prevent smoking. It should be controlled by a damper.

Windows and doors should be weather-stripped, preferably using factory-made units. Exhaust fans and kitchen range vents should have fitted back dampers that automatically close when not in use. Fireplaces should have glass doors and an independent source for combustion air. See the discussion of energy efficient fireplaces in Appendix F.

Without suitable measures to reduce infiltration, the loss of house energy through infiltration averages about 33 percent, with some older homes going as high as 60 percent.

Fortunately, sealing a home against air infiltration is a simple process if done during construction and it is relatively inexpensive, particularly considering the energy saved.

Most of the sealing is accomplished after the framing is complete and the electrical, plumbing and heating rough-ins have been finished and inspected. At this stage, an experienced sealing contractor can seal all of the holes and seams in the external side of the walls and ceiling with an expanding foam sealant. This is an excellent product for permanently filling large openings such as the gap between the frame of the window and the stud framing of the house and in caulking small cracks in selected areas most likely to leak.

Another technique is to wrap the entire exterior wall, over the sheathing before the siding is applied, with material such as Dupont's Tyvek or any of the other similar brands. These wrappings are paper-thin, very strong and will prevent the passage of air through the exterior walls without trapping moisture within the walls. The cost for this installation is very low, compared to the fuel savings for heating and cooling.

■ SOUND INSULATION

Thermal insulation of outside walls, floors and ceilings does double duty and is an automatic plus for reducing outside noise, such as passing traffic or airplanes. To reduce the undesirable effect of inside noise the same or similar type of insulation can be used in walls and floors. However, a vapor barrier is not needed.

Walls

Sound-deadening between rooms such as a bathroom and the living room or family room is desirable and can be obtained by using insulation batts between the studs. If even greater noise reduction is needed, a special insulation board can be added before the wall finish is installed. Another technique is to build what amounts to two separate walls, that is, separate stud lines with an insulation blanket. This added treatment and expense is seldom needed in most houses.

Pipes

If you have selected a metal pipe such as copper or most plastic types, the noise of water flowing can be reduced by having the plumber pack insulation material around the pipe, and where it goes through the framing or masonry walls to break the physical contact with additional packing. In other words, the pipe is isolated from the structure as well as possible.

Floors

Passage of sound through floors usually is not a problem for single-family one-story houses without basements; it is more typically a requirement for apartments and multi-floor houses. Noise transmitted through floors can be substantially reduced by installing insulation just below the subfloor between the joists. Also, the use of carpeting and padding on the second floor cuts down noise transmission to the spaces below.

Heating and Cooling

This appendix provides information to assist the reader in making the selection of a heating and cooling system for new construction. It describes the characteristics of the more conventional types of central heating and cooling systems, auxiliary heating and cooling systems and offers selected combinations of all types to meet the various requirements throughout the country.

■ OVERVIEW

The homeowner must consider the type of system, such as piped hot water or forced air for heating; determine the type of fuel to be used; find a suitable location for the equipment; and plan for distribution or delivery of heating and air-conditioning to the rooms. Your HVAC contractor can help you make these decisions based on study of your house design.

Most new houses are planned to have central heating. There are two basic types of central heating systems, one using heated water (steam systems now are little used in houses) delivered to rooms through pipes to convectors, radiators or radiant heat panels; and the other using forced air delivered via ducts to outlets in the rooms. Ducted systems have the capability of providing summer air-conditioning and thus do double-duty while water heating systems require a separate ducted system for summer cooling.

Piped systems require minimal space for the distribution piping, which usually can be concealed in finished rooms. Typical components of such systems are shown in Figure F.1. The ducted system requires much more space for routes

FIGURE F.1 ■ **Forced Hot-Water Heating System**

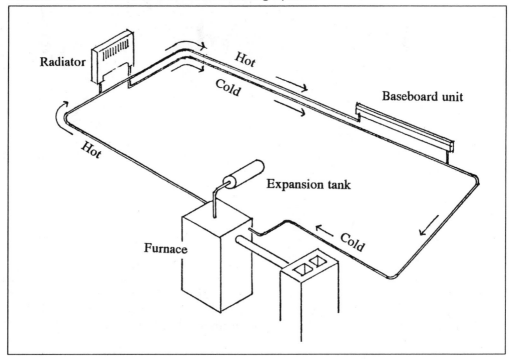

to the rooms. Because of their size, duct routes usually are planned below the main floor where there is a basement or crawl space, or above the ceiling if there is an attic. If it is necessary to duct up or down through a story, the duct location must be planned carefully so as to function properly in the system yet not create an awkward or obtrusive presence in a room. Desirable locations may be in a closet, chase or created duct space such as at the end of a hallway.

Equipment location should be planned for efficiency and ease of running pipes or ducts where needed. Usually, the shortest and most direct routes from equipment to rooms served are desirable to minimize energy losses along the way.

While piped systems have the capability of efficiently serving long pipe runs, the use of long air duct runs may necessitate using higher capacity equipment to offset energy losses. This adds to operating energy costs over the years.

In any type of system, a greater level of comfort is achieved if heat or cooling is delivered close to locations where energy losses or gains are the greatest. This means along exterior walls near windows and doors. When planning placement of furniture, keep this in mind. Furniture should not block outlets, radiators or convectors.

Poor distribution tends to create drafts, dead spots and uneven temperatures in rooms. This can be the case when ceilings are quite high, such as cathedral and two-story rooms, where there are large glass areas, and where the number or location of outlets, radiators and convectors is too limited. Thus, delivery locations should be well arranged to cover the room geometry.

In forced-air systems, it is necessary to have ducts that return the air to the heating and cooling equipment. Usually return registers or inlets are located away from supply outlets to enable good air movement through the room. A rule of thumb is, if supply outlets are low or in the floor, the returns should be high or in the ceiling and on the opposite side of the room, or vice versa. When a closed door interferes with air flow, it should be undercut one-half inch or more to ensure circulation.

The floor plan and the size of the house may affect the type and number of HVAC systems in the house. For example, a large house may best be heated and cooled by dividing it into different zones, each permitting a different level of heating, cooling or both. In some large houses, one zone may require heating while another zone needs cooling. These different zones may be created in one of two ways:

1. Install one large system with two independent circulating systems that furnish different levels of heat or cooling, using controls that regulate different parts of the house.
2. Install two smaller but independent systems, each with its own circulating system and controls.

For example, in a large one-story house, it often is desirable to have two zones, one for the bedroom area and the other for the general living area. Different temperatures thus can be set and savings in operating costs will be achieved. Another example where zoning is desirable is in a moderately large two-story house with separate zones for each floor, since load demands will be different on each floor.

This is particularly advantageous in forced-air systems supplying both cooling and heating. In the winter, the downstairs heating rises through the ceiling to the second floor; thus, less heat is required from the second floor system to satisfy its heating needs. In the summer, the reverse situation occurs, since the cool air needed to make the second floor comfortable descends through the open stairway to affect the main floor. Without zones, the upstairs would be overly warm in the winter and the downstairs overly cool in the summer.

In some houses, it may be desirable to use different types of HVAC systems for different zones such as a gas furnace for the main living area but electric resistance baseboard radiator convectors in the bedrooms where less heat is needed. This is another example of zoning flexibility.

For a piped water system, two zones can be created using one boiler and two circulating systems. A large-capacity forced-air furnace may be made to serve two zones by providing duct dampers to proportion the flow of air between two zones. The dampers may be operated manually or by a motor that is remotely controlled. However, zone operation of a large duct system does not function as economically as separate and independent systems, since the single large equipment produces the same output regardless of how a damper is adjusted or whether the full capacity is needed. If in doubt about the need or desirability of a zoned HVAC system, consult with a mechanical engineer or a knowledgeable contractor in the planning stage and avoid the problems trying to make corrections later.

Almost all modern systems, whether piped water or forced air, respond promptly to thermostatic controls. The air system usually reacts more quickly, and warm air or cooling may be felt shortly after the blower comes on. The piped water system takes somewhat longer to deliver heat to a room if pipes are long or have cooled down appreciably. For most residential systems, the thermostat senses room temperature and sends a low voltage signal to the equipment when the thermostat setting is within several degrees of actual room temperature. This spread of several degrees is necessary to avoid rapid cycling or periods of short operation of equipment, which is hard on the equipment and uses fuel uneconomically. Also remember that the equipment will last longer and operate more efficiently if it operates continuously, not on and off in rapid succession. When equipment capacity is determined, the design conditions for the expected outside temperature are taken into account, as are the insulative qualities of the house. Thus, the properly sized equipment will operate continuously at the low end of the outside design temperature. The better insulated house, which holds temperature better, also will minimize undesired frequent cycling of the equipment.

■ FUELS

The major use of energy in typical homes is for heating and cooling, some 45 percent of the total. About 15 percent more is used for hot water. Other principal uses are electricity for lighting (15 percent) and power for major appliances (20 percent). Thus, the type and efficiency of HVAC equipment and of hot water equipment together with the fuels they use are very important.

Choice of fuels includes the anticipated cost of energy in the future, but this is only part of the story. Other factors must be considered, such as local availability, regardless of whether air-conditioning is to be provided, and the advantages and disadvantages of types of systems for the given house.

Of the three most commonly used fuels today—electricity, natural gas and oil—for heating alone, electric-resistance type (either an electric-resistance furnace or electric-resistance baseboards in each room) is the most costly to operate. The cost to operate a conventional high-efficiency heat pump is dramatically lower and its heating cost is about the same as for natural gas. Oil heating generally is more expensive. Electricity in most areas is provided by a regulated public utility that offers the consumer the greatest stability of cost and availability. Natural gas also is regulated, but cost is more variable due to availability of supply. The price of bottled gas is determined by market conditions, and oil prices and supply are volatile and dependent on market conditions. During periods of energy crises such as occurred in the 1970s, this instability was very apparent.

Electricity

Electricity is readily available almost anywhere. From the standpoint of the homeowner, it is clean, leaves no residue and will not contaminate the atmosphere. It requires no chimney. The cost of electricity will probably go up or down along with the cost of fuels used to generate it. One of the greatest advantages of electricity as a fuel is reliability for the future, since it can be produced from almost any other type of energy—solar, nuclear, oil, gas, coal and geothermal. Thus, relying on electricity for house energy in times of energy crisis appears to be less risky than for other fuels. Also remember that all oil and gas systems require electricity to operate pumps and fans.

Oil

Today, oil is readily available. Oil is moderately clean if the burner is regularly serviced. Storage, preferably an underground tank, is needed. Oil-burning equipment does require a chimney.

Gas

Gas is available in two forms: natural and bottled, or liquid propane. Natural gas comes from the ground in a gaseous state, while propane gas is manufactured from crude oil. Natural gas is not available in many localities, especially in rural areas; liquid propane gas is available nearly everywhere, but its cost is higher. Gas is clean, requires no storage (except propane gas), but it does need a chimney or other approved vent. Gas can be used to operate heating and air-conditioning equipment, and domestic water heaters.

Coal

There are significant problems associated with coal, including its delivery and storage in the house, that the use of coal to fuel central house-heating systems is not recommended. In addition, coal requires a chimney; it is dirty before burning, during burning and leaves relatively large amounts of ashes, which must be disposed of. Depending upon availability in your area, coal might be a good choice for fueling auxiliary or back-up heating systems such as a fireplace or free-standing stove.

Wood

Like coal, wood is best used for back-up systems. If quantities of the hardwoods such as oak, locust, birch, beech, elm and ash are available at reasonable prices, the use of wood in an energy-efficient fireplace or stove as a back-up for other systems may be considered. The homeowner should realize, however, that substantial labor is required to place the unburned wood in storage, to move it to the stove or fireplace as needed and then to remove the ashes after combustion.

■ THE HEAT PUMP

The heat pump is one of the most innovative heating and cooling systems available today. It also is highly efficient. Heat pumps use refrigeration technology and are electrically operated. Inside, house air is ducted in a manner much like other forced-air systems.

The heat pump is the only heating system that does not make heat—it moves the heat already existing from the outside of the house to the inside when in the heating mode and from inside the house to the outside when in the cooling mode.

Air Source Heat Pump

The air source system (also known as an air-to-air system) can operate very effectively with outside temperatures of down to 25°F and above. Below this temperature range, its efficiency is reduced and the system will need auxiliary heat to maintain a comfortable heat level in the house. This auxiliary heat usually consists of electric-resistance heat strips built into the air handler unit. When signaled by an outdoor thermostat, these strips come on and reinforce the heat brought into the house by the refrigerant. Auxiliary heat also may consist of an oil or gas furnace installed as an integrated part of the heat pump system.

Some readers may have difficulty visualizing the extraction of heat from outside air that has reached a temperature of 25°F. Although it sounds unlikely, all cold air contains some heat. For example, the air at 0°F has 89 percent as much heat as air at 100°F. Heat is completely absent from the air only at absolute zero or

−460°F, which can only be approached in the laboratory. As the temperature goes down in cold winters, however, the air source heat pump begins to lose its ability to replace the heat lost from the house through its exterior skin at the same rate as the loss. When this "balance point" is reached (and it will differ from house to house because of the variations in construction, heat pump machinery and so on), auxiliary heat must be brought into the system.

Other Types of Heat Pump Systems

In addition to air-to-air (conventional) heat pumps, several other types of systems are avialable that utilize the ability of water or the earth in the heat pump cycle. These systems have been used for many years in both northern and southern climates. Although installation costs are greater than for conventional systems, the considerable savings in energy use by highly increased efficiency is offset usually in seven to ten years. If intrigued in their application, you should consult a professional engineer or HVAC contractor experienced in such installations. Ask for details and a cost comparison analysis for your particular situation. There are two basic types of such systems.

Water-Source Heat Pump   This type of system is used where well water is available in adequate quantity or where pond water exists that does not drop below 40°F in the winter. Sea water is not suitable because of the high concentration of salts. After the water is used in the heat pump cycle, it is discharged: this may be a problem. Open water sources also may contain debris and other contamination. However, there are innovative answers to these problems that may be appropriate to your situation.

Ground-Source (Earth-Coupled) Heat Pump   Even more widely used, this type of system has one or more closed underground loops (like an automobile cooling system) to recirculate the heat transfer fluid (usually water and antifreeze). See Figure F.2. The earth, which maintains relatively constant temperature year-round below levels influenced by surface temperature effects, is both the source and receiver of heat transfer, depending on the season. This system is more reliable and has fewer problems than water-source types.

Both types of systems are appealing to homeowners, not only for energy-saving advantages, but also because neither utilizes the noisy outdoor compressor of air-to-air systems.

The Heat Pump and Hot Water

Several heat pump manufacturers have developed an add-on device that permits the central heat pump to heat the domestic hot water as well as the house.

FIGURE F.2 ■ Ground-Coupled Heat Pump Systems

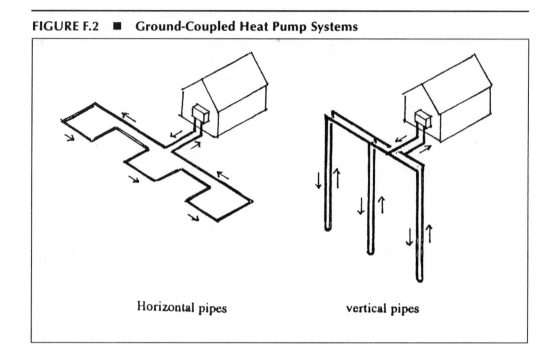

Horizontal pipes   vertical pipes

Domestic hot water is the hot water used for bathing, dish washing, clothes washing and so on.

In addition, some manufacturers market a small heat pump to be used solely for making domestic hot water. Check the cost of this device with a contractor and compare it with the cost of an electric hot water heater including operating costs to determine which is the best for you.

Efficiency and Other Characteristics

In judging the relative efficiency of different heat pumps systems from various manufacturers, compare the SEER (seasonal energy efficient ratio) and the HSPF (Heating Seasonal Performance Factor). For a high-efficiency air-to-air model, the SEER should be at least 10.0 and the HSPF should be at least 6.5.

Most heat pumps now, or will in the future, use environmentally friendly refrigerants. The older Freon-type refrigerants contribute to ozone depletion in the atmosphere. Unfortunately, new refrigerants are not compatible with systems designed to use older Freon.

With some early designs of the heat pump, during the cold season the hot air pumped into the house had temperatures below body temperature, 98.6°F, and thus occupants felt cold and perhaps uncomfortable to some (although the temperature of the hot air was well above the thermostat setting of 68°F to 72°F). The newer designs now available have largely eliminated this problem by providing warmer air (up to 15°F warmer) at greater efficiency during the heating season.

Today's state-of-the-art heat pumps are reliable and generally will perform as long as many non–heat pump systems.

Combination Systems

The combination of a heat pump with a gas or oil furnace can provide a more efficient central heating system than the single gas or oil furnace by itself due to heat pump efficiency. This can be particularly desirable in colder climates.

In a combination system, the heat pump operates unaided in its efficient operating range and the gas or oil furnace supplements or takes over the heating task when outside temperatures reach 28°F to 32°F and colder. In addition, the heat pump will provide air-conditioning in the summer at no additional equipment installation cost.

The initial cost of installing gas- or oil-fired systems in combination with the heat pump will be higher than either the gas or oil system with air-conditioning alone. To be economically sound, the annual savings in fuel costs should provide for a payback of this additional cost in not more than seven to ten years.

Since this combination system has a low operating cost, the payback requirement should be met easily if the house is properly insulated and if anti–air infiltration measures have been applied during construction.

■ DUCT WORK

All ducted systems require the efficient movement of air to and from locations served. Thus ducts should have minimal friction and minimal number of turns, and supply ducts should be insulated. Long runs of return ducts through unheated spaces also should be insulated. Two materials generally are used in making the ducts for forced-air heating or independent air-conditioning: fiberglass duct board and galvanized sheet metal.

Fiberglass Duct Board

This type of duct work makes a quiet system. It usually is assembled by using staples and tape, which do not give it the rigidity nor the ruggedness of the galvanized sheet metal. The fiberglass duct board provides insulation from noise and heat, however. It should cost about the same as the galvanized sheet metal wrapped with insulation. Flexible fiberglass ducts also are available for short branch runs.

Galvanized Sheet Metal

Metal ducts are put together using more positive means of fastening.

By itself, a sheet metal duct tends to be noisy. This noise can be substantially reduced, however, by lining the inside of the ducts with insulation material near the air handler, which also provides thermal insulation. The greatest noise comes from the air handler caused by the fan and motor, and the noise of the burner in combustion equipment.

■ AIR CLEANERS

Because of their duct network, forced-air heating and air-conditioning systems are ideal for electrostatic air cleaners; they can be installed as an integral part of the duct system. This may be important for occupants who are sensitive to air contaminants. They not only clean the air but tend to make it smell fresher, which is more important now with the sealing of houses and the reduction of fresh air moving into the house through the holes in the outer shell. For non-ducted systems, individual room cleaners that plug into an ordinary wall outlet can be bought. These are portable and some have renewable charcoal filters to aid in removal of smoke and other air contaminants.

■ HUMIDIFIERS

A house built with proper insulation and tight anti–air infiltration measures usually does not need a humidifier except where extremely low winter humidity is a problem. If your house has been constructed with no vapor barrier and has few or no anti–air infiltration measures, the air inside may become excessively dry because of the loss of room moisture. If so, higher temperatures will be needed to gain the same comfort as with moisture in the air. Should this be the case, consider the use of some sort of humidifier.

A humidifier can be installed directly into the duct system and hooked up to a water supply so that it will continually and automatically put the needed moisture into the air. The water should be relatively mineral-free, since mineral deposits in the humidifier will cause poor operation or early failure. An alternative is to use a separate distilled water source for the humidifier. A humidistat is used to control the humidifier, usually mounted adjacent to the house thermostat for convenience.

For houses heated with systems other than forced air, small portable humidifiers can be placed in appropriate rooms or areas throughout the house to accomplish the same thing. These also may be more practical where house water has high mineral content and added humidification is needed only occasionally. Distilled water may be used in the humidifier.

■ OTHER HEATING SYSTEMS

Radiant Heating

Radiant heating (heat directly radiated for the comfort of occupants) may be attained by installing pipe loops in the ceiling, floors or walls; panels of hot water coils; or embedded electric-resistance wiring. Design of these systems can be very tricky and should be undertaken only by one experienced in this field.

These systems depend primarily on radiation through the air for the passage of heat. Since radiant heat striking the occupant reduces body heat loss and increases comfort, the occupant will be more comfortable at lower temperatures compared to other systems, such as forced air and convection, assuming that system coverage is uniform. Radiant systems have several drawbacks, such as potential leakage from piped systems and a tendency to discolor the plaster after years of usage showing traces of pipe or wire locations. They also are inflexible if alterations or remodeling are contemplated. Electric radiant systems can have individual room thermostats.

Electric Baseboard Heat

Although operating cost is relatively high, electric baseboard heat is one of the simplest and least expensive heating systems to install. It is unobtrusive, almost noiseless and, depending upon the circumstances of its use, can be very efficient. Each room has its own control, permitting variations in the amount of heat provided and for economy of operation. If these controls are used properly and if the house has been well insulated and properly sealed against air passage, the cost of operation can be reasonably low. Maintenance costs for electric baseboard heat are the lowest of any heating system, since its units are dependable and long-lasting.

■ THERMOSTATS

All electrical and mechanical heating and cooling systems will have one or more thermostats wired to control the equipment. In a combination heating and cooling system, or a heat pump, a single thermostat can serve both heating and cooling modes. For add-on air-conditioning, usually a separate cooling thermostat is used.

Substantial savings in fuel can be realized by the use of a thermostat containing a control clock that automatically lowers the heat (setback) while the occupants are absent or sleeping. For example, a working father and mother with two school children could have an arrangement whereby the temperature automatically turns up to about 68°F a half-hour or so before rising, then turns down to

63°F after the last person has left the house, then back up to 68°F just before the first child returns from school and, once more, back to down to 63°F at the preset time for the night.

Savings also can be attained when air-conditioning is in operation by raising the temperature on the thermostat for those hours when the house is not occupied.

■ AIR-CONDITIONING

Nearly all of the forced warm-air heating systems are readily adaptable at modest additional cost to include air-conditioning. The heat pump automatically operates as an air conditioner, since the same machinery is used for both operations. The other forced warm-air systems are designed to accept transfer coils in the air handler for air-conditioning, using the same duct system for cool air distribution. The basic components are a cooling coil and a condensation collection pan with drain.

If your primary heating system is not a ducted type and you want central air-conditioning, it will have to be a separate system.

Do not install an oversized system in the hope of getting quick cooling. If oversizing is much greater than 15 percent, there will be a fast cool-down; however, the air will be saturated with moisture and feel clammy and uncomfortably cold. In a very large two-story house, zoned air-conditioning may be warranted. This usually means separate independent air-conditioning systems.

Central Air-Conditioning and Heat Pump Equipment

The most widely installed home central air-conditioning equipment is the split system, the outdoor part being the compressor unit and the indoor part, the air handler. These are connected by refrigerant tubing and wiring. Also available are combined one-piece units generally located in the foundation wall. Although one-piece equipment is less expensive, the system installation is less flexible; it is generally used in small houses where construction economy is necessary. Two-part equipment permits locating the indoor unit where ductwork and distribution of air are most efficient, and the noisy outdoor unit can be placed where least objectionable and away from bedroom and living areas. Two-piece equipment is relatively simple and practical to add to an existing forced-air heating system.

Air-to-air heat pumps also are made in split and one-piece equipment and have similar advantages and disadvantages.

■ LOCATION OF HVAC EQUIPMENT

If possible, locate the outdoor section of a heat pump or air conditioner away from decks, patios, bedroom windows due to noise and dryer vents due to lint and air contamination. Also avoid interior corners, which tend to accentuate the noise of the compressor. If your system is for air-conditioning only locate the compressor in the shade, since sunlight on the coils will unnecessarily increase the workload.

The indoor section can be located in the garage, a utility room such as a pantry or closet, the attic, the basement or the crawl space.

Wherever located, the ducts should be direct and as short as possible. If equipment is above living spaces, an auxiliary condensate drain should be provided to capture and drain overflow if the internal drain plugs up. If located in an attic, the duct layout should be planned so that the attic floor area is kept as open as much as possible for storage.

One other important potential drawback of an attic location is the noise made by the furnace and the fan. The noise transmitted through the ceiling framing is difficult to dampen and may be very disturbing. If framing conditions permit, the effect of structurally transmitted noise can be reduced if the equipment is suspended from the roof rafters. In any case, do not install this equipment directly over the bedroom area.

■ AUXILIARY HEATING AND COOLING

Up to this point, the discussion of heating and cooling has been of central systems for the whole house. Many different auxiliary systems may be ideal for solving special heating and cooling problems.

Through-the-wall air conditioners, heaters and heat pumps may be the best solution to the heating and cooling of an isolated part of the house or a part that is seldom used. If the design of the house allows the mounting of this equipment through the wall, the appearance is improved and there is no loss of the use of windows. The unit is only turned on when the room is in use. The chief objection to window or wall units is that they are noisy.

Small independent wall-mounted electric heaters with blowers are very effective for giving quick heat to a room, such as a bath, for short time occupancy and as a supplement to the main heating system. Electric heat lamps in the ceiling also provide similar heating. These can be timer-operated at a wall switch.

Water evaporation coolers for air-conditioning are very effective in hot, dry climates. They require less energy to operate than the conventional air conditioner and equipment cost is less. They need a more or less constant source of water, however, and are a potential source of objectionable biological growth, which can be health-threatening.

Ceiling paddle fans may be used to provide summer comfort even where high humidity is a problem since they move the air. They also are useful in helping to circulate air heated by a fireplace or stove in the winter. In houses designed with a cathedral ceiling the ceiling fan can be used to move the warm air that may accumulate in a pocket at the apex of the ceiling.

Whole house ceiling exhaust fans also are useful in providing comfort in the summertime where humidity is low. They should not be operated during cold weather, however, since they discharge the heated air to the attic and, hence, outside. If blown-in attic insulation is installed, these fans tend to stir up dust and move insulation particles. These fans have large blades and are noisier than paddle ceiling fans; the latter are almost completely silent at the lower speeds in quality models.

■ FIREPLACES

For centuries, the fireplace functioned as the principal means of heating a house and in later years as an auxiliary heating system. Charming as a fireplace is, unfortunately, it does not do the job very well. Depending on the use of room air for combustion, the fireplace can actually waste more heat than it generates. In modern homes, the room air used for fireplace combustion has already been heated by the primary heating system, and much of it is lost up the chimney. Therefore, rather than assist the primary system in its heating function, the fireplace increases the work load of the primary system. The installation of an outside air intake for a fireplace is recommended and is required by some building codes.

There are three basic types of fireplaces: the all-masonry, masonry/steel box and all-prefabricated fireplace.

The All-Masonry Fireplace

This type of fireplace, with a full masonry fire box and chimney, can be designed and built to meet the energy-efficient conditions as indicated earlier. Low maintenance and the beauty of the brickwork can enhance the overall house appearance. If you choose this option, be certain that you have a good design and that your mason has experience in building this type of fireplace. An outside air intake is advisable.

The Masonry/Steel Box Fireplace

This type of fireplace is similar to the all-masonry fireplace, except that the firebox is prefabricated steel encased in masonry. This type is somewhat less costly, and retains most of the other advantages of the all-masonry fireplace with regard to architecture and beauty. An air intake can be provided into the combustion chamber and the separate circulating vents can emerge from the front or to the side of the box.

The All-Prefabricated Fireplace

This is factory-made, with the only remaining requirement being the assembly and installation of the various parts. The system includes the firebox, usually with refractory tile liner, the flue pipes for the chimney in lengths of two, three or four feet, the chimney cap and related equipment. This type of fireplace has been on the market for some time and most framing crews are experienced in its installation. Its major advantages are that it can be installed directly on wood framing and a massive masonry foundation is not needed. The fireplace functions efficiently and is the least costly of the three systems. An example is shown in Figure F.3.

If your house has exterior wood, aluminum or vinyl siding or stucco, the enclosure around the exposed part of the metal chimney can be built using two-by-four framing (sized to complement the architecture of the house) covered with the same siding used on the rest of the house.

If your house is brick or stone veneer, this material is too heavy to be practical to use to hide the wood-framed metal flue. You may, however, use the factory-made artificial brick covers, but most do not look very attractive. If this is not appealing, your choice may be to select the all-masonry or the masonry/steel box fireplace, which has the brick chimney built from top to bottom.

The room-side wall finish on steel prefabricated fireplaces can be brick, tile, plaster, stucco or even wood. Within six inches of the fireplace opening the material must be noncombustible.

Gas-Fired Fireplaces

Prefabricated, efficient gas-fired fireplaces are available today with many choices. They are easy to install and are much easier to take care of than the wood burners. Some types can be installed directly against a plaster or sheet rock covered wall or on top of an existing wood floor. Look for the "zero clearance" type. Most of these fireplaces need a very simple "chimney" consisting of a short four-inch metal pipe installed horizontally through the exterior wall behind the fireplace to the outside to remove combustion products.

If public gas service is available in your area, you can hook up to it for the fuel supply. If not, bottled gas can be supplied from an exterior tank. Gas-fired stoves with similar characteristics also are available.

FIGURE F.3   ■   Energy-Efficient Fireplace Design

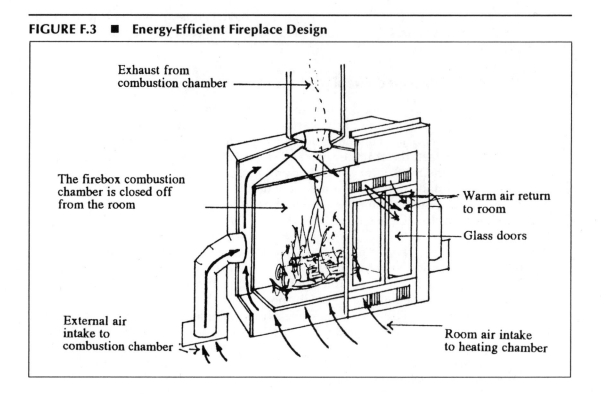

Exhaust from
combustion chamber

The firebox combustion
chamber is closed off
from the room

Warm air return
to room

Glass doors

External air
intake to
combustion chamber

Room air intake
to heating chamber

■ SUMMARY

Select your system and choice of fuel with care and plan installation based on awareness of how a system operates. Although much of a system is hidden and out of mind, it should be efficient and provide the desired comfort year-round.

Find out what types of systems are installed and serviced locally. Maintenance and service calls will be necessary sooner or later.

Also, review Appendix G on solar heating. Solar effects are always an influence and should be used advantageously.

Solar Heating

Since the 1970s, a lot of interest and attention has been given to taking advantage of solar power, especially for heating, and it is helpful to have a grasp of the principles and techniques involved, as well as their limitations. For example, any window through which the sun's rays pass is a source of solar heating, and the insulative treatment of windows, walls and ceilings obviously affects the extent of energy loss. These ideas are well known and often are taken for granted.

Solar energy is free; therefore, any time it can be used for efficient heating and cooling, use it. In the present state of the art, particularly in conventional houses, solar energy has its limitations; it may not be practical to produce economic and efficient heating in many house designs, and to the same extent in all geographic areas of the country. In most situations, a back-up heating system is required.

Solar heating systems are of two types: active and passive. These terms refer to how the systems function, with active systems requiring mechanical components to accumulate and distribute heat, and passive systems operating on natural principles alone without pumps, blowers or related controls. Often the virtues of both are combined.

■ PASSIVE SOLAR HEAT

A passive solar heating system uses three natural processes. First, the sun's energy radiates to the inside of the house through windows and glass doors, warming materials by conduction such as the floor, walls and other objects; these in turn reradiate the heat to warm the air of the cooler room. The warmed air then creates convection movement of the air.

The success of passive solar heating is based primarily on the proper design of the house. With the exception of the occasional use of low-powered electric fans to assist in air distribution, it does not use mechanical equipment. It is the most practical application of solar energy in the house. To function efficiently, however, the house must be designed specifically to use this type of heat in your locality. Any passive solar heating system will have the following components:

- The route by which radiant energy can enter the building. This usually consists of large glass or plastic window areas facing generally south or at least within 30 degrees of south and can be thought of as a collector. During the heating season, this collector should not be shaded by other structures or trees from about 9 A.M. to 3 P.M.
- One or more absorber elements, usually consisting of a masonry wall, the floor or a water tank. The absorber, a storage element, receives heat that has passed through the collector and gradually warms and holds it for later distribution.
- A distribution system by which the heat can leave the storage element and circulate through the living area. A strictly passive system would use all three methods of heat transfer, although convection and radiation are of greater importance. Some passive solar heating systems require the addition of electric fans to help circulate the warm air more efficiently.
- A control or regulation device to prevent the loss of heat from inside the house to the outside during no-sunshine periods, such as at night or on a cloudy day. Most heat regulators consist of movable insulating curtains. A control system also may include electronic sensing devices to signal a fan to turn on or to open or close vents and dampers that restrict the flow of heat.

Direct Gain

The simplest form of passive solar heat uses direct gain, illustrated in Figure G.1. Sunlight enters the house through the large window area, the collector, striking the walls and floor, where it is absorbed and stored. To be the most effective, the walls and floors should be built of masonry or other dense material to provide the amount of storage capacity needed. They also should be painted or covered with material of a dark color to improve the absorbing process. At night as the room cools, the heat, which is stored in the walls and floors, radiates into the room. Note also the insulation curtains at the windows, which should be closed at night and during nonsunshine days to prevent the loss of heat back through the collector. This is one of the drawbacks of the direct gain passive solar heating system. It gives the owner two poor choices: either lose the heat back through the collector or draw the curtain and lose the pleasure of daylight. Other

---

FIGURE G.1 ■ Direct Gain

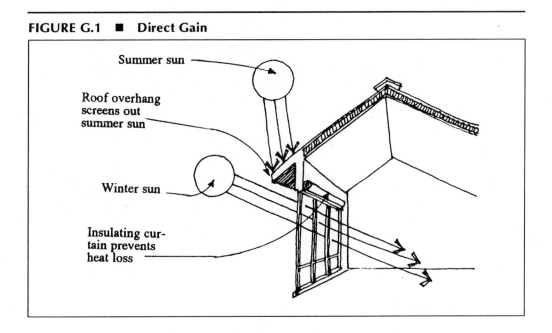

Summer sun

Roof overhang screens out summer sun

Winter sun

Insulating curtain prevents heat loss

---

limitations are the feasible size of the absorbers in the room, and the fact that the entering direction of solar energy changes each minute as the sun angle moves. Thus a wall that is warmed in the morning may receive no solar energy in the afternoon. Another limitation is the amount of heat that comes through the limited glass area.

Despite these limitations, and although this is the simplest passive heat system, it is the most practical for use in most home designs. The limitations mean that the passive system must be backed up by some other form of heating such as a conventional furnace, a heat pump or other heater.

Passive System Variations

Many variations of passive solar heating systems have been developed, but for most of these an experienced architect or engineer should be consulted for successful design. The guiding principles are the same as already described.

One design involves building a thick absorber wall inside the glass or window area, in effect, creating a compartment. Some of the absorbed heat then radiates directly into the adjacent room, and some is circulated from the compartment. This design is referred to as a Trombe wall system. In variations of this concept the wall may be replaced by drums or tanks holding water for absorbing heat. Obviously, introducing this type of system affects space planning, daylight and views.

Another design is called the solar greenhouse; it is like a plant nursery. Another design is the envelope house, which has an inner and outer envelope of construction, and heat is circulated within the two shells usually by fans to aid natural convection. The envelope house is expensive to build because of added construction cost. Also, careful planning is required to accommodate daylight and views.

In summary, even to a modest extent many features of passive solar heating methods can be adopted for significant results in the construction of houses today. Simply orienting windows to the south with a suitable heat storage method and controls of night losses at windows is one example. If carefully planned, the additional construction cost can be small and in time will be made up in fuel savings. In more elaborate systems with passive solar heating measures, the energy savings may surpass 80 percent.

■ ACTIVE SOLAR HEATING

An active solar heating system uses mechanical equipment to improve the collection and distribution of heat by using pumps and fans. There are two types of such systems: liquid-based and air-based, which designate the medium used to transfer the heat through the system.

The design of an effective active solar heating system to a particular plan is much more complicated than the application of passive solar principles; hence, the design should be tackled only by an architect, engineer or other person who has extensive experience in this field.

Due in part to cost as well as solving a house plan layout, the practical application of active solar heating systems is not as widespread as the passive solar techniques.

Like passive systems, in those periods when the solar heat source is not available, a back-up system is usually needed, but can be integrated with the active solar equipment for convenience and efficiency.

Active Solar Heat for Hot Water

Independent active solar heating systems are available for your domestic hot water. In most cases where the sun is not dependable, a back-up heating system will be needed. As with the active solar heating for the house, the system cost must be considered; it can easily exceed several thousand dollars, plus the back-up. However, local conditions may permit the installation of solar hot water heating systems at a cost which can be paid back in about five years, and thus economically attractive. Get some expert advice to determine whether the cost of the solar system makes this choice practical for your house. Also take into account your neighbors' trees (if in a wooded area) as well as construction that might interfere with solar collection.

Zoning Regulation

If your plan depends substantially upon passive or active solar heating, or on a combination of the two, check the zoning regulations for your area to ensure that further construction on adjacent property cannot block the sunshine from your lot and eliminate or reduce the capacity of your solar system.

Plumbing

Since most of the components of plumbing systems are not seen, we don't give them a lot of attention. Some basic knowledge is essential, however, as it affects planning and the selection of materials. While it is not intended to be a technical guide, this appendix will highlight important features upon which all plumbing systems depend for successful operation, and in most localities, the design and installation of plumbing systems are governed by a plumbing code.

■ THE PLUMBING SYSTEM

The two basic parts of house plumbing are the supply and waste removal systems. These systems are separated at the point of usage, the fixtures. This arrangement avoids contamination of the supply water.

The water supply system is under pressure to deliver water to fixtures, but thereafter the waste removal system depends on gravity flow to remove the water in most houses. Exceptions will be discussed later in this appendix.

The water source may be a municipal main or a private well where public water is not available. At the tap or connection to the public main, a cutoff valve and usually a meter are installed to measure the amount of water consumed. Almost invariably the water main and the supply pipe to the house are deep enough underground to provide protection against accidental damage from digging and freezing.

Inside the foundation, the house distribution system takes over. Sometimes another shutoff valve is installed here, which is capable of draining the house system should this be necessary for winterization or for plumbing repairs.

The house piping then routes the water to points of use such as plumbing fixtures, hose bibs where garden hoses may be connected, the water heater and other equipment. Because all of this piping is under pressure, the routing may be in any direction, providing that pipe sizes are adequate for proper flow. Each plumbing fixture served normally has supply cutoffs. These features apply to both cold and hot water piping.

All supply piping should be installed so that it is protected from freezing in climates where this may occur. Attic runs should be avoided, although those in the crawl space are less of a problem due to the warming effect of the earth beneath. If piping must be installed in outside walls or above a ceiling adjacent to the attic, the house insulation must be on the exterior side of the pipe.

The insulation of hot water piping is good practice when pipe runs are long, especially through such unheated areas as the crawl space or an unheated basement.

Supply piping may be either metal, usually copper, plastic or a combination of both. Plastic piping types are widely used in residences because the materials are cheaper and installation time (hence labor) costs are usually less than for metal. If left to the plumber, your piping system would probably be plastic, but check to make sure he or she is using the pipe you want.

Galvanized steel and iron pipe are seldom used as supply pipe in residences today, except for piping gas. Other types of pipe are easier to install and don't present rust problems.

Because of its stiffness, metal piping usually requires minimal support for long runs, although adequate brackets or clamps reduce noise transmission caused by water hammer vibration when faucets are closed suddenly.

Most metal piping will burst upon freezing, except flexible copper, which tolerates expansion. Once expanded, however, copper does not return to the original size and joints may leak.

Metal piping has the advantages of being relatively puncture-resistant, dimensionally stable and tolerant to heat if placed near ductwork or other heat sources.

Four types of plastic pipe are now widely used in residences for specific purposes. Customarily known by letter abbreviations, all are lightweight and chemically inert; they resist corrosion and permit smooth flow of water. Most types lack the strength of metal piping and are less stable in temperature changes than are metals and need close supports for long runs. Because plastics are better insulators than metals, they do not cool as quickly when used for hot water. A minor disadvantage of plastic pipe for use outside the house foundation is that plastic is more easily damaged by a sharp digging tool than is metal pipe.

The waste system also is known as the DWV (drain-waste-vent) system. In the language of the plumber, waste piping refers to lines that drain most fixtures except toilets, where it is called soil piping. Although DWV pipes are larger than supply pipes, they are not under pressure and use gravity flow instead. Their installation must be sloped for proper gravity flow of horizontal runs. Also, drain piping must be vented to prevent gurgling and sluggish flow.

Vent connections are almost always concealed in the wall or floor. Vent piping from an island sink will not permit the customary vent, so special wet venting is used and the fixture drain is oversized. Wet venting is not permitted for toilets.

Vent pipes usually are brought to the outside through the roof. To retain the full beauty of the roof, it is important that these vent pipes exit the house through the portion of the roof in the rear of the house or in other areas that are not awkwardly visible.

In houses with several bathrooms, especially two-story plans, DWV piping can be complicated. Turns and fittings in drain lines should be minimized, and curved bends are preferred to sharp turns.

Freeze damage is seldom a problem in drainpiping except at traps subject to below-freezing temperatures. If winterization is necessary, traps should be filled with a mixture of water and ethylene glycol (automobile antifreeze) or should be individually drained.

Cleanouts also are required in drain systems at sharp changes in direction where a plumber's router cannot pass. Through the cleanout the gradual accumulation of solids, grease, hair and other foreign objects may be dislodged. Typically, a cleanout is provided at the base of each vertical waste pipe (soil or waste stack), and at code-specified intervals of lateral piping. This also applies to the outside piping to the public sewer system or individual septic system.

The most common materials for the DWV systems are plastics, cast iron, copper, galvanized steel and wrought iron.

Advantages of plastic DWV drainpiping over metal types include lower cost for material and installation, light weight, which means it is easier to support and puts less of a load on the walls and floors than metal piping, and installation of vertical toilet soil lines within conventional two-by-four studs. The insulative quality of plastic permits grease wastes from kitchen drains to flow better without congealing and depositing in the pipe. Disadvantages are audible water flow noise, potential puncture damage, and possible gnawing by rodents.

Cast iron is still popular for its ability to dampen noise of rushing water in soil lines, but the material is very heavy, requiring strong supports about every four feet for lateral runs. Joints are of two types: hub or bell and spigot, and clamped type. The former, used in vertical three-foot soil lines, require oversize studs to accommodate the joints, while the latter will fit within two-by-four studs.

Copper is the rigid type and also can be accommodated within two-by-four studs. Its relatively thin walls make water flow noisier than in cast iron. It is used for vents and waste and soil lines. It is expensive, but is still the choice for quality homes.

Galvanized steel and wrought iron often are used for smaller waste lines and vents.

From where the drain line leaves the house, called the house sewer, any of the previously described DWV pipe and vitrified clay tile (if permitted by the local code) can be used running to the public sewer or the septic tank of an individual system. If a drain must be run under a driveway, cast iron is recommended because of its relative strength.

If your house plan and location of plumbing results in the lowest drain being below the nearby sewer level, you have alternatives to consider. One is to use an ejector pump with storage tank below the lowest drain, and pump to the sewer. Another is to drain all but the lowest fixtures by gravity to the sewer and use an ejector pump and tank only for the problem fixtures below the sewer line. This has the advantage of dependable gravity drainage for much of the house with only minor inconvenience should the electric power fail.

Several precautions are important in planning house plumbing systems. One is to avoid routes that are in or beneath a concrete slab, since access for repairs is impossible without tearing apart the slab. Also, once installed, the pipe cannot be insulated should this later prove desirable or needed. One exception to piping in slabs is where it is designed for radiant heat, in which case flexible copper tubing usually is preferred.

In any piping system, the fewer abrupt turns, the better the system. While supply systems function satisfactorily with abrupt turns, they can be a trouble source with DWV piping.

Observe where your water supply pipe and house sewer are buried. The few minutes it takes to plot them on a diagram may help in future problems by knowing where not to dig or plant a tree, or where to dig if leaks develop.

Don't make your choice of pipe materials solely on the basis of lowest cost. Consider where the pipes are located and what they do. Using different types of pipe depending on their advantages will make a better system than saying to the plumber, "Use plastic throughout." Pay particular attention to pipe runs that may be subject to freezing in climates where this may occur.

In planning bathroom locations, take into account that fixtures and piping can be noisy, so avoid putting plumbing in walls where this noise is objectionable. Also, if possible, avoid putting bathrooms over a dining or living room because of both noise and possible water leaks.

■ FIXTURES AND FITTINGS

While most of the plumbing is hidden, the fixtures and their fittings or trim are in plain sight. There is more to these selections than choosing units that look attractive and fit with your decor; functional requirements including performance, materials and overall quality also are important. As a rule, when you select fixtures *and* the fittings or trim (faucets for bathtubs, showers and washbasins), avoid cheap or bottom-of-the-line products unless you have a rock-bottom budget. Better units have more durable components and are less likely to leak or cause trouble.

Try to select from the same manufacturer. You will be assured of a better color match, and often you will get a better price from the plumber due to quantity buying from the same source.

To select your fixtures and fittings, go to one or more plumbing supply sources and take your time looking over the fixture types on display. Ask questions about the features. If units you like are special sizes, make sure that they will fit the plan. This is particularly important with bathtubs, shower stalls and whirlpool tubs. It will be helpful if you take along a copy of your floor plans for this purpose. Typical bath fixture sizes and symbols are shown in Figure H.1.

The fitting selection is done separately from the fixture selection with chromium plate being the most popular. Special decorator fittings are more costly. When considering fixture colors, make this choice carefully. White and bone color can be used with almost any bathroom decor, while colors like plum, rose and yellow make a strong fashion statement—you may tire of this.

Tubs, Showers and Tub-Shower Combinations

Choices for tubs are steel or cast-iron base with porcelain coatings and fiberglass or other plastic. The steel tub is the least desirable; it chips easily and sometimes will distort after installation, causing the ceramic tile to loosen around the tub or tub-shower enclosure.

The fiberglass tub, particularly when in a one piece tub-shower unit, has many advantages. It is easier to clean and tends to resist mildew better than the ceramic tile, but care must be taken to avoid abrasive cleaners, which scratch the finish. It also will bend under the weight of the body, and when the water is turned on and strikes the bottom of the unit it may be noisy.

A cast-iron or fiberglass tub may be combined with wall panels of acrylic, fiberglass, other synthetic or ceramic tile.

In making a choice of a tub enclosure, consider the ease of cleaning the paneled enclosure versus the greater decorative possibilities available in the ceramic tile. Fitting can be separate hot and cold faucets or one-piece mixing valve types.

FIGURE H.1 ■ Typical Bath Fixtures

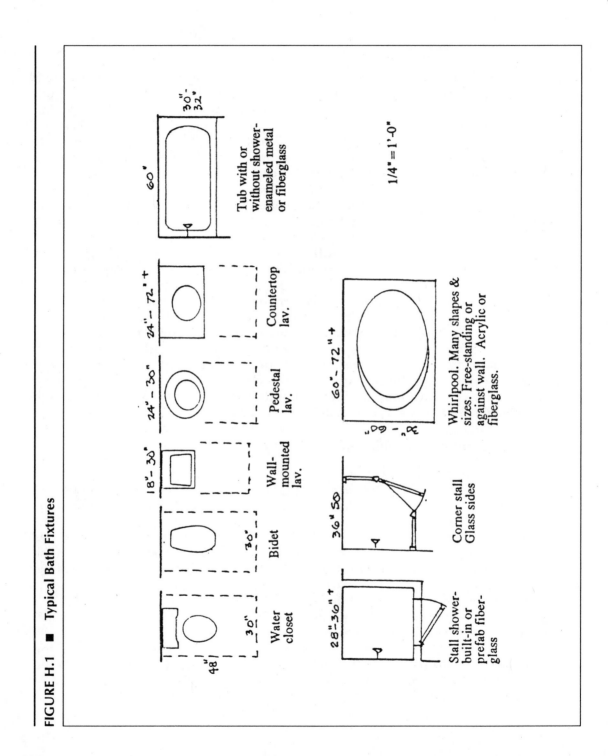

Water closet — 30", 48"

Bidet — 30"

Wall-mounted lav. — 18"–30"

Pedestal lav. — 24"–30"

Countertop lav. — 24"–72"+

Tub with or without shower-enameled metal or fiberglass — 60", 30"–32"

Stall shower-built-in or prefab fiberglass — 28"–36"+

Corner stall Glass sides — 36" 50

Whirlpool. Many shapes & sizes. Free-standing or against wall. Acrylic or fiberglass. — 60"–72"+, 30"–60"

1/4" = 1'-0"

Stall showers (without tubs) offer the choice of the acrylic and fiberglass units versus the ceramic tile. Tile will be more expensive, although it permits designs with special configuration such as round and oversize stalls. With fiberglass, you must select from the sizes and colors made by the manufacturer.

Water Closets (Toilets)

Most manufacturers make water closets from low cost to very high cost. The typical residential unit is made of vitreous china in white, bone and decorator colors, and is floor-mounted with the outlet directly beneath. The best buy is usually in the middle of the price range and should be low water usage (about 1.6 gallons). For water economy, install this type. Some units have very low noise levels, but these are usually expensive. Some are one-piece; others have a wall-mounted tank separate from the commode. For elderly people, high-rise water closets are available, although standard toilets usually can be fitted with an extension seat.

Bidets

Widely used in Europe, the bidet for feminine hygiene is finding a greater number of users in America. Most are made of vitreous china and are available in styles and colors that coordinate with water closets. The fixture requires both hot and cold water supply and proper drain. Bidets are floor mounted and require access space along both sides (approximately 30 inches in overall width). Location is a matter of personal choice, but many prefer to have the bidet and water closet close by.

Lavatories

The most popular lavatories (washbasins) are the china lavatory mounted on or dropped into a plastic laminated vanity top. Decorator types are available in the shape of a seashell and other patterns. Round and oval-shaped bowls are the easiest to clean. The porcelain-finished cast-iron lavatory is still available, but is not very popular, since it requires a metal mounting ring, making it harder to clean.

The one-piece marbleized bowl and countertop is very popular because of its appearance, ease of cleaning and low cost. Other popular plastic materials such as Corian, are made with the color all the way through the material, and tops can be sawn for accurate fit to walls. They are more expensive than marbleized material.

Wall-mounted lavatories come in china and enameled iron, and a range of sizes. They are most suitable where space is limited and the bathroom must be compact. Larger units may have legs at the front. Most wall-mounted units have minimal deck or top space for soap and toiletries.

Pedestal lavatories have been in and out of fashion. Most of the models available today are expensive decorator types with unusual shapes or exotic appearances. As with many wall-mounted types, deck space usually is limited. Some pedestals conceal the piping, and some can be positioned next to the wall with others free-standing.

Fittings, like those of tub and shower can be separate hot and cold faucets, one piece with individual hot and cold handles, and one-piece lever or pull-and-turn type.

Kitchen Sinks and Laundry Tubs

Kitchen sinks are available in various sizes and are made either of stainless steel, solid plastic or porcelain-finished cast iron. The selection is one of personal preference with the option of one, two or three sections or bowls. The most widely selected is the twin bowl of stainless steel with overall size of 33-inches wide by 21 inches.

The more expensive line of the stainless steel sinks have more chrome alloy, which provides better looks and a reduced tendency to water-spot. Otherwise, there is little difference for home use. Most are coated on the bottom for sound deadening.

Porcelain sinks tend to gradually roughen and possibly chip when given hard usage.

Most laundry tubs are made of fiberglass or stainless steel. They have a deep bowl to hold more water than the average kitchen sink. If, however, the location, size and shape of an auxiliary kitchen sink is acceptable for laundry use, it will give you an extra, more versatile sink for doing other chores. In this case, one side of this second kitchen sink should be a deep bowl with the other shallow.

A hospitality or bar sink is generally stainless steel, although decorator models are available with exotic finishes and fittings. This small sink is usually equipped with a gooseneck spout for easy filling of a pitcher.

Kitchen and laundry fittings are generally of a more utilitarian type than those in bathrooms. For a kitchen sink, a swing spout is most useful, and many food preparers also like a pull-out spray attachment. As with lavatory fittings, kitchen fittings may have separate hot and cold water faucets, one-pieced units with separate hot and cold handle, and lever or wand-type handle. Chrome-plated brass is the most popular finish. Laundry tub fittings are generally more utilitarian. Kitchen sinks and laundry tubs usually are fitted with strainers at the drain. Some fittings are now made with inside plastic components or bodies, but all metal types probably will not last longer nor be less troublesome.

Bath Vanities

Bath vanities are cabinets usually provided by the same source as the kitchen cabinets. The choice of style, finish, material and color is a matter of personal choice and may be used to complement bathroom decor.

The normal height of an installed vanity with top is about 32 inches. This is low for a tall person, for whom a 36-inch counter height might be preferable. Ensure that vanity height fits the user.

Sill Cocks

A sill cock or hose bib is an outside cold water tap for lawn watering and other outdoor uses. You should have at least two; one on each side of the house; one should be convenient to the garage. You will need even more for a very large house so that your garden hose does not need to be excessively long and hard to handle. In cold areas where freezing is a problem, sill cocks should be the freeze-proof variety. These are self-draining, provided the hose is not left attached in freezing weather.

Hot Water Heaters

Hot water heaters are available for gas, oil, electricity and special types associated with a heat pump or solar heat.

A standard 52-gallon water storage type heater is recommended minimum capacity for a family of four living in a two-and-a-half–bath house. If you feel a need for additional capacity (long showers and several consecutive laundry loads), then a larger heater may be needed. Gas heaters recover more quickly than electric, but if electric is your choice specify a quick-recovery type. An alternative choice is the "point of use" water heater at or near the fixture location. This type of unit is controlled so that it rapidly heats water upon demand (when the faucet is turned on). They do not store hot water.

You can have the hot water heater hooked up with a timer set so that the heat comes on late at night to properly meet the demand for the following day. Some power companies offer reduced rates for off-peak usage and provide the related controls. Check this with your local company.

Hot water heaters should be located near the area of major demand to reduce the energy waste in running the water long distances and to reduce the aggravating waits. If your house has two major demand areas, install two smaller hot water heaters with one near each of these areas. The additional cost for the material will be made up by the energy saved in a few years. You also will have a hot water system, which is not only more convenient to use, but more efficient, since less water and electricity are required.

If you locate the hot water heater in an unheated area, add an additional insulation blanket to the sides and top (if gas heat, do not insulate the top).

Most plumbing codes require a relief valve to prevent dangerous bursting. Each hot water heater should have a drain line to the outside to take away water that is discharged. Another optional precaution is to install a protective drain pan under the water heater to catch seepage should the heater tank develop a leak. It also should drain to the outside. This drain is especially important where the heater is located in a finished area with wood flooring. Generally, do not install a hot water heater in an attic that is subject to freezing.

Clothes Washers

As part of your contract, have the plumber install an in-the-wall box for the water cutoffs and for faucets and drain. This box will dress up the installation and provide protection to the plaster or drywall. It is worth the small additional cost. Some wall boxes also have provision for the electric outlet.

■ SEWAGE DISPOSAL SYSTEM

If your lot is served by a community sewage system, you only have to hook up to this system. If no public or community sewage system is available, you will have to install on your lot an individual system designed for the local conditions, including the porosity of the soil. The system that you choose probably will have to be approved by the local health authorities.

Septic Tank and Drain Field

Where public sewage systems are not available, this is the most widely used residential system, providing the subsoil percolation or absorption is satisfactory. An illustration of a typical septic tank is shown in Figure H.2.

The three principal components are as follows:

1. The concrete septic tank, which collects the sewage from the house; into which the solids decompose; and from which the liquid or effluent passes on to the distribution box
2. Next, the smaller distribution box which controls the liquid sewage and distributes it evenly among the several drain lines
3. And finally, the subsoil drain lines (drain field), which carry the effluent to the various parts of the field, where it is absorbed into the soil through a filter bed generally of crushed rock or gravel

FIGURE H.2 ■ Septic Tank System

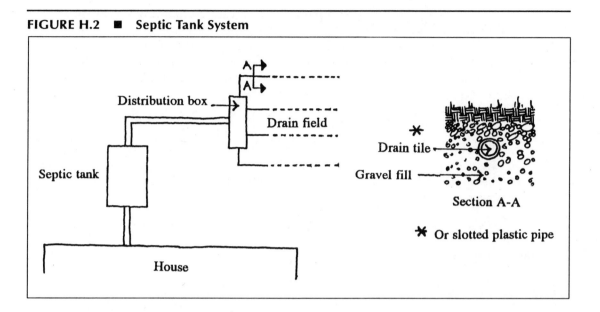

The specifications for this system usually are determined by the local health department. After analyzing the soil and considering the size of the house (usually the number of bedrooms which determines in large measure the number of people that could be expected to live in the house), the health department will issue a septic permit, which will include the size of the tank, the number of subsoil drain lines, their length and the width and depth of the trench for each line.

The area to be used by the septic system should be cleared of all trees and other heavy growth to ensure that the system's capacity will not be reduced by future damage from roots. Weeping willow trees, in particular, have a way of working their roots into the pipelines and clogging them.

Check your lot size and house location to ensure the following:

- The lot will provide enough room to accommodate the house and the septic system. If the lot is sloped, the septic field generally will be on the downslope (low) side of the house.
- If your plans require a water well, there is enough room to provide a minimum lateral separation of 100 feet between the well and the nearest point of the septic system, as required by most codes.

- The size of the lot should permit the movement of machinery (primarily a backhoe and a small bulldozer) to the septic area after the foundation of the house has been built. If this is not possible, install the septic system before you begin the foundation. If a septic tank must be pumped later, most pump trucks have long hoses to reach most locations.

Where soil perk (capability to absorb sewage liquid) is too poor for a gravity absorption drain field, it still may be possible to install a pressurized slow release system. In this system, the same quantity of fluid goes into the soil, but through smaller openings in the drainpiping under pressure over a longer period of time.

In this type of system, proper design is critical and early consultation with the local sanitary department is essential. Usually, it must be designed by a sanitary engineer.

Sand Filter Disposal System

If the soil conditions of your lot do not permit the use of a subsoil drain system, you might consider installing a sand filter system if permitted in your locality. These are miniature sewage systems that operate on principles similar to the large public utility systems and discharge water that is close to being drinkable. Their efficiency is not related to soil conditions, but they require a place to drain the discharge. They are more expensive than the subsoil drain system.

Electricity

The design and installation of electrical systems are controlled by electrical codes in most areas. The homeowner, however, has a number of options and choices for features that he or she may wish to include. They are described in this appendix.

■ ELECTRICAL SYSTEMS

In most localities, it is possible and desirable to have underground service to the house, since overhead wires are unsightly and underground service usually is less susceptible to storm damage. In some subdivisions, underground service is provided at no added cost. Usually, this no-cost arrangement applies where all subdivision customers are served by underground systems, and pad-mounted transformers are provided. Elsewhere, the customer is assessed extra for underground service. Check with the local electric company.

The electric meter should be located where it is inconspicuous yet accessible for reading. Usually the house electric panel must be within ten feet of the meter and the panel should be in a convenient location in the event a breaker should trip. Suggested locations are the garage or utility room. Most residential service is 110/220-volt single phase, and typical appliances and residential equipment are built to operate on these voltages.

When your electric service is installed, the capacity will be based on anticipated initial loads with reserve for the future. Your local power company can advise on service capacity and also on insulation standards for an all-electric house. Since all-electric houses draw greater loads than those with gas or oil heat and gas appliances, your electric service will be determined by the type of anticipated energy losses, equipment and appliances to be used.

House wiring today usually is copper, although aluminum cable is commonly used for the outside service line to the house. Copper wire of appropriate size is more efficient than aluminum and avoids the problem of failure and fire hazard at outlets and switches, which at one time was a problem with aluminum wiring systems. This now is not a worry, since installation of wiring must conform to codes and in most jurisdictions the systems are inspected by the local electrical inspector. In most residential wiring, the type of wire known as Romex is used with two conductors and a ground wire. Wiring in metal conduits may be required where runs are exposed and subject to damage. Conduit runs are more expensive.

The majority of house electrical systems are known as line-voltage systems (110/220 volts), in which the lights, switches and equipment are connected directly to the line voltage wiring coming into the house. A typical room may require 100 feet or more of wiring.

FIGURE I.1 ■ Line-Voltage and Low-Voltage Systems

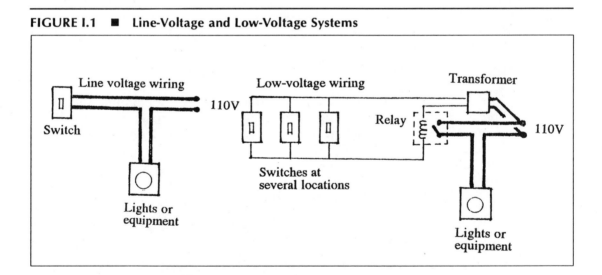

A second type, used for many years, is the low-voltage system (12 to 24 volts). Both of these systems are illustrated in Figure I.1.

Note that the low-voltage system uses a transformer and a relay in conjunction with smaller low-voltage wire. Much of the circuitry consists of the smaller low-voltage lines. In large, spread-out houses, this low-voltage system may be more efficient and flexible, since heavier line-voltage wiring is reduced and voltage losses are less. Multiple switching (one light controlled by several switches in different locations) is easier to install with low-voltage switching. The relays in low-voltage systems must be accessible, since they occasionally fail and must be repaired or replaced.

For the typical residence the line-voltage system is generally the more economical system to install. Check with your local electrical contractor for advice.

■ LIGHTING

Interior Lighting

Two principal types of lighting are area lighting, such as the chandelier in the dining room, and local or task lighting, such as for reading at selected chairs. Most area lighting is inadequate for local task lighting.

The simplest area lighting is by one or more ceiling lights, but the brightness of the lights often creates unpleasant glare. Overhead area lighting fixtures can be shaded or provided with diffusers (usually glass or plastic to reduce the amount of glare), but these cut down somewhat on the effectiveness of the light delivered. Where overhead lighting is essential, and if ceiling construction permits, recessed lights may be used. The light source is partly cut off from view as one moves farther away, which means less uncomfortable glare. This type of lighting is more popular and appropriate for contemporary houses but also can be effective in traditional designs. Where ceilings are below attics, certain approved recessed light fixtures must be used to allow insulation to be placed around the fixtures; otherwise, the fixture holes are a source of energy loss. Several common and popular types of recessed area lighting fixtures, including cove lighting, where the lamps are behind a baffle or valence, are shown in Figure H.2.

Local and task lighting may be provided by table and floor lamps and, where appropriate, by built-in fixtures such as under-cabinet lights in a kitchen or sconces (wall bracket lights).

Basic lamp types used in residences are incandescent and fluorescent. The former type generally produces a warmer light, is available in many sizes and lamp types and is a point source. Several may be grouped in a display such as around a bathroom mirror fixture. A point source has the primary disadvantages of causing glare (if the lamp is visible) and casting shadows of any object in its path. Fluorescent lights, on the other hand, provide spread-out sources of light and, compared to incandescent lights of equal brightness, create less glare and provide nearly shadowless light.

Three other advantages of fluorescent lamps are that they produce less heat, emit about two to three times as much light as incandescent lights of equal wattage and last many times longer. The large, usually ceiling-mounted fluo-

FIGURE I.2   ■   Types of Lighting

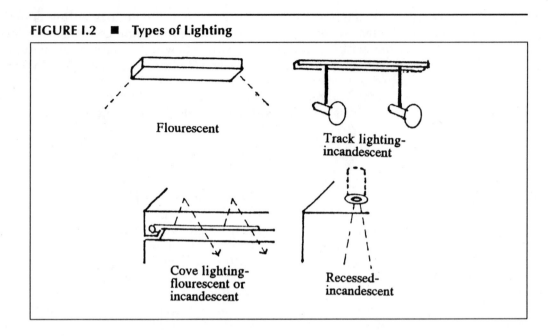

rescent fixtures, however, are unattractive in homes (too commercial-looking), except for good lighting in kitchens, bathrooms, workshops and other areas that need full light coverage. Special-shaped long-lasting fluorescent lights are available as replacements for some incandescent bulbs for many floor and table lamps, and save energy.

The high-intensity halogen bulb with the same wattage produces a brighter light than the incandescent bulb and has a longer service life. It is useful in special fixtures, where bulb changing is relatively difficult.

All types of lighting fixtures should be accessible for changing lamps. Often a step stool or stepladder will be needed. If dramatic and other interesting lights are placed very high up, such as over a stairway, use of special ladders may be needed. Keep this potential problem in mind when designing your home.

Switches and Receptacles   A room's light switch should be near or convenient to the room entrance. Rooms with more than one entrance should have switches at the principal entrances, using three-way switches for two locations and four-way switches if more than two locations. The amount of wiring for four-way switches becomes considerable, however, and their use should be kept to a minimum. This is a situation where the low-voltage system is more practical.

In some rooms such as a living room, family room and bedroom, it may not be desirable to have an overhead or other light permanently wired. Instead,

duplex wall outlets (two outlets in the same receptacle) can be split and separately wired so that one outlet is always "hot" and the other controlled by a wall
switch, as shown in Figure I.3. This is desirable where the outlet at the always hot
location is needed continuously, such as for a clock, and the other outlet used for
a lamp that is turned on only when the room is in use.

FIGURE I.3 ■ Hot and Cold Outlets

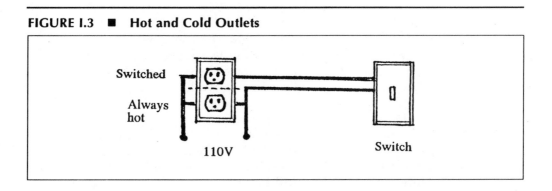

Special switches for closets are available, which conveniently operate as the
closet door is opened and eliminate a conventional switch, which for aesthetic
reasons would be unattractive.

Where multiple switches are located close together, it is more attractive to
gang (combine) them in a common outlet box with a common cover plate.

Switches are available in regular snap or spring action, and the quiet type,
which makes no noise when operated. The colors of standard switches, wall
outlets and plastic cover plates are ivory, brown and white. If room decor is
planned in advance, the best compatible switch and outlet color or finish (such as
mirrored glass or polished brass) can be selected. Primed metal cover plates also
can be ordered and finished on the job by painting with desired colors or covered
with wall paper.

Wall outlet receptacles or duplex outlets should be located so that no point
along a wall is more than six feet horizontally from an outlet (in many localities
this is a building code requirement). Thus, on a long wall outlets will be spaced
not more than 12 feet apart. Also, most codes require an outlet in any short wall
greater than two feet wide. In general, locate outlets where you need them,
including two side by side such as in the kitchen over the countertops. Two
outlets together are better than a tangled network of extension cords. Determine
your furniture arrangement before construction so you will know in advance
where wall outlets should be. Check these locations again before wire is installed
and changes or corrections are easy to make. Avoid switch locations that will

interfere with desired decor such as hanging pictures. Standard switch height is about 46 to 50 inches above the floor. Where a wheelchair user is to be accommodated, this height also is satisfactory.

Residential duplex outlets usually are located about 12 inches to 18 inches above the floor along walls and above counter height in kitchens, laundry and near washbasins in bathrooms. For architectural decor reasons, outlets may be installed horizontally in the baseboard, where they are less conspicuous and can be painted to blend in with the baseboard. Outlets may be needed in bookshelves or cabinets for stereo, TV and VCR.

To provide for the easy use of vacuum cleaners, rug cleaners and other appliances occasionally used in each room of the house, one suggestion is to provide an outlet at the entry door switch or at least one nearby. The appliance then can be much more easily plugged into a clearly available outlet rather than into a low-mounted wall outlet, which is often blocked by a table, chair or sofa.

Most electrical codes require use of ground-fault outlets in bathrooms, kitchens, laundries, exterior outlets and wherever a shock hazard from dampness or water may be probable. These special outlets are made to immediately cut off the power and prevent electrical shock should a harmful electrical leak occur.

Outside receptacles should be protected with a weatherproof cover and located where sheltered from rain and snow. Outside receptacles should be installed at screen porches, decks and other points to serve an electric lawn mower, leaf blower and other yard equipment.

Discuss with your electrician any special electrical requirements you anticipate and ask that the location of all switches, receptacles and lighting outlets be marked before any wiring is installed. In this way, you can check locations and rearrange or move outlets without the expense or trouble of reinstalling wiring.

Outside Lighting

For security and other purposes, many homeowners want outside floodlights mounted on eaves or other high places around the house. Decide if you want all floodlights switched together, in groups or singly. Outside door lights should be provided at each entrance doorway and may be required by code. These may be wall-mounted or, if an overhang or porch ceiling is above the door, some type of overhead light. If a house is remote from the street or a walkway is long, you may want to install one or more post or yard light connected by underground wiring. You also may want to consider lighting in gardens and terraces to illuminate shrubs, flowers, trees and walks. Usually, the most convenient location for switching such lights is adjacent to the door to these areas.

Photocell switches are available to automatically activate outside lighting at nightfall and deactivate it in the morning. Another choice is timer switches which can be set for "on" and "off" at selected times during the night, but these have to be reset if the power fails and as seasons change during the year.

If you intend to illuminate large lawn areas, install equipment for using mercury or more efficient sodium vapor lamps. Both create distinctly colored light but are more efficient than incandescent lamps, and are available in sizes from 40 to 1000 watts with the 175-watt size being equivalent to 300 watts of incandescent lighting. Make sure that your outside lighting plan will not be a nuisance to your neighbors. Incidentally, fluorescent lamps are not very practical outdoors, since cold temperatures seriously affect their output.

To automatically control any electric circuits such as the outside security lights or any other outside or inside lights and outlets, you can install an add-on system called X-10 Technology. The system can be programmed to operate regardless of whether the house is occupied. It consists of a master control station plus small modular controls at each device to be controlled, such as a light, coffee pot or electric fan. The system transmits the controlling signal over the house wiring system so it does not require separate wiring. Plug-in portable outlets also are available. The control components can be installed when the house is being built or retrofitted later. The control station can be plugged into any outlet such as in the bedroom. Some have battery backup and thus permit moving the control station to another location without memory loss. The battery backup also means that the self-contained digital clock and control settings will not be lost in the event of a power failure.

■ OTHER ELECTRICAL SYSTEMS

Security Systems

Many wired security systems are available; take time to investigate the advantages and disadvantages most compatible with your needs. Battery backup systems are desirable if power failure is common or if electric lines might be cut by a burglar. Some systems are quite sophisticated and expensive, but simple systems can be purchased at reasonable cost. A better installation job can be done before the house is closed in. Some of the system areas available follow:

- An outside perimeter system to signal entry at doors and windows or to detect glass breakage
- Detection of a moving person inside the house
- A light beam photocell system to detect anyone or thing passing through the beam
- Audible alarms for the system

- A method of deactivating the system as you enter the house
- A telephone dialer transmitting to a monitoring service
- Special outdoor fixture lighting devices that automatically turn themselves on by detecting movement of a person within the sensing range of the light, and then turn off a short time later (These special lights also may be activated by the wind blowing large bushes or trees and by the movement of deer or other large animals. Some also can be turned on manually when it is desired to intentionally light the outside of the house. Thus, they may replace all or part of the standard outdoor lighting.)

To assist you in determining which of these systems is best for you, you may want to deal directly with one of the firms or services specializing in security.

Fire Detection

Fire or smoke detection systems of some type should be installed in all homes. Some building or electrical codes require them. Smoke detectors should be wired with back-up battery operation in new construction. They generally are installed at a high location in or near bedrooms to provide warning when most needed and several may be needed in a large house.

Individual battery-operated units also are available and can be added to a home at any time. Most are equipped with a "low battery" audible or visible warning so you can replace a weak battery yourself.

Fire detection also can be picked up on an automatic telephone dialer to alert a surveillance monitor.

Door Chimes

Door chimes or other announcing systems are a necessity in most homes. These are low-voltage systems and should be installed before walls are closed in. Most are operated by a transformer, which can be located in a closet, the garage or the attic. Some chimes can be programmed to give a different signal for each door provided with a push button. Lighted buttons should be used so they can be more easily found in the dark.

It is difficult to hear doorbells or chimes when you are operating clothes washers, dryers and other loud appliances. If your home is spread out, you might need additional bells or chimes installed in rooms farther away from the front door.

Intercoms and Built-in Stereo

Built-in intercoms and stereo systems are available with many options.

One of the most useful is a speakerphone at the front door over which a caller can identify himself or herself. Also available are TV cameras and monitors that show the person at the door.

In a large or spread-out house, an intercom may be helpful between remote rooms.

If you do decide to install a sound system, the wiring should be run before walls are closed in.

Telephone Wiring

Telephone wiring should be planned in advance. Usually the local telephone company provides wiring up to the house or to a terminal at the house. Interior wiring may be done by the owner or contractor or installer, you decide.

Simple telephone systems usually require only the proper wire connected to outlet boxes where phones are desired. While personal choice varies, most people want a phone in the master bedroom, in or near the kitchen and elsewhere for convenience. In recent years cordless phones have become popular and can be used anywhere in the house and in the yard within the range of the unit. Check with your phone company for specific information and suggestions.

Most homeowners need only a single line, but a second or third may be desirable if you have a home-office fax machine or want a separate children's line. Also, security systems may require a separate line.

Television Wiring

In a new house it is desirable to prewire TV for cable or a house antenna. If TV cable service is available in your area you should check with the cable company for particulars.

For homes without cable, a rooftop rotating antenna with built-in house wiring is an asset, especially if "rabbit ears" on the TV set do not produce a quality picture.

Emergency Generators

Although little used in homes, emergency generators may be a good investment where power outages are common. Since capacity of home-size generators is limited, it is impractical to serve the whole house. Thus, you should install special wiring to a limited number of lights and important equipment, such as the refrigerator and freezer and possibly to a security system.

Some systems may be elaborate and automatically activate when power failure occurs but residential systems usually require manual starting and switching to the emergency circuit. Energy sources for emergency generators are usually gasoline motors or natural gas (LP gas in areas where natural gas is not available).

The selection of generator capacity and installation of the system can be determined by the electrical contractor or seller of the equipment.

■ THE "SMART" HOUSE

In recent years, electrical techniques have been developed that can greatly increase the convenience for control of the house electrical system appliances and other features. Several industrial organizations are now promoting different versions of this new technology. Basically, these are control systems that can be programmed to do things ordinarily controlled manually throughout the house, such as control of lights, appliances, equipment and the home security system. For example, the HVAC system may be made "smart" by responding to changing weather to conserve energy while no one is at home, or one may telephone the house while away to actuate the thermostat and have the lights turned on before returning, or to be sure that the stove is off before you have left.

Another example replaces the function of many different cables presently installed to provide service for power, television cable, audio systems, intercoms, telephone and security systems. A single multi-wire cable is installed, which allows you to hook up any or all of these devices at any wall socket. Each device will have its own "smart" module that ensures that only the correct connections are made.

Most of these systems have a feedback system to indicate what is working. In addition, the system can be designed to provide controls as to the timing of the operation of individual elements. For instance, in the morning you can set up the system to turn on the coffee pot 20 minutes before you get up and with the radio or television turned on to wake you up.

The capabilities of the developing technology are numerous. If this interests you, consult with the local power company, an electrical engineer, architect or electrical contractor who has experience in this area for help in determining just what elements and type of system you might want in your house.

House Plans

■ SOURCES FOR HOUSE PLANS

Although this book is a comprehensive guide to making decisions in the selection of a quality plan, it does not sufficiently educate the reader to actually make the drawings. The many aspects of house design must be brought together using the experience of capable and professional skills.

You may find a number of sources or utilize the house plans: services, architects, designers and builders.

Plans Services

A wide diversity of plans is available from plans services, featuring nearly every style and size of home desired. Many newspapers carry a plan-of-the-week, and at newsstands numerous magazines and catalogs are filled with house designs. Some feature specific styles, such as all-traditional, while others include a wide range of styles, many with novel features and appeal such as dramatic interior spaces.

These publications show floor plans and usually one or more photo-like illustrations showing the character of the designs. Also, room sizes and overall square footages generally are given. Carefully consider these dimensions to see if they meet your needs. Overall square footages provide a yardstick to determine if the design seems to fall within your budget.

You can evaluate a design for its strengths and possible weaknesses as covered in this book, such as efficient use of space, arrangement of rooms, traffic patterns and relationship to the lot. Although leafing through magazines and catalogs is time-consuming, the effort is well worthwhile. Do not skimp on making comparisons and choices, especially if this is your first venture into planning a house.

When you find a design you feel is satisfactory, send for a set of working drawings (the drawings used by the builder or contractor). When these arrive, you will have detailed information for further study. Then you can picture how rooms will be furnished, study the features included in the design and try to determine how easy or difficult it may be to adapt the design to your lot.

When using mail-order plans, take into account that not all are prepared with the same degree of thoroughness and skill. This is a nonregulated industry. Some plans services provide fully developed and detailed drawings including specifications and materials lists, while others offer outline plans to which you or your builder will have to supply much additional information. Carefully read the descriptions of what is included in your order. With any set of stock plans, you or your builder will still have to check locally on zoning and code matters and restrictive covenants, and generally follow through on selection of products to be used such as windows, lighting and plumbing fixtures, and HVAC systems. In some cases, you may want to seek the help of an architect or professional designer.

The cost of mail-order plans usually is modest, some several hundred dollars a set and often with discounts on additional copies. You will need three or more sets. To the extent that these plans can be used with no or minimum modifications, they usually are the most economical sources for obtaining house plans. It helps if you can go somewhere to see an already-built example of your preferred design. Using mail-order plans is not the same as going to a car dealer to select from current models on display.

Architect-Prepared Plans

For the greatest degree of detail and accuracy in the planning and building process, you may want to employ an architect. The architect works closely with you to incorporate ideas and requests, and sifts through often bewildering choices of suitable products. The architect prepares the working drawings and specifications. The architect also can provide services on the bidding and construction phases of the project, and assists in the selection of decorative finishes, plumbing and electrical fixtures, HVAC systems, built-in designs and sometimes furniture designs and unusual features such as unique stairways and fireplaces.

If you use a local architect, he or she will be familiar with the zoning ordinances and building codes, and can assist in meeting requirements of restrictive covenants and property owners' associations.

Architects receive professional training and are licensed by each state. Building design is their occupation. Most plans services employ or are directed by architects. Some architects are known for a distinctive style and this hallmark may be to your liking, such as in traditional designs, others in contemporary and some in both. Before employing an architect, have an introductory meeting. Ask to see examples of his or her work and get answers to essential questions such as what you can expect in the working relationship and particulars of business arrangements. Some architects will work with you as a consultant for design or other particular help you may need.

Architects' fees will be considerably higher than the cost of plans purchased from plans services. This can be misleading, however, since fees are a fraction of the overall building costs. In the long run fees are quite reasonable, taking into account that greater savings realized by skillful and innovative planning, space utilization and recognition of potential costly problems that can occur if important factors are misjudged or overlooked. Architects generally practice independently of builders and contractors, and for this reason their services are not tied to particular products and materials. You and the architect become a team.

Designer Plans

In many localities, professional house designers provide planning and design services. In some states they are certified or licensed, a reassurance that they meet desirable standards of ability and service. Some have worked with architects or design services before becoming independent designers. Some are affiliated with or employed by builders or contractors who specialize in custom designed houses. Either way, the designer offers individual attention.

Using a designer employed by a builder can be advantageous if you neither need nor want the broader services of an architect but still seek the personalized approach. The builder-affiliated designer usually is obliged to provide designs under the builder's supervision with the condition that the prospective homeowner engage that builder, a package arrangement.

On the other hand, independent designers, like architects, prepare plans directly for you without tie-ins to any builder. Depending upon state or local regulations, designers may be regulated as to what services they can provide. You should discuss particulars with the designer, ask to see examples of his or her work and find out about business arrangements. Fees of designers vary widely based on services provided. Some fees are figured on house square footage, and others may charge hourly rates.

Builder-Supplied Plans

Many builders can provide plans from plans services, or from an architect or designer with whom they customize designs, or from an in-house designer as described earlier. Most small-volume builders (who build only a few houses a year) offer stock plans from plans services that they have found to be reliable and popular. In talking to a builder, seek flexibility on his or her part to accept your wishes and plans of your own choosing.

Some builders provide plans at no charge as an inducement if you are willing to contract for their building services. This arrangement can be quite attractive to a prospective homeowner, although it is important to recognize that the cost of preparing plans is absorbed in the builders' costs, just not charged as a separate item. If you decide not to proceed with construction, usually you will be charged a fee only for services rendered. Ask about this and any other arrangements offered. As with an architect or designer services, ask to see examples of previous work before committing.

Many small-volume builders will work with you in making minor changes to a set of stock plans. If they have design experience or employ a designer, the results may be quite acceptable. This situation can be advantageous, since the drawing changes and building can be done as a single package.

In summary, consider the sources of plans that best suit your circumstances, needs and desires, and to what extent help will be needed. Take into account the value of your own time in the planning and building process.

The best use of stock plans is if they do not require significant changes. If you want individual attention and design requirements are involved, employing an architect or an independent designer may be the best decision. These choices also permit obtaining competitive construction bids. Or the package arrangement of a builder who can offer design help is another choice.

For personalized services be sure that you have a clear understanding (preferably in writing) as to what will be provided, and that fee arrangements are worked out on an agreeable basis.

INDEX

E